Angelus Novus, 1920, by Paul Klee.

The Israel Museum, Jerusalem

Graven Images

Series Editor
Leonard V. Kaplan
University of Wisconsin, Madison

Graven Images was born in discussions of the various post-structuralist assertions of intellectual hegemony within the realm of post-modern discourse that led to attempts to redefine a space for the sacred in the face of post-modernist materialism. **Graven Images** will focus on the clash between post-modern theorizing and the urge to transcendence as it illuminates the status of culture and the law.

Titles in Series:

Cognitive Justice in a Global World, edited by Boaventura de Sousa Santos

The Law Before the Law, Steven Wilf

The Law Before the Law

STEVEN WILF

LEXINGTON BOOKS

A division of
ROWMAN & LITTLEFIELD PUBLISHERS, INC.
Lanham • Boulder • New York • Toronto • Plymouth, UK

LEXINGTON BOOKS

A division of Rowman & Littlefield Publishers, Inc.
A wholly owned subsidiary of The Rowman & Littlefield Publishing Group, Inc.
4501 Forbes Boulevard, Suite 200
Lanham, MD 20706

Estover Road
Plymouth PL6 7PY
United Kingdom

British Library Cataloguing in Publication Information Available

Library of Congress Cataloging-in-Publication Data

Wilf, Steven Robert.
The law before the law / Steven Wilf.
p. cm.
Includes bibliographical references.
1. Jewish law—History—To 1500. 2. Jews—History—To 1200 B.C. I. Title.
BM520.52.W54 2008
296.1'8—dc22 2008014163

ISBN-13: 978-0-7391-2313-3 (cloth : alk. paper)
ISBN-10: 0-7391-2313-0 (cloth : alk. paper)
ISBN-13: 978-0-7391-2314-0 (pbk. : alk. paper)
ISBN-10: 0-7391-2314-9 (pbk. : alk. paper)
eISBN-13: 978-0-7391-3051-3
eISBN-10: 0-7391-3051-X

Printed in the United States of America

™ The paper used in this publication meets the minimum requirements of American National Standard for Information Sciences—Permanence of Paper for Printed Library Materials, ANSI/NISO Z39.48–1992.

To My Parents

Contents

Preface

This study began as an exploration in what occurs *before* a foundational moment of law giving. My goal was to explain how we think about those norms which exist prior to the imposition of unequivocal higher law, and to understand how we might resolve the many difficulties involved. A law-giving moment—be it the giving of the Torah at Sinai, as discussed in this book, or the framing of the United States Constitution—creates dilemmas. On one hand, legal decision making relies upon claims to persistence. Legitimate legal authority comes from precedent, and for many legal institutions and doctrines prior to this century, it also derives from claims of deeply rooted ancient norms. On the other hand, foundational moments create rupture, sweeping away the past.

The subject of this book is about a particularly complex relationship between legal precursors and a law established after a founding moment—the problem that pre-law poses in Jewish law. To be sure, Jewish law is an exemplar of the pre-law problem—only more so. The founding moment, the giving of the Torah at Sinai, is shrouded in claims of untouchable authority. Sinai is seen as the apotheosis of divine legislation, and subsequently as the fountainhead of legal legitimacy. Seeking to ensure compliance with received norms, later generations have portrayed Sinai as the sole source of Jewish law. At the same time, however, an alternative tradition of Jewish jurisprudence evokes the pre-Sinai progenitors of the Jewish people, the Patriarchs and the generation of the Exodus, drawing them into later legal debates. Indeed, the actions of the Patriarchs are seen as an exemplary model for how all subsequent generations of Jews should acquit themselves. As the classic Talmudic phrase suggests, "the ways of the Patriarchs (or forefathers) are a sign to the children." Both the *lex scripta* of Sinai and the customary *lex non scripta* of earlier pre-Sinai generations therefore contend as competing sources of binding legal authority. What is the meaning of the pre-Sinai legal past in light of the tension between following the demands of earlier custom and the dramatic giving of written law at Sinai?

Let me begin by stating what this book is *not* about. It is not an historical study which employs critical Biblical scholarship to examine the framework of *actual* pre-Sinai law. It is not a literary analysis of Biblical motifs. It is most certainly not a theological work operating within a received religious tradition. Instead, *The Law Before the Law* explores the *imagined* world of pre-Sinai legalism. A very long tradition of speculation, of conjecture, and even of outright fantasy has been spun around reconstructions of this imagined archaic Jewish law. Since these speculations build upon themselves, I have chosen to unpack them as clustered readings whereby the chronological arc of the Biblical narrative is followed as the source of sites of memory for persistent legal ideas.

This book traces a narrative of pre-Sinai law from Adam to Noah and the generation of the Dispersion; through the various challenges faced by the Patriarchs; and, ultimately, to the collective law giving experienced by the Israelites as they left Egypt. Though a good deal has been written about the revelation at Sinai, hitherto little has been done to describe the character of pre-Sinai law. Partly, this lack of attention reflects the fact that sources have been scattered, often among disparate Jewish traditions. The aim of this book is to stitch together the wealth of comments about the formative period of Jewish law and fashion them into a coherent narrative, retelling the story from Creation to Sinai from a distinctly legal point of view. Such a narrative, I hope, will tell us about what law looks like to legally-trained observers away from the momentous commanding voice of law giving. This is an enterprise of recovering a submerged legal world. On one hand, later commentators describing the law before the law saw it as the necessary grounding which readied the people for law-giving at Sinai. On the other hand, and this is a more provocative line of enquiry as I suggest at the end of this introduction and throughout the book, pre-Sinai law was posited as a counterpoint to Sinai which was different in many ways from Sinai itself, and therefore constitutes a counter-legal history.

What animates this book is not simple curiosity. I want to emphasize the normative currency of this project as well. The fundamental jurisprudential problem of how to deal with time and rupture, with *before* and *after*, exists in a number of other legal systems. The oft-told Constitution-centered history of United States law, for example, sounds remarkably like the revelation at Sinai. There is a moment of law giving, the Constitutional Convention; its inscription as written higher law; ratification by the people as a whole; and the tracing of all ordinary law to this singular source. So much American law hangs like a mountain dangling by a hair—to borrow a Talmudic image—upon the debates and decisions of Constitutional framers gathered in Philadelphia. How often are we reminded that the Constitution serves as our scripture?

Nevertheless, courts make occasional reference to pre-existing common law habits of mind. Particular common law rules are either accepted and integrated into the existing legal framework or, alternatively, rejected as vestigial remnants of the past with little relevance for current problems. As much as we proclaim the trumping power of the Constitution, we are aware of the continuing relevance of Anglo-American legal principles in interpreting Constitutional norms. The common law *before* the Constitution is preserved as a kind of architectonic of American law, a set of shifting geologic plates which remain hidden beneath the seemingly unified crust of the Constitution. Until we feel their rumbling movement at various times, our consciousness of these deeper layers recedes.

Other legal systems have dismissed their earlier law as largely antithetical to contemporary norms. Take Islamic law, for example. Islamic jurisprudence includes the concept of *Jāhilīyah*, which refers to the period prior to the establishment of Islamic law, and has come to epitomize a time bereft of true law. Instead of being rooted within Islamic values, social governance in this early period was founded upon man-made norms. Although technically archaic law, twentieth-century Islamic legal scholars have seen *Jāhilīyah* constantly reappearing in various guises even into the present time. Indeed, modern Western norms, imported from alien legal sources and adrift from a traditional religious nomos, are sometimes described as *Jāhilīyah*. Every faithful Muslim retains a duty to resist the re-imposition of this archaic law.

No doubt there are many different approaches to the law before the law—legal norms prior to a covenanting moment. Sometimes these norms are allowed to remain intact and granted dispositive legal weight; sometimes, as was done with the reception of common law in the early American republic, they are sifted; sometimes examples of pre-law are dismissed out of hand as recondite legal relics; and sometimes, as with *Jāhilīyah*, they are abhorred. In all cases, earlier norms, with their claims to legal authority across time, pose significant challenges to the sense of seamlessness for contemporary law. As this project developed what increasingly interested me was the struggle between the demands of an over-arching narrative of a single law giving, with its pretensions of a unified history and unassailable claims for law's doctrinal coherence, and a pervasive historicism which sought to unravel the neatly formulated tale of an all-encompassing foundational moment. The stories we tell about law, I believe, do not emanate solely from grand narratives; but through quieter, though equally insistent contradictions, which appear as law evolves over time, and especially when there are rifts between one period and the next, between the *before* and the *after*.

This book should be read as jurisprudence *in situ*. Much like Isaiah Berlin's hedgehog and fox, there are two contrasting types of jurisprudence. The first kind of jurisprudence is crystalline, almost geometric. It outlines rules and sub-rules, relentlessly following their logical outcomes. Personified by figures like Bentham or, especially, Hans Kelsen, hedgehog jurisprudence seeks to uncover fundamental universal principles which stretch across discrete legal cultures. This type of jurisprudence often reflects a stubborn disregard for much of the complexity of human social interactions. Largely prescriptive, its weakness is also its strength. For doing one thing well, in the manner of Berlin's hedgehog, it can impose a clear vision despite a myriad of conflicting details.

The project of the law before the law belongs to the fox species of jurisprudence. Foxes, Berlin tells us, know many things. There are fewer comforting verities and a great deal of detail. Law plays itself out through the confrontation of the decision-making legal mind with the fabric of legal doctrine. Law is sometimes vested with official power, sometimes not; sometimes in accordance with a rational application of clear legal principles, sometimes encumbered by various psychological claims which pull in opposite directions. The fox perspective is law *in situ*, rooted in facts. As seen in the works of Blackstone, Oliver Wendell Holmes, or, in our own time, in Michael Sandel's *Democracy's Discontent* and Robert Cover's *Justice Accused*, experience, not logic, is its touchstone. Historical jurisprudence of this sort uncovers its own truths, but these are often difficult to neatly categorize.

The Law Before the Law takes us not simply backwards towards legal doctrine distant in time and place—but to an observation point where the debates over law themselves were speculative, and not immediately binding. The locus is the imagination. As a lawyer, I at first found this most troubling for I was trained to address real legal rules in settings such as courts, where power and law intersect. This book seeks to uncover what people very different from us believed—to step inside the imagined *nomos* of the other and to utilize interpretive tools radically different from our own, but never, as a result, to be captured by the insistent voices of their beliefs. In the end, I discovered the need of Jewish law and perhaps other legal systems as well to confront troublesome jurisprudential and psychological issues in a laboratory of ideas, a carved out protected space. *Before* and *after* are not simply points along a chronological continuum. They are heuristic tools for challenging legal authority simultaneously from within the tradition, its very past; and, since this past is a distant vista whose remoteness sharpens the comparison, from without.

I have stressed the comparative dimension in this brief introduction because I wanted to underscore how the pre-law problem—the existence of law prior to a law-giving moment—is a commonplace of many legal systems. However, in order to fully plumb thickly imaginative renderings of law, I have chosen to focus solely upon one legal system, Jewish law, and the problem of how Jewish commentators view the significance of Jewish law existing prior to Sinai. The comparative dimension of pre-law will remain in the background as we unpack the particular debates found in nearly two millennia of Jewish legal storytelling. Such an investigation requires a great deal of internal textual footwork. The essence of Jewish law—as with all legal systems—is in the details. These details take us to the minutia of religious and civil norms, to extraordinarily fantastic anachronism, and to legal structures which might seem at first glance absolutely peculiar to Jewish law. But, I hope, that even as this book is caught up in this web of detail, the reader will think comparatively about larger questions of law and justice. To borrow a phrase from Emmanuel Lévinas, Jewish legal culture constitutes "a particularism that conditions universality."[1]

I will address in the first chapter some of the methodological problems of embarking on such a study. However, it is important not to lose sight of the fact that the legal commentators we will be studying were engaged in a jurisprudential project themselves. Even as Jewish legal scholars undoubtedly embraced fealty to the idea that Torah came from Sinai, they envisioned a different law prior to this founding moment, a legalism more oral, more customary, more discretionary, and, above all, more concerned with the psychological question of how a norm bearing person is created than can be found in the blunt assertion that a law is obligatory because it was given to Moses at Sinai. The discussion of pre-

Sinai law, then, is not a flight from the reality of instant cases. It is the journey to a place where law itself—away from the lengthening shadow of the law-giving moment—can experience its own revelation.

Note

1. Emmanuel Lévinas, *Difficile Liberté: Essais sur le judaïsme* (Paris: Edition Albin Michel, 1963), p. 315.

Acknowledgments

In the introduction to his book, *Present at Sinai*, which constructs a poetics of law-giving, Israeli novelist and Nobel Prize laureate Shmuel Yosef Agnon thanks my great-great grandfather, Solomon Wilf, for his Hebrew writings on Jewish non-legal material. Like Agnon, I have benefitted from numerous written sources, and I have strongly felt the flow of the cross-generational debates that characterizes much of *The Law Before the Law*. These virtual conversations have been wonderful. But I most appreciate the comments of many living friends and colleagues. Those involved already know their identities, and how much I owe them. I have benefitted enormously from the suggestions of Jonathan Boyarin, Arye Edrei, Steven Fraade, William Hallo, Zeev Harvey, Marilyn Katz, Leonard Kaplan, Ranon Katzoff, Thomas Morawetz, Howard Needler, Peter Ochs, Jeremy Paul, Richard Ross, George Savron, Jonathan Schofer, Nanette Stahl, and Suzanne Last Stone. Albert Baumgarten made what probably has been the most useful suggestion I have ever received when publicly presenting my research. Carol Weisbrod read my manuscripts in various early incarnations, and over the years has been an endless source of wisdom. Special thanks are due to Judith Miller, whose friendship has meant so much to me. Michal Zamir provided able research assistance and Janet Kelly prepared the manuscript. Parts of this book have been presented at a gathering of the Jewish Law Association at Zutphen (Netherlands), Yale Law School, and the Tel Aviv University Faculty of Law. This book could never have been written without the Yale University Libraries and the strong support of the University of Connecticut Law School. I feel privileged to be part of an institution which values legal scholarship in the broadest of terms. Final revisions of the manuscript took place while I was visiting at the Law Faculty of Hebrew University.

My family has been warmly supportive of this book. I would like to thank my parents, Morris and Selma Wilf, my mother-in-law Shifra Epstein, and Sara, Moses, and Lily. My late father-in-law, Morris Epstein, a noted scholar of medieval Hebrew legends, had his own engagement with imaginative traditions. Special words of appreciation are due my wife, Guita. Her gifts are legion—and tangible.

Steven Wilf
New Haven
Jerusalem

Abbreviations

Tractates

ARN	Avot de-Rabbi Natan
Avot	Avot
AZ	Avodah Zarah
BK	Bava Kamma
BM	Bava Mezia
BB	Bava Batra
Ber.	Berakhot
Beẓ	Beẓah
Eruv.	Eruvin
Git.	Gittin
Ḥag.	Ḥagigah
Hor.	Horayot
Ḥul.	Ḥullin
Kid.	Kiddushin
Men.	Menaḥot
Pes.	Pesaḥim
RH	Rosh Ha-Shana
San.	Sanhedrin
Shab.	Shabbat
Yoma	Yoma

M.	Mishnah
T.	Tosefta
B.	Talmud Bavli

Other Sources

Gen. R.	Genesis Rabbah
Exod. R.	Exodus Rabbah
	Midrash Rabbah, ed. Aryeh Merkin, 11 vols. (Tel Aviv: Yavneh Publishing House, 1986).
Mek.	Mekhilta de-Rabbi Ishmael, ed. Jacob Z. Lauterbach, 3 vols. (Philadelphia: Jewish Publication Society, 1933).
Mek. [Horowitz]	Mekhilta de Rabbi Ishmael, ed. Ḥayim Shaul Horowitz and Israel Avraham Rabin (Jerusalem: Wahrman Books, 1970/71).
MT	Maimonides, Mishneh Torah. Citation references follow the Yale Judaica Series.
PR	Pesikta Rabbati, trans. William G. Braude (New Haven: Yale University Press, 1968).
PRE	Pirke de-Rabbi Eliezer (Jerusalem: Eshkol Publisher, 1982/83).
PRK	Pesikta de-Rav Kahana, ed. Bernard Mandelbaum (New York: Jewish Theological Seminary, 1962); Trans. William G. Braude and Israel J. Kapstein (Philadelphia: Jewish Publication Society, 1975).
Tanḥuma [Buber]	Midrash Tanḥuma, ed. Solomon Buber (Vilna, 1885).
TdE	Tanna de-Bei Eliyahu, ed. Meir Friedman (Vienna, 1902), trans. William G. Braude and Israel J. Kapstein (Philadelphia: Jewish Publication Society, 1980).

Chapter One

Why Legal Prehistory Matters

For every constitution there is an epic, for each decalogue, a scripture.[1]

Jewish law begins at Sinai. Or so we are commonly taught. How is it possible to ignore the dramatic power of the law giving moment? On the third day, as morning dawned, there was thunder, and lightning, and a dense cloud upon the mountain, and a very loud blast of the horn, and all the people who were in the camp trembled.[2] Moses delivers the Tablets of the Law to the people waiting below. The gates of revelation open for an ever so brief span of time, and then close—leaving behind a written scripture which will be the foundation of all positive law, written and oral; and, with the closure of revelation, legal lacunae which may be addressed through interpretation.

The received narrative of Jewish law flowing like a great river from divine legislation to its elaboration in the Talmud and onwards to the interpretations of the great legal academies of the Near East and Europe, and even to the legal scholars of our own time, is an epic tale of continuity. It establishes the core of Jewish historical identity as the keepers of the collective memory of how the law becomes manifest in this world. For a people who believe in a transcendental God and who for millennia were exiled from their land, firmly grounded legal authority has become a touchstone. Sinai creates a law which extends beyond territorial sovereignty. Moreover, the concept of Sinai deflects criticism of the law as mutable, subject to historical contingency, and as simply another species of rule making like any other insubstantial product of the human legal imagination. Judah Ha-Levi calls the giving of the Torah at Sinai a second act of creation.[3] Nineteenth-century German-Jewish thinker Samson Raphael Hirsch describes the Torah as the only constitution which did not emanate from the people whose law it would form. If the Jews are unique, and of this Hirsch had no doubt, it was because their law was uniquely handed down to them.[4]

All beginnings, even the most seemingly unassailable ones, pose difficulties. While some major Jewish thinkers valorized Sinai as the beginning of Jewishness, others concerned themselves with the problems raised by this conception. What did the law look like prior to Sinai? How do we reconcile the fact that the members of the founding generations of pre-Exodus Hebrews, such as Abraham, were considered progenitors of the people even though they predated the receiving of the Torah? Twentieth-century German-Jewish philosopher Isaac Breuer, a descendant of Hirsch, claimed Kant was limited because he had not stood at Mount Sinai, and therefore had to be content with devising the idea of law to fill the lacunae where the law itself should have been.[5] However, the Patriarchs themselves, Abraham, Isaac, and Jacob, shared Kant's difficulty. While the Patriarchs were said to have followed the law, they did so without witnessing the revelation at Sinai. This perceived missed experience prompted quite different responses from commentators. Sometimes the Patriarchs were anachronistically represented as being bound by the same norms as ordinary observant post-Sinai Jews, presaging later developments in Jewish oral law; sometimes they were said to have differed in their obligations from those later established. According to the latter interpretation, the Patriarchs were seen as encompassing an independent set of normative standards with a vast amount of discretion.

Beyond whatever rules were followed, the Patriarchs—and this, we shall see, is the argument of a number of medieval and early modern commentators as well as the subject of our current inquiry—were viewed as grappling with the *idea* of law. Later generations of commentators needed to understand how law as a system of thought worked, delving into such basic jurisprudential questions as the ways norms become binding, the scope of discretion in legal decision making, why certain approaches to statutory interpretation are legitimate and others are not, the character of judges, and how law changes. But the idea of law was not conceived out of thin air. Instead, it was examined within the context of two closely related comparisons.

First, as has been suggested, it was explored through gazing backwards in time to earlier incarnations of Jewish law. What were the legal responses of pre-Sinai historical figures to the challenges they faced? In this fashion, law was simultaneously rooted in context—Abraham, for example, had a defined and certain past punctuated by those events described in Biblical scripture; and remarkably free of the constraints of legal doctrine since the pre-Sinai background was an immense canvas which left a great deal of room for commentators to embroider their own details. This usable legal past covered a good deal of historical ground. It included all those who experienced standing *before* Sinai, including the Patriarchs—Abraham, Isaac, and Jacob, the generations who suffered Egyptian captivity, and those Israelites who made their way through the Wilderness to the place where the Torah ultimately would be given. Reading these historical texts as legal guides was as much an exploration of law *in situ* as any case analysis. Indeed, it was easier to plumb the shared qualities of law when the context was *elsewhere* in the historical past rather than in the midst of a troubling case with flesh-and-blood litigants.

The difference between one past and another within the context of Jewish law itself, then, was one move towards comparison. A second approach might be found through probing the rival forms of legalism in the world before Sinai. In addition to archaic Jewish statutes, law was said to come in a variety of non-Jewish guises: the law of Adam which, as we shall see, was truly the introduction of basic legal forms in the world; the code of Noah, binding upon pre-Sinai Jews as well as non-Jews; the legal foundations of the generation of the Tower of Babel; the law of Sodom; and the legal regimes of other peoples encountered by the Israelites around the time of the Exodus such as Egyptian slave law or the unsettled habits of the peoples of the Wilderness. These might be distinguished from one another, each representing a different alternative to Jewish law.[6]

Commentators often saw Adam as the model of ingenue legalism. Not long after his creation, Adam was faced with legal choices which required employing his endowed interpretive capacities although he lacked sufficient guiding precedent. Noahide law was the most important of the comparisons for it showed how another set of statutes, ordered into a code, might exist parallel to Jewish law. As will be explored later, the Noahide code was an invented tradition describing the law of the *other*—familiar in its outline, but seen as incapable of creatively expanding like

Jewish law.[7] The law of the Generation of the Tower of Babel and the law of Sodom might be juxtaposed to each other. With its demand for a single legal language, Babel represented for many commentators a universal, even authoritarian binding law. It was established purely for the purpose of social control. Sodom's jurisprudence was the opposite. It was said to be filled with so many malleable interpretive moves that its citizens became skilled in perverting the very notion of justice. If Babel's law was rigid, Sodom's allowed for a dizzying spectacle of topsy-turvy legal interpretations.

There was one more posture towards law which Jewish commentators whole-heartedly rejected. Perhaps even worse than the perversion of statutes in their eyes was the denial of any sort of legal norms. The peoples of the Wilderness—a society bereft of the most rudimentary attachment to the rule of law—represent the frightening specter of antinomianism. Within the visage of these rival legal systems, then, lies an entire arsenal of legal ideas not to be emulated, such as untutored approaches to norms, rigidly cramping the power of legal analysis to expand upon statutes, harsh discipline, interpretive wiliness, or heedless antinomianism; but sometimes there also exists a sense of the common principles of law which traverse particular legal systems. Whether as a jurisprudential counter-example from one's own legal past or as a parallel example from a different legal regime, gazing face-to-face at the other law demands self-consciousness.

The Meaning of Multiplicity

There has been a growing recognition that Jewish law, and indeed all law, must be seen as marked by pluralism and a diffuse sense of power animated by a complex relationship between the individual and social norms.[8] Grounding the authority of Jewish law upon a unitary moment of revelation, ironically calls into question the transmission of this law after Sinai. How do we account for controversies over substantive aspects of Jewish law? Or even differences through time or across communities? Both medieval and modern commentators, not surprisingly, remain haunted by the fact that so much law seems to come from somewhere other than the instance when the Torah was received through Moses, and this single law giving has engendered plural interpretations which seem inconsistent with a narrative describing the uncorrupted transmission of law arising from a solitary revelatory occurrence. Controversy, so troubling to medieval commentators even as its pluralism is celebrated by moderns, seems ever more striking in the face of the model of a single, overwhelming moment of law giving.[9]

As a result of this dilemma, the archetype of law giving at Sinai itself has become more complex. Moshe Halbertal recently has shown how three approaches emerged in the middle ages to accommodate legal disagreements within the framework of a unitary law giving. The first is a retrieval model. Embraced by twelfth-century Spanish scholar Abraham Ibn Daud, and in our own time by David Weiss Halivni, it presumes the perfect transmission of both written and oral law to the people standing at Sinai itself, and imperfect transmission in later generations. The corruption of inherited traditions compels later scholars to correct errors through recovering the Torah's original meaning. Halivni depicts the heroic figure in this paradigm as the redactor of legal texts. A second model, the cumulative approach espoused by Maimonides, postulates that interpretive and analytic tools were granted along with written and oral legal traditions, and that differences of opinion reflect competing outcomes in the course of employing these hermeneutic methods.

The third model is the constitutive approach, which Halbertal identifies with Nachmanides, who died in 1270, and the early fourteenth-century Talmudist Yom Tov ben Abraham Ishbili, more commonly know as Ritba. According to this view, properly constituted legal authority within each generation is vested with the prerogative to establish unprecedented legal rules. The *halacha is* what accepted authority says it is. Such a constitutive approach provides for an open-ended creation of new law. Change will largely be incremental since courts with legitimate authority are well aware of the importance of preserving inherited legal traditions, and therefore will be conservative in their judgments. However, the constitutive approach also poses a challenge to thinking of law as limited by the past. Our task, so it is claimed, is not to restore what was lost in the transmission from Sinai. Rather, the very imperfection of the original law giving provides for opportunities to express multi-vocalism in legal interpretation.[10] The investment in these competing models by medieval and modern commentators was enormous. For the problem of legal difference after Sinai informed not only theological questions about God's intent, but also engendered different ways of deciding real legal issues.

All these models explain pluralism within the framework of Sinai. Nevertheless, there exist alternative skeins of tradition which recount the law *before* the giving of the Torah. Scattered through a vast literature of commentaries, these alternative traditions focus less on the notion of a discrete instance of law giving, with its divine law giver at center stage, and more on the multiplicity of law absent a grand foundational moment. Of particular relevance are those multiple episodes when law is received prior to Sinai.

Take, for example, the debate over when the Jews were commanded not to eat the sciatic nerve. According to the Biblical text, this charge was issued to Jacob, and thus the narrative origin of the law pre-dates Sinai. Such timing poses a problem because there was no functioning system of kosher laws at this time. Other dietary restrictions, including those regarding the eating of milk and meat together or methods of ritual slaughter, will be described in the written Torah which the Israelites receive only generations later. How, then, did commentators interpret the chronological instance of this law giving—was it in the time of Jacob or did the injunction need to await the arrival of Moses?

To answer this question posed by traditional interpreters of Jewish law, let us turn to the narrative framework of the commandment not to eat the sciatic nerve. Prior to meeting his brother, Esau, for the first time in many years, Jacob readies himself and his family for the looming confrontation. Jacob anxiously anticipates Esau's response. Esau presumably still resents the loss of his birthright and might seek revenge through violence. Strategically dividing his camp, Jacob returns unaccompanied to the other side of the ford of the Jabbok. The night is one of waiting. However, even as he wrestles with his fears as he awaits the next day's encounter, a strange event takes place marked by a phantasmagoric wrestling match. *Jacob was left alone and a man wrestled with him until the break of dawn. When he perceived that he could not overcome him, he struck the socket of his hip; so Jacob's hip socket was dislocated. . . . Therefore, the Children of Israel are not to eat the displaced sinew on the hip-socket to this day.*[11]

How does the narrative relate to our question? It seems to tug in two directions. On one hand, Jacob's skirmish with the stranger is the root reason for establishing the prescription; on the other hand, this passage is written in a retrospective literary style as an etiological tale describing the source of the binding ordinance for the *Children of Israel*, those who would assume the rule as part of the receiving of the Torah at Sinai, *to this day*. Similarly, Talmudic rabbis seem torn about the chronological origins of the legislation. R. Judah states that the law forbidding the consumption of the sciatic nerve was binding on the descendants of Jacob at this very moment. According to his view, the mysterious figure of the wrestler disappears and Jacob is left with both a limp and a new statute which obligates his offspring across the generations.

The rabbis disagreed. They argue that the narrative simply explained the reason behind a commandment which *later* would be given as part of the kosher laws proclaimed at Sinai. Narrative legitimates, accounting for the meaning behind law—and especially a law as peculiar as this one; but, the rabbis seem to claim, it has no legal validity until the rule of the sciatic nerve becomes an established norm along with other dietary commandments after the receiving of the Torah. It was the rabbis' retort to R. Judah which so neatly summarizes the pluralism inherent in the idea of pre-Sinai law. "How could it be that the Torah was given multiple times?"[12] But, of course, this was precisely what R. Judah was suggesting.

This Talmudic debate reminds us that Jewish law appears as a drama with many acts. There are, as we shall see, multiple moments when norms are introduced prior to Sinai. Different historical contexts serve as backdrops, a shifting *mise-en-scène*; and, of course, with changes in the scene new actors come onto the stage. Claims to plural understandings of law are easier to make in such a context when the idea of a unitary moment of law giving has collapsed, and there are a variety of legal experiences emerging from very different times and places.

Personality and the Primacy of Orality

The account of Jacob's encounter with the angel invokes a vivid image—the displacement of the bone within the joint. In a metaphoric sense, law giving has dislocating effects. It alters the self. The various descriptions of pre-Sinai law focus largely upon the psychology of receiver, rather than upon the law giving itself. These are stories of rupture, containing both successful instances of obeying rules in times of adversity, and also recalling the frailties and failures involved in seeking to recast human desire to fit the exacting demands of law. Law and personality are thickly interwoven and interdependent. Coursing through the narrative of Adam's transgression; the twin catastrophes of the Flood and the loss of a common language after the fall of Babel; the vicissitudes of the Patriarchs—their fragile legal transmission in the midst of an entangled family romance; and the emergence of a Jewish nation through the crucible of Exodus, Wilderness, and Revelation must be seen a single, momentous problem. How can human beings, frail and mutable, accommodate the obligations, tasks, and responsibilities of their creator—not merely through obedience, but through becoming architects of the *nomos* themselves?

Telling the stories of pre-Sinai legalism tries to answer this question by seeing law as an habituating mode of thinking. It should come as no surprise that one of the major themes in various commentaries on the law before the law is how personality traits emerged which allowed for assimilating the law into the core of the individual's being. Without the creation of a norm-bearing personality capable of internalizing norms, sifting custom, crafting reasoned legal interpretations, and imposing the order of law upon the natural world, the Torah's laws would exist merely as parchment barriers, and would be ineffectual in either persuading or compelling adherence. Only the emergence of a common law mind, as a preface to Sinai, can serve as a receptacle for the revelation which follows. Read this way, the narrative leading to Sinai is not simply a story—as if this would not be enough—of nation building and religious realization; nor indeed is it even a narrative describing the articulation of a legal code. For many later legal readers of the Biblical text, it is about how to devise a norm-bearing person, one capable of enduring the tremendous burden of legal obligation not just for the extraordinary moment, but within everyday life; thereby, making divine law fixed and permanent in this world. The path to revelation must therefore be said to begin with election.

In other words, as commentators seem to suggest, a kind of legalism *had to predate revelation*. I offer this argument in the strongest of terms because it so clearly contradicts a rival and dominant trickle-down theory of law, viewing legalism as beginning with the establishing of unassailable higher law principles. According to this view, these principles are inscribed in nearly immutable foundational documents; explained through the decisions of judges, with whom interpretive authority is vested, or through official commentary; and only later do these interpretations shape the behavior of ordinary citizens. What is the basis for this misunderstanding? Trained as so many of us are to identify norms with the official institutions of law, it has been difficult to conceive of legalism absent the mystique of a law-giving moment; outside the boundaries of binding norms; or even without traditional notions of sovereignty where law devolves from an act of command. At the core of this commonplace lies what I believe is the false identification of law as inevitably flowing from foundational narrative.

To turn Robert Cover's syllogism on its head, *nomos* precedes narrative. Cover suggests that normative judgments are rethought when fitted within "a narrative of constitutional redemption" which he often identifies with a foundational tradition emerging from a unitary law giving. Legal interpretation, he argues, combines myth and storytelling, as well as rules, to establish a meaning unique to a particular community.[13] But what we see in the Biblical accounts of the pre-Sinai *nomos* are disorienting, raw encounters between individuals and the demands of unfamiliar law. Here is a legalism which does not come from enveloping myths, comforting interpretive boundaries established through the meta-narrative of the single law giving moment, or a sense of coherence and shared values. Instead, there is an overwhelming sense of danger. The problem is how to embrace the law without an injurious loss of autonomy. If divine legislation was followed as God's perfect will, depriving its recipients of an interpretive posture, the law would be nothing but the command of a superior to an inferior. Obedience would become bondage. It cannot be that receiving law means a mere mechanistic subordination to rules. The highest possible stage in legal culture is when we recognize that we must control ourselves. As a consequence, the nurturing of the *nomian* personality, with its commitment to legal interpretation circumscribed by an internal sense of duty, simply may have found the commanding voice of the Torah overwhelming. Revealed written law had to be stayed until an unwritten legalism could shield the heart from relentless command. This led a number of commentators to a most unorthodox conclusion: Torah in its origins is an oral law.

Over a century ago, Yehuda Leib Alter, the well-known Hasidic Rebbe of Ger, similarly questioned the primacy of written law. In the very first page of his Biblical commentary, entitled *Sefat Emet*, he argues that the acts of the Patriarchs, Abraham, Isaac, and Jacob, embody the power of God. But this power must be expressed through normative actions, commitments, and ordinary behavior in order to establish the norms of Jewish law. The very foundation of the written Torah, Alter wrote, was "therefore dependant upon human narrative." In short, and here is Alter's theological radicalism, oral law—the stories of the Patriarchs—precedes written law. All the Biblical sections that tell of the Patriarchs exist to show how Torah was fashioned out of their actions.[14] What kind of legalism is Alter suggesting? It is one where law flows—slowly and through encounters with everyday life—as a kind of unfolding awareness, a growing consciousness, until oral norms become fixed in an authoritative scriptural canon. This is quite a reversal from the traditional apologetics for oral law as a later interpretive response to the lacunae found in written revelation.[15]

Alter is not alone in suggesting oral law conditions the written law. He is joined by a rather surprising jurisprudential bedfellow, Philo of Alexandria. An urbane first-century Hellenistic Jew with a Platonic predisposition, Philo portrays Abraham as an embodiment of the unwritten law (*agraphos nomos*). He valorizes unwritten law because it is not law "inscribed on monuments nor on leaves of paper, which the moth destroys, but on the souls." The individual who observes the unwritten law should be praised since "the virtue which he displays is freely willed."[16] As we shall see, Greek thinkers showed a strong preference for oral rather than written law. Later commentators also represented pre-Sinai law as more fluid. Nachmanides, a thirteenth-century commentator who will be central in the exegetical task of uncovering a pre-Sinaitic legalism, described how God *purposely* imparts oral knowledge in order to prompt the study of law rather than its straight-forward observance. According to Nachmanides, Abraham constructed a taxonomy of Jewish law. From clearly defined pre-Sinai principles Abraham would derive a full-bodied post-Sinai understanding of norms, including the reasons behind the commandments and their mystical secrets.[17]

These figures did not see the law's orality as a response to gaps in the written text. The problem was more than the mere intelligibility of statutes. Mystics and philosophers alike shared a concern with what lies beneath the outer garb of legal rules. What are the common principles, or even ultimate truths, behind the commandments? How do these alter the consciousness of those performing them? For example, the nineteenth-century Lithuanian Talmudist Ḥayim of Volozhin, who might be considered both a mystic and a philosopher at the same time, declared that pre-Sinai law was not binding. Instead, the Patriarchs had a surprising amount of individual discretion to decide whether, in particular circumstances, they should follow a *halacha* or not.[18] The Torah was simply a guidepost for these early generations. In the time before Sinai, the law might be followed or ignored, depending upon the perception of whether it would draw the individual closer to God. Pre-Sinai Jewish law, a number of commentators seem to suggest, is more concerned with shaping legal consciousness than the alternative conception of law fixed by command.

Exegesis, Non-Linear Time, and the Legal Imagination

From the outset, we must confront the methodological implications of creating a legal history of the imagination. What I mean by legal imagination is something less than a unified, coherent jurisprudence; but something more than a general cultural stance brought to law.[19] If law was simply the command of a superior—such as a political or even divine authority—to an inferior, then there would be little need for the imaginative impulse other than to create legitimizing narratives. In fact, under circumstances of pure obedience, imagination would be a suspect faculty, compromising compliance.[20] If, however, law is primarily about law thinking, then imagination should be fostered. The story of the law before the law provides an ocular for seeing the many ways in which the legal exegetical project relies upon the imagination—as a place to express wonder; to resolve the contradictions found in the canon; to engage in radical displacements of time and space; and to be playful with legal analysis before investing it with normative power.

Jewish law is a superb laboratory to examine the legal imagination at work for a number of reasons. The enterprise of constructing law or *halacha* has always been matched with an impetus towards non-legal material or *aggada*.[21] The latter genre creates the space for tugging at the limits of legal constructs. Much of the Jewish legal imagination is embedded in its territory of words piled upon words: in midrash and rabbinic explanations, and in Biblical commentary. Despite the sometimes overdrawn contrasts which have been made between *halacha* and *aggada*, traditional rabbinic legends are filled with self-consciously legal casts of mind. Moreover, the Jewish legal imagination has flourished because as a consequence of the vicissitudes of exile it has been spared the brunt of the coercive power of a state legal apparatus. With its luxuriant textual landscape—*aggada*, and the distance of that landscape from the state, exegesis provides a chance to peer inside the Jewish legal mind when it is most unencumbered, and thus provides insight different from legal codes, responsa, or other more commonplace historical sources for Jewish law.[22]

No doubt the Biblical text itself—both a narrative and a legal code intermingled—demanded an investigation into the law before the law. An astute reader certainly would recognize that the pre-Sinai tradition is full of norms. Noah knows precisely how to distinguish between clean and unclean animals for the purpose of offering sacrifices.[23] The narratives of Abraham's war with the five kings; Judah and Tamar; the destruction of Sodom; and the rape of Dinah only make sense in the context of pre-existing norms. After all, as has been pointed out, how does Cain know it is wrong to kill Abel?[24] Why should Joseph have scorned the advances of Potiphar's wife as a *great wrong* and a sin against God, if there was no divine law?[25]

But the phrasing of the question looking backwards from the present—did the Patriarchs observe the Torah?—should give pause. Much of this interpretive thrust is patently anachronistic. It recast the primal religious narrative of Abraham into a code of law. As we shall see, a particularly famous rabbinic dictum claimed Abraham knew all the detailed laws of the Sabbath down to even those technicalities added late in the Talmudic period. There are other well-known examples of anachronism as well. Abraham, Isaac, and Jacob set aside tithes.[26] Rashi, a medieval exegete, describes how Jacob studied in the Yeshiva of Shem and Eber.[27] Drawing upon rabbinic sources, Rashi also narrates how Joseph distracted his brothers by dispatching them with an issue in *halacha* to contemplate during the return journey to their father. The issue derives from a passage in Deuteronomy which, of course, had not yet been written, outlining the requirement to break a heifer's neck in response to an unsolved murder. The subject matter both hinted at questions of collective responsibility for the pseudo-murder of Joseph, and was intended to distract the brothers from engaging in divisive arguments about casting individual blame.[28] How do we deal with such unsettling chronological shifting? Some have suggested that readers should ignore modern conceptions of linear time, and see these junctures within the framework of panchronism where before and after becomes immaterial.[29]

However, the commentators we shall discuss did not believe time could be indiscriminately intermingled in the service of interpretation. The very problem of the law before Sinai emerges only because there *is* a sense of order in time, a before and after Sinai, and anachronism is used selectively as a self-conscious added layer of analysis. For example, this might be seen in the well-known rabbinic tale of Moses not understanding the purpose of the crowns inscribed above the letters in the Torah. He is told that in the future Rabbi Akiva will derive multiple laws from them. Ill at ease, Moses is reassured when he learns that Akiva claims these laws were given to Moses at Sinai.[30] Moses knows the Talmudic era sage, Akiva, even though the former is born over a millennium earlier—here is the panchronism; but we recognize Moses's puzzlement as he encounters a later legal tradition—and hence the anachronism. Such a denial of linear time speaks to the theoretical utility of imagining such an encounter. Through occasionally breaching the ordinary order of time we can learn how one persuasive authority might respond to another. Tradition might be challenged by tradition. In fact, that is a classic mechanism for a jurisprudence rooted in tradition to initiate change.

For modern jurisprudence, the rule of reason or new information emerging from social science research arguing for a better functioning regime might lead to new laws. However, tradition creates its own ruptures. It draws upon competing memories of customs; remembered dissents in legal decisions; and the legitimacy of common practice or recalled alternative authority. Traditional jurisprudence churns up past diversity in order to create pluralism in the present.[31] Rabbinic, medieval, and even traditional modern commentators were working with the instruments of their own devise, and it is not unlikely that the exegetes were themselves aware of their anachronism; but suspended their disbelief in order to discover deeper truths. If they can live with this anachronism, so can we.[32]

Before we embark upon trying to reconstruct the story of the law before the law, it would be useful to proffer one example of how the fluid thinking about time in legal exegesis brings into relief the problem of competing sources of law. During the strife with his brothers, Joseph was said *to bring evil reports about them to their father.*[33] While the Biblical text does not make clear what precisely was the content of these evil reports, R. Meir in *Genesis Rabba* says Joseph related to Jacob the suspicion that his brothers consumed the limb of a living creature. This action directly violated one of the Noahide code's seven statutes.[34] Binding upon all the descendants of Adam, the Noahide statutes should have been followed by the brothers as well. Given all the offenses which the brothers might have committed, however, it is difficult to understand R. Meir's comment. Why report the violation of this particular commandment and not another?

According to Judah Rosanes, a seventeenth-century commentator from Constantinople, Joseph rejected a lenient position proffered in the Talmud—a Talmud which would not be composed until several millennia later. In the Talmud, R. Shimon ben Lakish permitted a Jew to eat organs removed immediately after proper kosher slaughtering, even though the carcass may still show some reflexive action, since the moment of severing the windpipe constitutes the legally determined time of death. For non-Jews, obligated under the Noahide statute not to eat the limb of a living animal, there are a variety of methods of slaughtering. Therefore, only the actual cessation of bodily motion constitutes the animal's death, and gentiles as a result are forbidden to consume its organs. R. Pappa, who heard this ruling, was astonished. For it posed an instance where Jewish law was less exacting than the law applicable to gentiles.[35]

Rosanes presumed, with the kind of anachronistic flourish which we have been describing, that Joseph was aware of this Talmudic debate. According to Jewish law, the brothers were permitted to consume organs from a properly slaughtered animal still experiencing reflexive action, and that is precisely what they did. However, Joseph believed the brothers should have been strict in this matter through conforming to the local practice, which was Noahide law. The question concerning the actors in this story is whether it is enough to obtain legal permission for a usage from a future oral law authority or should behavior comport with local norms so as not to create an imputation of impropriety. After all, while the brothers—in this peculiarly anachronistic world—may have been able to look centuries ahead to the debates in the Talmud, others could not. Peering over a wall, perhaps, or even from local gossip, their neighbors might learn about the origins of the meat being served and surmise that the brothers are violating the Noahide commandment. A clue identifying this disagreement was said to be embedded in the Biblical language itself. For when the brothers return Joseph's coat smeared with blood, they stated that *an evil creature has devoured him*.[36] The word *evil* from *evil report* is combined with the word *creature* from the prohibition to eat the limb of a living creature.[37]

Presenting the bloodied coat to their father, the brothers are hinting at what is truly a classic problem in the conflict of law—which of two potentially binding sources should the Patriarchs follow? Sometimes the relevant authority was local law with its reference to the Noahide commandments, sometimes the oral law with reference to a particular legal opinion raised by one of the sages in a much later controversy. Perhaps this interpretation of the *evil report* reveals the divisions of the rabbis and later commentators as they recovered the fabric of archaic Jewish legal norms. For it portrays even the Patriarchs finding themselves mired in debate over defining what is meant by the law before the law.

The Problem with Founders

Let me be clear. The exegetical turn to imagined archaic law is meant to recover traditions of interpretation. It does not seek to depict what may have been the actual law followed by Abraham, Isaac, Jacob, and the Jews in the Wilderness. This book focuses upon imagined law to the exclusion of describing actual law. I want to make three caveats about my approach from the outset. First, it sidesteps the tradition of comparative scholarship. It ignores, quite purposefully, an admirable body of research which has sought to reconstruct what might be known about existing pre-Sinaitic law from a series of close readings of the few available Biblical texts within the context of comparative Near Eastern sources. Conceiving early Jewish law as corresponding to archaic legal systems, be these those of Mesopotamian origin or surviving primitive legal systems, lies outside the scope of this book's project. Secondly, I am not—like so many who have embraced the literary turn to Biblical studies—willing to read the Bible as *sola scripta*, as if it remains a pristine text untouched by generations of readers.

Nor does this book, thirdly, serve to pigeonhole the responses of commentators into neat historical periods. Instead, it is about the elasticity of legal thinking, shifting—perhaps in even dizzying ways—back and forth between different commentators across time. I would be naive not to recognize that this approach violates the norms of historicism which are so deeply entrenched among academic researchers of rabbinic Jewish texts since, after all, an historical approach was once critical for distinguishing scientific scholarship from traditional forms of study. But this is an old battle. As Walter Benjamin remarked, historicism now has become a somewhat comforting verity which strings together past moments, narrating "the sequence of events like the beads of a rosary."[38] While this book elucidates the problem which time poses for law, and weaves together fragments from commentators which recount pre-Sinai law into a coherent chronicle, it is self-consciously anti-historicist insofar as it primarily seeks to map the boundaries of a sophisticated debate which takes place across the pages of Biblical commentaries. Its impulse therefore is dialogic—affording a sense of this ongoing conversation by contrasting one commentator with another, often choosing the figures which provide the sharpest counterpoints. The core question for this book is how the text is read as law—rather than the comparative, literary, or historicist issues surrounding questions of authorship.

No doubt it is true that the cultural baggage of commentators does define the way readers think about the law before the law. Consider, for example, the issue of whether Abraham knew, and obeyed, post-Sinai law. By rendering Abraham's legal knowledge as oral, Philo seeks to reconcile Hebrew traditions of a revealed written law with the Greek preference for *lex non scripta*. Nachmanides suggests that Abraham analyzed the commandments in the style of a medieval exegete engaged in the project of uncovering their underlying purposes, *ta'amei ha-miẓvot*. Almost certainly, such an approach must be understood as influenced by medieval Spanish Jewish controversies about the role of philosophy. When, in nineteenth-century Eastern Europe, Ḥayim of Volozhin valorizes Abraham's study of the law over his practical observance, he is making a pointed claim about the primacy of Talmudic analysis to his Hasidic opponents.[39] But what interests me here is recovering the dialogue itself, and, for the most part, I have chosen not to break the flow of the conversation and pause to situate commentators in the particular cultural framework of various periods.

It is not simply that later commentators are looking for legitimacy through invoking a founder such as Abraham. Founders, I would argue, pose problems because they highlight rupture as well as continuity. Let us look again at Abraham—this time as seen through the eyes of Jehiel Weinberg, an influential mid-twentieth-century European figure who bridged tradition and modernity. Living a significant portion of his adult life in Berlin, Weinberg was certainly aware of the challenges posed to Orthodoxy by the historical perspectives of German-Jewish scholarship, and especially through the critical examination of the past known as the *Wissenschaft des Judentums*. Perhaps in response to the *Wissenschaft*'s critique of legend, and its replacement with rational history, Weinberg straddled the issue of how much law Abraham knew. In a legal *responsum*, he concluded that Abraham knew the Torah; but at the same time it was impossible for him to have followed those symbolic commandments—such as the eating of certain foods at the Passover *Seder*—which serve as mnemonic devices to recall the Exodus from Egypt or other prospective historic events since these occurrences had not yet happened.[40]

Even though Weinberg's comments might be situated within the framework of modern discomfort with the anachronism of presuming pre-Sinai knowledge of the Torah, they should also serve as a warning not to draw hasty conclusions from rough historical contexts. For, strikingly, Weinberg's argument has its roots in a work of early tenth-century

Babylonian philosopher Saadia Gaon, whose own controversies concerning the validity of existing practice led him to assert the solidity of the chain of oral tradition from the Jewish past to his own time. In Saadia's case, it was the Karaites who challenged the authority of *lex non scripta*. Conceding that there is historical change in the course of transmission, Saadia distinguishes the law of Abraham from the law of Moses. The two laws are one and the same—and we cannot argue that Abraham's law was abrogated by Sinai.

However, Moses did add certain precepts, such as the eating of unleavened bread during Passover. Saadia's example of *matzah*, the same as Weinberg's, hints at the fact that Weinberg drew upon Saadia's idea that symbolic commandments constituted a later addition. Saadia explains the introduction of these commandments as being similar to the case where a person escapes, and then vows to undertake the obligation of fasting on the anniversary of that day.[41] Such an obligation only makes sense to those who have experienced the event. Commandments meant to prod memory are different from other statutes.

Both Weinberg and Saadia agree that there were limits to Abraham's knowledge. Certain laws are eternal, others—like statutes ordaining mnemonic rituals—are contingent and emerge in the course of events. Abraham knew the law, but only eternal legal norms and those which were directly commanded him. Weinberg's approach, with all its nuance, reflects more than another sally in a polemical battle over Jewish responses to modernity. But it also is more than simply an echo of Saadia. Aware traditional Jews touched by modernity, like Weinberg, would recognize the implication that Abraham had a different psychological posture towards *halacha*. No matter how carefully Abraham considered the purpose of law as a reflection of divine will, he lacked the full historical memory of the law's meaning as it unfolds across time. Abraham lived not just before Sinai—but before *Wissenschaft* as well. He could not fully grasp the mutability of law. Abraham may be familiar to us in his observance; but he cannot think about law with our past directed gaze. We, moderns, shoulder the consequences of thinking about the law before the law with the disenchantment born of our awareness of legal evolution.

Nomos and New Testament

Why did commentators grapple with such a hard question as whether the Patriarchs followed *halacha*? It simply was a problem which could not be ignored. Jewish history began with the Patriarchs, Abraham, Isaac, and Jacob, who were idealized as devoted servants of God well before the giving of the Torah.[42] Traditional commentators *had* to know what Abraham was commanded.[43] Ascertaining Abraham's knowledge might be a way of uncovering the archeological foundations of Jewish law, and perhaps even a means to trace how Jewish legalism evolves. Moreover, as Elias Bickerman wrote, in its plain meaning "the Torah itself denies the antiquity of Mosaic law."[44] Commentators were well aware of contradictions within the Biblical text that needed to be resolved. These are of the kind that have troubled schoolboys for generations. The behavior of pre-Sinai figures did not comport perfectly with post-Sinai Jewish law. How did Abraham serve a meal of milk and meat together, and still keep a proper kosher home? Why could Jacob marry two sisters when such a pair of unions is prohibited under *halacha*?[45] To both endow founders with the role of being exemplary illustrations of divine service and then for them to breach even ordinary legal norms posed seeming dilemmas which had to be addressed. It is, after all, part of the exegete's task to create a seamless web of Jewish legalism in scripture itself.

To be sure, the conundrum of Abraham's relationship to the law could have been dealt with differently. Paul, for example, must be read as both within the tradition of delving into the law before the law, and defying it as a radical proponent of a competing conception of Sinai as rupture. He learns from the example of Abraham prior to Sinaitic revelation that grace alone, the Patriarch's status within the covenantal framework, accounts for divine favor. There is no absolute need for the law. Borrowing Paul's metaphor, Abraham is not a contracted laborer who reaps a reward for fulfilling legal obligation.[46] Paul's reading of the Abraham narrative assumes that the central purpose of law is obedience. What is obedience without threat of punishment? And what is punishment, but coercion? "Law can bring only retribution, and where there is no law there can be no breach of law."[47] Paul inverts the Jewish idea of law as the *sunnum bonum*. His sharply antinomian solution to the problem of pre-revelatory law, of course, is one that could not possibly work for rabbinic Jews: valorizing Abraham's freedom from law, and severing the covenant—in Paul's terms the divine promise made to all those who are righteous, including those from all nations, whether or not they obey the law—from Sinai itself.

Paul, of course, was appropriating the Jewish legal narrative of the time before Sinai to turn against Jewish legalism itself. Transgression only exists where there are rules. The root cause of Adam's disobedience was the introduction of law into Eden, the very command not to eat from the Tree of Knowledge. Similarly, Paul sees Abraham as a prelapsarian figure. The fall of his descendants from their state of grace came through bestowing upon the Jews a revelatory law which would inevitably be violated. By establishing commands, Sinai creates a crushing burden of binding obligations "so that no one may have anything to say in self-defense, and the whole world may be exposed to God's judgment."[48] Paul draws upon the traditional language of the prosecutor in Biblical and post-Biblical literature, often identified with Satan, where arguments mustered against Israel are countered by a defense attorney. In Jewish sources, the defense is often that the Jews have faithfully executed the commandments. Prior to the Exodus from Egypt, for example, Israel seemed unworthy. The defense raised was that they had performed two commandments, circumcision and the Passover sacrifice, as part of their claim that they merited redemption.[49] Paul has inverted this metaphor. The law is the prosecutor, an accuser who points to all the commandments not discharged.

Paul is convinced that establishing a *nomos* inevitably results in failure. At the bottom of every Mount Sinai lies a golden calf. "In the absence of law, sin is devoid of life."[50] The rediscovery of a robust pre-Sinai legalism, then, is unconsciously or consciously a Jewish rebuttal to Christian antinomianism. Jewish commentators would find more law, not less. They would uncover archeological strata of legalism prior to the giving of the Torah at Sinai, dispensing with Paul's notion of a past untouched by law. Most importantly, this law was recast as embodying the power of interpretation rather than obligation. Abraham was transformed from Paul's antinomian figure into a exemplary legal scholar. Jewish tradition insisted Abraham knew all the law. Abraham's acts of kindness, and God's reward, were not extra-legal; instead Abraham drew every action into the process of bringing norms to the world. Indeed, the rabbis believed law enveloped the narrative before Sinai. If Paul would cast law out of Eden, the Jewish response was to find it before and after revelation in the very marrow of the Biblical narrative.

The Reading for the Fifth Day

How do we rediscover imaginings of earlier law? The Rabbis left an intriguing road map in the form of a text from an exegetical midrash compiled in the period of the Talmud, the *Mekhilta*. Before making our way to the *Mekhilta*, we first must look at the source upon which it is based—the description of the covenant enacted at Sinai to mark the giving of the Torah. Let us begin, then, with the Biblical passage:

> And Moses wrote all the words of the Lord, and rose up early in the morning, and built an altar at the foot of the mountain, and twelve pillars corresponding to the twelve tribes of Israel. And he sent the young men of the Children of Israel, who offered burnt offerings and sacrificed peace-offerings of oxen to the Lord. And Moses took half the blood, and put it in basins; and half of the blood he dashed against the altar. And he took the Book of the Covenant, and read it within the hearing of the people; and they said: "all that the Lord has spoken we will do and obey." And Moses took the blood, and sprinkled it on the people, and said: "Here is the blood of the covenant, which the Lord made with you in agreement with all these words."[51]

Outlining the Sinai covenant, the Biblical passage depicts a sacrificial ceremony, a set of readings, and the assent of the parties—with the people consenting by saying they *will do and obey*, and God, presumably, accepting the offering. As we shall see in the last chapter, when we return to a discussion of the covenant, there is a disagreement among commentators about when the Sinai covenant occurs—whether it is prior to the giving of the Tablets of the Law at Sinai or after the law has been delivered to the people. The evidence from the *Mekhilta* below clearly supposes the covenant anticipates revelation and fixes it as part of the three day preparatory period preceding the receiving of the Torah. But, even assuming the covenant as a precursor to law giving, what precisely happened when the covenant was established? The *Mekhilta* seeks to elaborate upon the laconic Biblical text:

> *And the Lord said unto Moses: "Go to the People and Sanctify them today."*
>
> This was the fourth day of the week. *And Tomorrow*. This was the fifth day of the week. *And be ready against the third day*. This was the sixth day of the week on which day the Torah was given. And what did Moses do on the fifth day? *He got up early in the morning and built an altar under the mountain* (Exod. 24:4). . . . *And he took the Book of the Covenant* [*Sefer ha-Brit*] and *read in the hearing of the people* (Exod. 24:7). But we have not heard from what he read to them.

> R. Jose the son of R. Judah says: from the beginning of Genesis up to here. Rabbi says: He read to them the laws commanded to Adam, the commandments given [to the Jews shortly before the Exodus] in Egypt, and at Marah, and all the other commandments which they had already been given. R. Ishmael says, at the beginning of the matter, *The land shall observe a sabbath of the Lord. Six years may you sow your field* (Lev. 25:2-3). [He read to them] the laws about the sabbatical years and the jubilees, the blessings and the curses [Lev., chap. 25]. What does it say at the closing of the section? *These are the statutes and ordinances, and laws.* (Lev. 26:46)
>
> They [the people as they heard the reading] said we accept all these upon ourselves. He [Moses] took the blood and sprinkled it on the people, as it is said: *And Moses took the blood and sprinkled it on the people* (Exod. 24:8). He said to them: Now you are bound, held, and tied; tomorrow, come and receive all the commandments. All these acts were performed on one and the same day.[52]

The initial conundrum for the *Mekhilta* is what happens on the fifth day of the week, the second day of the three day period. During the fourth day of the week, the Jews are initiated into the covenant. It is the beginning of a three day period of abstinence imposed in order to prepare themselves for the revelation. On the sixth day, paralleling the day of man's creation in the Genesis narrative, the *Lord will come down in the sight of all the people, on Mount Sinai.*[53] This is the day when the divine glory will be manifest, when the emanation of God will be seen face-to-face. Marked by thunder and lightning, and the blast of the horn, the Jews receive the Torah on this day. If the fourth day is the beginning of revelation and the sixth day its apotheosis, then what is the purpose of the fifth day? The Biblical text offers only one word; it is "tomorrow." The midrash seeks to fill this lacuna by suggesting that the fifth day, as well, has a profound significance. The answer is intriguing: between the day where the Jews are set apart (like priests) as holy and the day for directly receiving the law (like prophets) lies a day where *both* take place—when they receive the law through a series of readings, and when they are sanctified as the holiest of objects.[54]

The fifth day, then, is a day of binding the Israelites through sacrifice and reading. At the moment of the sprinkling of the blood, the Jews become bound to a covenant of revelation. Here is another binding as powerful as the binding of Isaac. Multiple words are used for binding: the Jews are now "bound, held, and tied" by their obligation to the law.

But this commitment—this sacrifice of self and material goods to preserve a legal system—substitutes for the sacrifice of their lives, functioning in much the same way as an animal sacrifice serves as a proxy for its contributor. The people's particular sacrifice entails continual submission to the rule of law *after* a covenant has been established, and as a consequence the command shifts from the voice of a superior to become a very part of their being.

Perhaps this explains the focus on the other medium of making the covenant, the readings. which are notably referred to as the *Book of the Covenant*. For just as the ritual of sanctifying through blood suggests the commitment of the inner self so does reading mark the moment when the normative legacy has been internalized by the listeners. Reading is a kind of partaking. Prior to the sacrifice and reading, the people say all God requires, *we will do*. But after the reading of the fifth day is completed, the response becomes *we will do and we will hear*.[55] The divine commanding voice has been domesticated by the law. No wonder the *Mekhilta* exclaims "all these acts were performed on one and the same day."[56]

What are the readings for the fifth day? This is the core question the *Mekhilta* poses. The issue here is somewhat akin to choosing the readings for the weekly portion to be publicly read in synagogue—a task assumed by the scholars of the Talmudic period. But the question of choosing readings is even more consequential in this particular case. According to one opinion in the Talmud, the Torah was given as a sealed text at the time of its completion shortly before Moses' death. For almost the entire period in the Wilderness, from the time of the giving of the Torah at Sinai until the Israelites were about to cross into the Land of Israel, the only law they had was oral with the exception of the brief readings of the *Book of the Covenant*.[57]

The *Mekhilta* offers three different opinions about its content. R. Jose proposes reading from the very beginning of creation until the revelation at Sinai.[58] Essentially, he is suggesting reading Genesis and about half of Exodus. Although this proposition at first glance seems rather lengthy, it may not be, considering that the entire day was available for these readings. Clearly, R. Jose seeks to focus on the *narrative* of the law. Creation and the Patriarch narrative cycles unfold as a prologue to the revelation at Sinai. R. Jose's reading traces the arranging of the natural world; the establishing of primordial man and woman in the garden, their transgression, and exile; the flood; the emergence of the central role of the Patriarchs, Abraham, Isaac, and Jacob; and the immanence of God in history as he takes the Jews out of slavery. The two divine roles—as creator in Genesis and as redeemer in the Exodus—establish the duty to accept the law. Those who emphasize the significance of meta-narratives for law are, in a sense, the heirs of R. Jose.

R. Ishmael advances the idea of reading *positive law*. His suggestion is to read for the fifth day two chapters of Leviticus, including the agricultural laws regarding the sabbatical year and the jubilee, the law of bonded labor, and the section dealing with the blessings and curses. This section also details limitations on the alienation of real property and mechanisms for redeeming ancestral land. Perhaps the reason for this choice is the framing of the selection. It begins with *And the Lord spoke unto Moses at Mount Sinai, saying speak to the children of Israel, and say to them: when you come to the Land which I give you* (Leviticus 25:1) and ends with *these are the statutes and ordinances and laws, which the Lord made between Him and the children of Israel at Mount Sinai by the hand of Moses* (Leviticus 26:46).

This should not be considered a pragmatic introduction to binding law. These agricultural statutes will not be applicable for some time as the Jews remain in the desert for nearly forty years. The law of the sabbatical year was enforced only after the conclusion of the conquest of the land of Israel, which would take an additional twelve years. Mandating a return of land to its original owner, the law of the jubilee only becomes applicable upon the subsequent forty-ninth year since it occurs only after seven cycles of seven years. Indeed, it might be a little over a century after Sinai when the first jubilee year will be observed. While agricultural legislation may be a very tangible law—full of concrete regulations which would be applicable to most male Israelites—it seems ironic to choose this reading for a nomadic people in order to provide a foretaste of the soon to be received law. Nevertheless, it was this particular set of injunctions which were chosen to be taught in this solemn moment. Why?

In some ways, these laws—detailed and practical—embody a hidden narrative. R.Ishmael's selection details the punishment—destruction of the land and exile—which shall come as a consequence of forsaking the commandments; and also the promise of redemption as God remembers his covenant with the Patriarchs and those whom he brought out of Egypt.[59] The Jews will receive the Land of Israel and a set of commandments. Like Adam, who violated the injunction not to eat the fruit of the Tree of

Knowledge of Good and Evil, they risk punishment and exile if they transgress. The focus on the land was not accidental. It was, then, a repetition of the primordial command to Adam. If the land will be cultivated according to *halacha*, then *the land will give its fruit and you will eat your fill; and you will dwell securely on it.*[60] However, if the Jews on the land were to act towards the law in a *casual fashion* (*be-kari*), God will unleash a *casual fury (be-ḥamat keri*). Failure to follow the law would result in a repetition of Adam's exile, and also rupture the patriarchal covenant focusing on the promise of the land and the surety of redemption.

The *Mekhilta* calls these readings *The Book of the Covenant*. For R. Jose, the covenant is a jurisprudential narrative from creation to law giving; for R. Ishmael, it is the acceptance of the detailed positive law pertaining to settlement upon the land, a sample of the many commandments which will be received at Sinai, and the threat of sanctions if these commandments are not followed. However, for our purposes, the most significant of these three alternative selections of the reading is the one suggested by Rabbi or, as he is also known, Judah ha-Nasi. His readings are nothing less than a summary of the law before the law: Moses "read to them the laws commanded to Adam, the commandments given [to the people of Israel shortly before the Exodus] in Egypt, and at Marah, and all the other commandments which they had already been given." To reinvoke a list of commandments given *prior* to the revelation is to focus on the appropriation of law by the Israelites. These were no newcomers to the idea of law. Instead, as R. Judah Ha-Nasi's readings remind us, there were multiple law giving experiences. In a series of stations—of revelatory moments—the Jews with each station experienced an internalization of normative thinking until they were fully prepared to accept the Torah itself.

Perhaps the three positions in the debate about the readings reflect different approaches to the exhortation to *be ready against the third day* (the day of revelation). What is the optimal *preparatory* reading? R. Jose situates the law within an historical tale tracing the path from Eden to Sinai. The historical narrative readies its listeners for revelation. Jews can accept the law because they are responding to the will of their creator, who created them, who redeemed them from slavery, and who nourished them in the Wilderness. In return, they offer obedience. The covenant between the Israelites and God is founded upon an exchange of benefits, contractual consideration, on each side. In contrast, R. Ishmael's reading of the basic agricultural laws established after entering the Land of Israel provides a foreshadowing of what will be required of all future Jewish generations. Such a reading sees the common law of the people, the *lex terrae*, as truly the law connected to land. The covenant can be binding because there is fair notice, a full and complete disclosure of the burden of *halacha* within the context of a settled society. Judah ha-Nasi, finally, shows the Jews that they have previously internalized a significant portion of law. Allegiance has already been guaranteed through the very actions of their ancestors—Adam, the Patriarchs, and even their own accomplishments in the Exodus and the Wilderness. The Sinai covenant is simply a further step in the process of assimilating divine law. It must be understood as a part of a process, a pattern of law giving activity over time, and not as a unique event.

None of these different approaches alone seem adequate to the task of preparing the Jews for the full burden of the commandments. While all three readings reveal something of the nature of binding legal authority—describing either how it was experienced or will be experienced, there truly can be no full disclosure in the midst of revelation. God, the lawgiver, remained only partially revealed; the full scope of the law's precepts were only partially disclosed. The history of law, the foretaste of just a few legal rules, and even the recapitulation of earlier instances of law giving from a time when they were perhaps not fully binding cannot tell the people what the commandments would be like to experience as an ironclad duty. Listening to injunctions is very different than having to live under their restrictions. Most certainly, the sense of how the law might evolve was not shown to the people. Being aware of the hermeneutic legal methods taught before and after Sinai does not divulge the extent to which they will be used. This is not surprising. For the Jewish people through interpretation will define, shape, and remake the law in their own image.[61]

This book is an attempt to offer a more complete account of the biography of this law making than has been proffered by a straightforward recapitulation of the Sinai narrative. It asks the question how did the Israelites become norm bearing? What psychological transformations needed to take place for this habituation to legal rules? How should we understand the layered archeology of Jewish law? And, ultimately, does the uncovering of pre-Sinai law spawn competing versions of law to the reception of the Torah at Sinai? As we shall see, one advantage of picturing law as materializing slowly over time, is that it allows an opportunity for the interpretive impulse to emerge—an impulse which may have been cribbed if law giving was circumscribed to a single overwhelming revelatory moment. This is a far step from Paul's notion of the law as autocratic. Instead, autonomous human agency is pivotal. By locating law as part of their innermost selves well before Sinai, the Jews ultimately envisioned themselves as able to domesticate a divine written code, bringing to bear the resilience of oral law, the creativity of human legal interpretation and judgement; and a fealty which could survive the absence of a state. No wonder pre-Sinai law, as evidenced by the many scattered references, was something of a preoccupation for commentators.

Nevertheless, the plethora of comments concerning the pre-Sinai *nomos* are so diffuse as to have impeded hitherto their being woven into a narrative. Here the discussion of the *Mekhilta* is of critical importance. Judah ha-Nasi's set of readings for the *Book of the Covenant* can provide a badly needed roadmap to the rabbinic conceptions of the law before the law. These assigned readings, we recall, are "the laws commanded to Adam, the commandments given [to the Jews shortly before the Exodus] in Egypt, and at Marah, and all the other commandments which they had already been given."[62] We shall follow this list of law giving events in their chronological order. However, we are not bound to the *Mekhilta* as an exacting guide to the scope of pre-Sinai law. This study follows the path of later exegetes and dwells on those passages which have elicited the most debate.

Three verses—one about the law of Adam and Noah; one concerning the commandments given at Marah, but also including a discussion of the Exodus laws; and one about all the other ordinances the Israelites were given at Sinai—form the backbone of our narrative. A fourth verse, which describes the commandment to remember Sinai, also will be discussed. In a sense, then, this book is at its most basic level simply an exegesis of these four Biblical verses. But, as shall be clear shortly, these verses create the backdrop for a wealth of discussions taking place over nearly two millennia about pre-Sinai law, and indeed elicit even broader debates probing the very nature of law itself.

The first verse, discussed in the next chapter, is from the Eden narrative. It describes the instruction to Adam not to eat of the Tree of Knowledge of Good and Evil: *And the Lord God commanded man, saying from every tree of the Garden you shall surely eat; but of the Tree of Knowledge of Good and Evil you shall not eat.*[63] Here, Jewish tradition found the first legal command. As we shall discuss, exegetes examined this injunction in detail to identify how God sought to create a norm-bearing being, endowing humankind with the ability to obey, interpret, and transmit norms. This was seen as a raw encounter between one person and one statute. Nevertheless, commentators sought to abstract the idea of law from this narrative. Obedience-interpretation-transmission proved to be a general requirement for all laws. Adam's failure—and the first *exempla* of executing judgment—links law with punishment.

Moreover, Chapter II will look at what it means to establish not simply rules, but a code of law. Exegetes used this single verse enjoining the fruit of the Tree of Knowledge of Good and Evil to elaborate an entire legal code for non-Jews, the seven Noahide commandments. Looking at the Noahide code as an archaic legalism intimately bound to pre-Sinai traditions, we will ask the question of why commentators thought it was unable to develop into a robust a legal system like the *halacha* itself. The Noahide code is both a particular inheritance of Jewish law and a step-child supplanted through later legal developments. In a sense, exegetes offered a common law reading of the Noahide code rather than the natural law interpretation which has been propounded in our own times.

The narrative of the Tower of Babel is explained as a legal response to the trauma of the Flood. In order to avoid divine punishment, its architects sought to construct a system of enforcement where law would be nothing more than simple obedience. This first section, then, underscores the difficulty of becoming a law bearing being. While man was faced with *nomos* from his very beginning in the form of the original command, it was hard to develop the personality which might weave its way between the Charybdis of blind obedience and the Scylla of legal interpretation as an instrument of desire. For that reason, the establishment of a flourishing legal system will await the generation of the Patriarchs.

The second verse includes the phrase: *Inasmuch as Abraham obeyed Me and kept My charge; My commandments; My laws; and My teachings.*[64] Exegetes proffered this passage as evidence of the legal knowledge of Abraham and the other patriarchs. In Chapter III, entitled *Did the Patriarchs know the Torah*?, we will parse the scope, source, and obligatory nature of Abraham's law. What aspect of Jewish law was Abraham said to observe? Was this law distinctly pre-Sinai in character? What did exegetes mean when they claimed that Abraham observed the entire Torah down to the last detail of rabbinic oral law? How did the foundational generation weave their way through a variety of legal sources—customary law, direct divine commands, the Noahide code, and the prospective Sinai code—and fashion a coherent legalism?

The idea of law emerged from the initial charge to Adam; but there is no word for law, only the language of command and punishment. Abraham first evokes the root of the word for law when in the midst of the discussion over the pending destruction of Sodom, he asks *shall the judge of all the earth not perform* [just] *law.*[65] In the eyes of rabbinic and medieval exegetes, Abraham is not simply the progenitor of the nation, but also the father of Jewish law. He must grapple with the same triptych which challenged Adam: obedience, interpretation, and transmission. However, Abraham was portrayed as engaging a dense fabric of legalism without losing his sense of bearing. Abraham put the issue of obedience to rest with the extraordinary subordination of both desire and legal interpretation through the binding of Isaac. While Adam did not have one word for law, Abraham in our verse is identified with a four-fold bundle of phrases for law—charge, commandments, laws, and teachings. Much of this chapter parses these four terms of art.

From this multiple understanding of law comes a full-bodied interpretive power. According to various commentaries, Abraham learns the ethos of judging as an apprentice to God as magistrate in the narrative of the destruction of Sodom, reconciling justice and law, and learning deliberate judgment. In this narrative, Lot serves as a counter-model of how not be a judge; and Sodom as a counter-model of a society grounded on unjust law. Abraham, moreover, is portrayed as classifying law; creating a systematic jurisprudence; probing into the rationales behind norms; and manifesting a desire to engage in the abstract study of law as an idea. Beyond obedience and interpretation, Abraham's legal transmission nevertheless appears fragile. In some ways, this is because it is bound with the overall problem of succession—who will receive the birthright—which bedevils the Patriarchs. Four theories of transmission are customarily proposed for Abraham. He is seen as a link in an oral tradition; as receiving law in a prophetic or revelatory manner directly from God; as relying largely upon the use of hermeneutic rules and reasoned analysis; or as communicating written legal expression. This chapter concludes through an examination of the exegetical thrust behind choosing one or another of these modes of transmission.

A legal tradition for a single individual, even one as remarkable as Abraham, by its nature seems perishable. Addressing the continuing issue of legal transmission, Chapter IV, *The Giving of the Commandments at Marah*, maps how the law was envisioned as transformed from a familial patrimony to the cultural heritage of an entire people. This chapter begins with the numerous commandments concerning the Passover *Seder* in Egypt, showing how the company of celebrants forms a model for governance. However, most of this chapter concerns Marah, an encampment of bitter waters in the Wilderness, where the Jews were said to adopt a form of governance for civil society. The *explicatio textus* unpacks the verse describing the receiving of law at Marah: *And* [*Moses*] *cried to God; and God showed him a wood, and he cast it into the waters, and the waters became sweet; and there He made for them a statute and an ordinance, and there He tried them.*[66] This verse is interpreted by exegetes as nothing less than a kind of pre-revelation to Sinai. Parallels were drawn to the decalogue. Though often half-forgotten as an episode, the people at Marah were said to have received ten pre-Sinai commandments.

What is the nature of this foreshadowing of a much grander revelation at Sinai? Why anticipate the unveiling of the law? What commandments were said to be given there? An analysis of the commandments at Marah suggests that commentators saw a requirement for a psychological transformation as the Israelites made their way towards Sinai. This chapter examines in detail the debates over the identity of these commandments, which the Talmud claims numbers ten, including the seven Noahide commandments plus three others—the command to establish a legal system, the Sabbath laws, and the injunction to honor parents. The charge to keep the Noahide code reflects a backwards gaze to pre-Sinai legalism while Sabbath observance points forward to a charge at Sinai. Embedded within the debate over the nature of the Marah commandments is a discussion of the difference between substantive and procedural rules; the issue of what makes law binding; and a discussion over how law establishes civil governance. Marah also marks the beginning of law in action as the Israelites enact the commandment of Sabbath through the gathering of manna.

Finally, the last substantive chapter, *Law as Collective Memory*, describes the laws given at the very moment of the revelation of Sinai, including the establishing of boundaries around the mountain and sexual abstinence. It also looks at the first law granted after Sinai in order to understand how revelation turns into ordinary law making. However, most of the focus of the chapter is upon unpacking one ambiguous verse: *Only be careful for yourself and be very careful for your soul, lest you forget the things your eyes have beheld, and lest you remove them from your heart all the days of your life; and make them known to your children and your children's children the day that you stood before the Lord your God at Horeb.*[67] Is this Biblical dicta, a simple exhortation, or is there indeed a legal obligation to remember Sinai which should be enumerated among the traditional count of six hundred and thirteen commandments? As we shall see, Nachmanides saw this as a binding commandment; while others, including Maimonides, understood the verse as merely hortatory.

This final discussion should illuminate the significance of revelation for those who come *after* the event. What is the role for interpretation of law after a law giving moment establishes an unquestioned higher law? How does Jewish law retain its vitality and authority even after the stunning immanence of Sinai? What is the normative purchase of memory? This verse requires a reliving of the experience, an evocation of the sense of standing at Sinai. Even generations later, the now *nomian* personality should be transformed through awe. But the verse also permits, indeed commands, discretionary legal innovation as part of a personal transmission to the next generation. One's children and children's children must sense what it is like to experience law giving multiple times through receiving new norms in the course of everyday life. It is the Sinai command which ensures that Sinai represents open-ended law giving, not closure. In short, this commandment, which has had little attention paid to its significance, keeps the law before the law alive.

Notes

1. Robert Cover, "Nomos and Narrative" in Martha Minow, Michael Ryan, and Austin Sarat, eds. *Narrative, Violence, and the Law: The Essays of Robert Cover* (Ann Arbor: University of Michigan Press, 1992), 96.

2. Exod. 19:16. In his authoritative work on Jewish law, Israeli Supreme Court Justice Menachem Elon succinctly describes the prevailing view of revelation as the first moment in establishing Jewish legal norms: "The Torah revealed at Sinai—the Oral as well as the Written Law—is both the supreme value of Jewish law and the source of *halakhic* authority; and everything in the Torah is 'binding on all Israel.'" Menachem Elon, *Ha-Mishpat Ha-Ivri* (Jerusalem: Magnes Press, 3rd revised edition, 1988), II:945, translated as *Jewish Law: History, Sources, Principles,* transl. by Bernard Auerbach and Melvin J. Sykes (Philadelphia: Jewish Publication Society, 1994), II: 1145. For a general

description of this historical unfolding, *see* N.S. Hecht, et al., eds., *An Introduction to the History and Sources of Jewish Law* (Oxford: Clarendon Press, 1996).

3. Judah Ha-Levi, *The Kuzari,* I, 91, trans. H. Hirschfeld (New York: Schocken Books, 1964) 63; trans. Yehudah Even Shmuel, *Sefer Ha-Kuzari* (Tel Aviv: Dvir Publishing Co., 1972), 30.

4. Samson Raphael Hirsch, *The Pentateuch*, trans. Isaac Levy, 6 vols. (Gateshead: Judaica Press, 1973), Exod. 19:10-13.

5. Isaac Breuer, *Concepts of Judaism*, ed. Jacob S. Levinger (Jerusalem: Israel Universities Press, 1974), 277. Breuer's comment may be read within the Jewish response to German idealism and Kant's stigmatizing of Jewish law as consisting of commandments bound to material concerns rather than a moral categorical imperative. *See* Michael Mack, *German Idealism and the Jew: The Inner Anti-Semitism of Philosophy and German Jewish Responses* (Chicago: University of Chicago Press, 2003), 142-48. On Breuer's belief that Jewish law exists in a plane beyond functional or historically contingent norms, *see* David N. Myers, *Resisting History: Historicism and its Discontents in German-Jewish Thought* (Princeton: Princeton University Press, 2003), 137-40.

6. This book will not discuss the rabbinic motif of an eternal, preexistent Torah. The idea of the Torah being created prior to the creation of the world, which may be found in such rabbinic sources as *Genesis Rabbah* 1:4 and B. Pes. 54a, and Kabbalah, does not describe Torah as a detailed legal document, but rather as a cosmologic blueprint revealed only later at Sinai. *See Encyclopedia Judaica*, s.v. "Torah, Origin and Preexistence," by Warren Zev Harvey.

7. An invented tradition is "a set of practices, normally governed by overtly or tacitly accepted rules and of a ritual or symbolic nature, which seek to inculcate certain values and norms of behavior by repetition, which automatically implies continuity with the past. In fact, they normally attempt to establish continuity with a suitable historic past." Eric Hobsbawm and Terence Ranger, eds., *The Invention of Tradition* (Cambridge: Cambridge University Press, 1983), 1.

8. Carol Weisbrod, *Emblems of Pluralism: Cultural Differences and the State* (Princeton: Princeton University Press, 2002), 178-210. Tamar Ross, *Expanding the Palace of the Torah: Orthodoxy and Feminism* (Boston: Brandeis University Press, 2004), provides a sophisticated reading of how novel roles for women within Judaism prompts new thinking about the relationship between legal norms and social change.

9. Perhaps the most striking discussion of the plurality of Jewish law is a classic text is PR 21, which proffers a conception of a multi-faceted law emerging from Sinai. This section also recognizes the problems and possibilities inherent in legal controversies. Moses is portrayed as concerned with the difficulty of rendering practical legal decisions about what is pure and what is impure given the different results from hermeneutic analysis, while R. Tanhum

bar Hailai states that legal indeterminacy has the advantage of allowing teachers to propose competing opinions about the law.

10. Moshe Halbertal, *People of the Book: Canon, Meaning, and Authority* (Cambridge: Cambridge University Press, 1997), 45-71, where citations for the medieval sources may be found. *See* David Weiss Halivni, *Revelation Restored: Divine Writ and Critical Responses* (Boulder: Westview Press, 1997) for a modern exploration of the problem of legal transmission.

11. Gen. 32:25-33.

12. B. Ḥul. 101b.

13. Cover, *Nomos and Narrative*, 166. While not wishing to overstate my disagreement with Cover, I would add that I am skeptical of over-arching legal meta-narratives. Meta-narratives, or master narratives, are problematic in two ways. First, they presume that there is a shared set of intent or values which can be articulated across an entire social group. As such, meta-narratives require an understanding, frequently imposed, of the meaning behind law. Such meaning is often unclear. If it does not reject the positions of a considerable minority of views, secondly, the meta-narrative is overly capacious—being so broad as not to offend. However, in those cases where the meta-narrative encompasses contested values, it may be imposed to curb a much richer discourse. *See* Suzanne Last Stone, "In Pursuit of the Counter-Text: The Turn to the Jewish Legal Model in Contemporary American Legal Theory," *Harvard Law Review* 106 (1993): 813-94. A classic example of the dominant use of the meta-narrative is Michael Walzer, *Exodus and Revolution* (New York: Basic Books, 1985), where he draws upon a Biblical meta-narrative, what he calls Exod. politics, to create a restorative political movement which is also aware of human frailties.

14. Yehuda Leib Alter, *Sefat Emet* (Jerusalem, 1970), 2 vols., I: 5. Alter sees the actions of the Patriarchs as encompassing the written law. Alter uses the phrase *talui be-ma'aseh ha-adam*. *See* also the comment of Rabbenu Baḥyya, Gen. 18:19, "the words received in tradition from the Patriarchs which are not written in the Torah are like the written law [itself]."

15. The traditional notion of oral law as providing explanations for lacunae in the written law may be seen in the opening passage of Maimonides' *Mishneh Torah* I, i : "All the commandments which were given to Moses on Sinai, were given with their interpretation. . . . This interpretation [*perush*] of the Torah was not written down, but it was commanded to the Elders, to Joshua, and to the rest of Israel." The *locus classicus* describing oral transmission is, of course, M. Avot 1:1. Such valorization of the oral law is distinct from those proffered by a variety of other traditional sources, including the traditional explanation that it is the identifying badge of the Jews as the written law becomes the shared heritage of both Jews and Christians. *See* the introduction of Moses of Coucey, *Sefer Miẓvot Ha-Gadol*; or even Profiat Duran's contention that the simpler version of law in its oral form, with less textual controversies, allows more time to engage law in a *vita activa*. Isadore Twersky, "Religion and the Law"

in Isadore Twersky, *Studies in Jewish Law and Philosophy* (New York: KTAV Publishing House, 1982), 201-11. Izbica-Radzin Hasidism poses another example of radical Hasidic reworkings of Abraham's Torah, *see* Shaul Magid, *Hasidism on the Margin: Reconciliation, Antinomianism, and Messianism in Izbica and Radzin Hasidism* (Madison: University of Wisconsin Press, 2003).

16. Philo, *De Specialibus Legibus* [*On the Special Laws*], trans. F.H. Colson and G.H. Whitaker (Cambridge: Harvard University Press, 1985), IV: 289, VIII: 101-2. Ephraim E. Urbach, *The Sages: Their Concepts and Beliefs* (Jerusalem: Magnes Press, 1975), 2 vols., 286-314. There is some controversy about Philo's use of the term *agraphos nomos*. At times, it may refer to customary habits and practices in general and in other instances more specifically to Jewish oral law as a parallel source of law to the *lex scripta*. John W. Martens, "Unwritten Law in Philo: A Response to Naomi G. Cohen," *Journal of Jewish Studies* 43 (1992): 38-45.

17. *See*, for example, Nachmanides, Gen. 26:5.

18. Ḥayim of Volozhin, *Nefesh Ha-Ḥayim,* 1:21.

19. For a similar approach to imagination to the one I am suggesting here, *see* Paul Veyne, *Les Grecs ont-ils cru à leurs mythes?* (Paris: Editions du Seuil, 1983). Most legal history is about law as internal intellectual history—its doctrinal autonomy, and an almost genealogical transmission of legal norms (statutes or institutions such as courts) within official decision-making structures; or, alternatively, it is about law-and-society—the functional or constitutive relationship of law and the outside world. But a history of the legal imagination steps away from the circumscribed boundaries of traditional legal history's interiority and the functionalism of law and society. Instead, the legal history of the imagination focuses upon how law is envisioned, formulated, and represented as a cultural artifact independent of its inscription in adjudicating processes or binding injunctions.

20. *See*, for example, the classic enunciation of the legal positivist reliance upon hierarchy where law is defined as "a rule laid down for the guidance of an intelligent human being by an intelligent being having power over him" in John Austin, *The Province of Jurisprudence Determined*, ed. Wilfrid E. Rumble (Cambridge: Cambridge University Press, 1995), 18.

21. While using *aggada* as the source for a legal history may be unusual, the notion of breaking down the boundaries between *aggada* and law has a lengthy pedigree. *See*, for example, Ḥayyim Nachum Bialik's canonical essay, *Halacha and Aggada*, trans. Leon Simon (London: 1944; Jerusalem: Ibis Editions, 2000). Abraham Isaac Kook, *Ha-Rayah* (Jerusalem: Mosad Ha-Rav Kook, 1984) 103, 4 vols., I: 123. Steven D. Fraade, *Nomos and Narrative Before Nomos and Narrative*, 17 Yale J. Law & Human, 81 (2005).

22. Historian Jacob Katz demonstrated how *responsa* literature uncovers the change over time with Jewish law, underscoring both its complexity and the way law serves as a window into social change. However, Katz focuses largely

upon *actual* legal transformation. What I am suggesting here is a broadening of legal history source material beyond codes and *responsa* to the realm of commentary in order to unpack the way law is conceived. A collection of essays, Jacob Katz, *Divine Law in Human Hands: Case Studies in Halakhic Flexibility* (Jerusalem: Magnes Press, 1998) provides a sample of the methods Katz employed. Steven Weitzman, *Surviving Sacrilege: Cultural Persistence in Jewish Antiquity* (Cambridge: Harvard University Press, 2005) discusses the use of the imagination as a repository of cultural strategies for ancient Judaism.

23. Gen. 8:20. Gary A. Anderson, "The Status of the Torah before Sinai: The Retelling in the Damascus Covenant and the Book of Jubilees," *Dead Sea Discoveries* 1 (1994): 1-29. Anderson claims that the Priestly source "systematically maintains the fiction that the Patriarchs were ignorant of the Sinaitic laws." Jon D. Levinson, "The Conversion of Abraham to Judaism, Christianity, and Islam" in *The Idea of Biblical Interpretation: Essays in Honor of James L. Kugel*, ed. Judith H. Newman, Hindy Najman, and James L. Kugel (Leiden: Brill, 2003).

24. David Novak, *Natural Law in Judaism* (Cambridge: Cambridge University Press, 1998), 34. Cain's awareness is clear from his own admission: *My sin is too great to be forgiven* (Gen. 4:13). Of course, it is possible to distinguish between ethical norms and legal norms, and to argue that Cain was aware of the former, not the latter. *See* James K. Bruckner, *Implied Law in the Abraham Narrative: A Literary and Theological Analysis* (London: Sheffield Academic Press, 2001), 11-50.

25. Gen. 39:9. James Kugel, *Traditions of the Bible: A Guide to the Bible as it was Read at the Start of the Common Era* (Cambridge: Harvard University Press, 1998), 224. In the *Book of Maccabees*, Joseph is praised for having "kept the commandment, and [therefore] became Lord of Egypt." 1 Maccabees 2:53.

26. PRK 10:6. The proof text for Abraham, for example, is Gen. 14:22, *I have lifted up my hand to the Lord* where *lifting up* connotes a heave offering.

27. Rashi, Gen. 25:22. According to traditional sources, a yeshiva existed from the time of Abraham through the period of the enslavement in Egypt and the wilderness. "Abraham, our father, was a member of the yeshiva, as it is said, *And Abraham was old* [*zaken*] *and stricken with age* (Gen. 24:1). The word for an elderly person [*zaken*] is identical with serving as a scholar in a yeshiva. B. Yoma 28b. Moreover, Rebecca was described as consulting the sages of Shem and Eber concerning her troubled pregnancy. Gen. R. 63:6.

28. This is based upon a pun on the Hebrew text. In the verse, *and they* [Joseph's brothers] *related to him* [Israel] *all the words of Joseph that he had spoken to them, and he saw the wagons* [*ha-'agalot*] *that Joseph had sent to transport him, then the spirit of their father Jacob was revived* (Gen. 45:27), Joseph provides wagons as transportation for his brothers. By doing so he also furnishes hope again for his aging father who has long been paralyzed with

grief over Joseph's presumed death. According to Rashi, the wagons (*'agalot*), punning with *'eglah*, afford a sign of the last subject studied together by Joseph and Israel: the *'eglah 'arufa* (the broken-necked heifer). The *'eglah 'arufah*, is an expiatory ritual authorized by a court which requires the killing of a heifer when a murder occurs outside of a town by unknown hands (Deut. 21:1-9). At the same time, the idea of the *'eglah 'arufa* intimates the need to atone for collective guilt regarding Joseph's sale into slavery. *See* also Gen. R. 94:3.

29. The term *panchronism* comes from Max Weinreich, *History of the Yiddish Language*, trans. Shlomo Noble (Chicago: University of Chicago Press, 1980), 208-9. Sacha Stern has argued that the "concept of time as an entity *per se* was alien to the ancient Jewish world-view," and that, unlike ancient Greece, pre-medieval Judaism focused upon events or processes. Sacha Stern, *Time and Process in Ancient Judaism* (Oxford: Littman Library, 2002), 1-25 and 124-28. *See also*, Sylvie-Anne Goldberg, *La Clepsydre: Essai sur la pluralité des temps dans le judaïsme* (Paris: Albin Michel, 2000), 11-35.

30. B. Men. 29b. According to PRK 4:6, "matters which were not revealed to Moses at Sinai were revealed to R. Akiva."

31. H. Patrick Glenn, *Legal Traditions of the World: Sustainable Diversity in Law* (Oxford: Oxford University Press, 2000), 1-55. Glenn presents a theory of traditional jurisprudence across societies, arguing that legal tradition creates a well-spring for pluralism which is relevant today. Part of the project here is to extend a legal historical analysis to archaic law where the traditional is most clearly elaborated. *See* Rudolfo Sacco, "Mute Law," *American Journal of Comparative Law* 43 (1995): 455-68.

32. Jed Rubenfeld, *Freedom and Time: A Theory of Constitutional Self-Government* (New Haven: Yale University Press, 2001), 3-44 and 91-244, suggests that legal systems draw upon precedent in order to establish binding norms which reflect commitments over time. But this creates tensions between the insistence upon recognizing the legal or political power of the past over the present while creating Constitutional moments which reflect ruptures in time.

33. Gen. 37:2.

34. Gen. R. 84:7. In addition to the accusation of eating from the limb of a living animal, the *midrash* suggests two others possibilities: Joseph disparaged the sons of the maid-servants for their inferior social status, calling them slaves, or, alternatively, that the brothers were setting their sights on the local women. The poetic justice, of course, is that as a result of any of these evil reports, Joseph would experience three parallel afflictions. His garment would be torn as if he was consumed by a beast; he would be enslaved in Egypt; and Potiphar's wife would set her sights upon him. James L. Kugel, *In Potiphar's House: The Interpretive Life of Biblical Texts* (New York: HarperCollins, 1990), 79-84.

35. Judah Rosanes, *Parshat Derakhim* (Jerusalem: Yitzhak Ochana, 1995/6), 15-16. B. Ḥul. 33a. I appreciate Professor Ranon Katzoff sharing with me his citation to the Rosanes commentary. This wonderfully dialectic conflict of

law argument has had a remarkable genealogy of its own. In his autobiography, David Weiss Halivni describes how in the midst of the destruction of Hungarian Jewry, a fellow Jew, Joshua Heschel Friedmann, asked him to repeat this comment in his name. According to Friedmann, the tables will be turned when Joseph will later choose to follow the more lenient Talmudic law when he suggests that the thief of his goblet be enslaved and not put to death rather than the stricter local custom. The power of the comment in Halivni's account of the Holocaust is that it highlights the need to understand the suppleness of Jewish law within the context of those human frailties which emerge in difficult times. David Weiss Halivni, *The Book and the Sword: A Life of Learning in the Shadow of Destruction* (New York: Farrar, Strauss, and Giroux, 1996), 119-23.

36. Gen. 37:33.

37. Rashi, Gen. 37:2.

38. Walter Benjamin, *Selected Writings*, ed. Michael W. Jennings, vol. 4 (1938-1940): *On the Concept of History* (Cambridge: Harvard University Press, 2003, 397.

39. Ḥayim of Volozhin, for example, stated that it was permissible for the Patriarchs to erect private alters wherever one wished and charge interest prior to Sinai. Even though these were both outlawed under Jewish law. Indeed, he argues that charging interest to fellow Jews was an act of kindness since it made capital available to those in need. Ḥayim of Volozhin, *Ruaḥ Ḥayim* (Jerusalem: 1993/4), 1:2.

40. Jehiel Jacob Weinberg, *Shealot u-Teshuvot Seridrei Eish*, 2 vols. (Jerusalem: Jehiel Weinberg Institute, 1998/9, II: 497 (responsa 53). Weinberg had to address both a modern sense of linear time and authoritative traditional sources, such as M. Kid. 4:14, which assert that Abraham knew the Torah in its entirety. More generally, on R. Jehiel Jacob Weinberg, *see* Marc Shapiro, *Between the Yeshiva World and Modern Orthodoxy: The Life and Works of Rabbi Jehiel Jacob Weinberg* (London: Littman Library, 1999). Other commentators, as well, fashioned distinctions among the different commandments—claiming some were observed prior to Sinai, while others were not.

41. Saadia Gaon, *Sefer Ha-Emunot ve-De'ot* 3, translated as Saadia Gaon, *The Book of Beliefs and Opinions*, trans. Samuel Rosenblatt (New Haven: Yale University Press, 1948), 162-3. On Saadia's role as champion of tradition, *see* Robert Brody, *The Geonim of Babylonia and the Shaping of Medieval Jewish Culture* (New Haven: Yale University Press, 1998), 244-48.

42. The idea of pre-Sinai figures as models for Sinai legalism may be seen in the Mekhilta's comparison of Joseph's character with the Ten Commandments, Mek. 1:176-81.

43. Not all Jewish thinkers embraced the idea of pre-Sinai legalism. Both Samuel ben Meir (Rashbam), a son-in-law and disciple of Rashi, and Maimonides rejected the idea that Abraham's actions constituted Torah. On Maimonides position, *see* Ẓevi Hirsch Chajes, *Torat Avot* (Zulkew: Saul Meyerhoffer, 1836),

24-28. However, it would be overly simplistic to argue that anachronism was alien to Jewish rationalists. The appropriation of Abraham has echoes even outside of traditional Jewish exegesis. Isaac Baer Levinsohn, an *haskalah* historian portrayed Abraham as a fellow *maskil* who was knowledgeable in the fields of astronomy and philosophy. Shmuel Feiner, *Haskalah and History: The Emergence of a Modern Jewish Historical Consciousness* (Oxford: Littman Library, 2002), 181.

44. Elias J. Bickerman, *The Jews in the Greek Age* (Cambridge: Harvard University Press, 1988), 294. We will return to Bickerman's argument about the law before the law in the Conclusion.

45. According to midrash, Cain married his own sister since there were no human beings alive other than Adam, Eve, and their descendants. This early incestuous act was granted through God's mercy. Sifra, Lev. 21:17. However, later possibly incestuous acts by the Patriarchs pose difficulties. Although Biblical law (Lev. 18:15) specifically bans sexual relations between a man and his daughter-in-law, Judah's union with Tamar, who previously had been the wife of two of his sons, will ultimately result in the royal dynasty of David. To explain this conundrum, the Book of Jubilees suggests that the first two marriages were never consummated, and therefore since these were not legally valid, no incestuous act occurred. Jubilees 41:27-28. A similar argument is made in the *Testament of Judah* in the *Testament of the Twelve Patriarchs,* 10, 1-6. *See, also,* Hindy Najman, *Seconding Sinai: The Development of Mosaic Discourse in Second Temple Judaism* (Leiden: Brill, 2003), 49-50.

46. Romans 4:3-4. Gary A. Anderson, The Status of the Torah in the Pre-Sinaitic Period: St. Paul's Epistle to the Romans in *Biblical Perspectives: Early Use and Interpretation of the Bible in Light of the Dead Sea Scrolls*, ed. Michael E. Stone and Esther G. Chazon (Leiden: Brill, 1998), 1-24.

47. Romans 4:15. Paul's understanding of himself as heir to Abraham makes sense within the context of the Jewish tradition of pre-Sinaitic legalism, and qualifies the idea of Paul as completely rejecting the inheritance of Jewish law. For a discussion of Paul's inheriting Abraham's legacy, *see*: John Gager, *Reinventing Paul* (Oxford: Oxford University Press, 2000), 136-37.

48. Romans 3:19.

49. Mek. 1, 33-34.

50. Romans 7:8.

51. Exod. 24:4-8.

52. Mek., 2:209-11.

53. Exod. 19:11.

54. Nachmanides, Exod. 24:1, however, states that "all these acts were performed on one and the same day," which means that the events described for the fifth day actually took place on the day after the giving of the Torah.

55. Exod. 24:3 and 7.

56. Nachmanides, Lev. 25:1, suggests the sprinkling of blood only occurred at the time of the first covenant prior to the destruction of the tablets (when Moses saw the Golden Calf). A subsequent covenant was performed with the appropriate readings when Moses readied the people to accept the *second* set of tablets. However, Nachmanides claims, there was no need to offer a sacrifice and sprinkle the people with blood, since the second covenant was simply an acceptance of the first covenant. Nachmanides further assumes a special importance for the blessings and curses in the second covenant for these create a greater promise of adherence to the law.

57. B. Git. 60a.

58. Rashi, Exod. 24:3: "Moses wrote down [everything] from creation until the giving of the torah; he also wrote down the commandments which were commanded at Marah." The term *Sefer ha-Brit* or *Book of the Covenant* is used one other time in the Bible, *see* 2 Kings 23:1-3 where it refers to the scroll Josiah discovers during the repair of the Temple. In both cases, the book is an exposition of laws beyond the major body of statutes received at Sinai.

59. It is possible that the tradition of R. Ishmael's reading survived in some traditions. *See*, for example, Jubilees 50:1-4: "And I told you about the Sabbaths of the land on Mount Sinai, and I told you about the jubilee years in the Sabbaths of years; but its year have we not told you till you enter the land you are to occupy."

60. Lev. 25:19.

61. Isaiah 42:21.

62. Mek. 2:209-11 Gen. 2:16. In fact, as we shall see, this verse establishes both a positive grant of authority to eat of the fruit of the various trees of the Garden, and the prohibition against consuming of the fruit of the Tree of Knowledge of Good and Evil.

63. Gen 2:16.

64. Gen. 26:5.

65. Gen. 18:25. Indeed, the one earlier use of the term for law, *mishpat*, comes in a place name. *And the Horites in their Mount Seir, until El-Paran, which is by the desert. And they returned, and came to En-Mishpat, which is Kadesh* (Gen. 14:7), which supports the claim that commentators believed law prior to Sinai had to be revealed even when not clearly discussed. Rashi, for example, offers two explanations for the name *En-Mishpat* or well of judgment. It refers either to the waters of Meribah, where Moses and Aaron would be judged in the future. Or, alternatively, it was a place of judgment for the inhabitants, presumably under the strictures of the Noahide code.

66. Exod. 15:25.

67. Deut. 36:9.

Chapter Two

In the Beginning Was the Nomos

> *And the Lord God commanded man, saying from every tree of the garden you shall surely eat; but from the Tree of the Knowledge of Good and Evil you shall not eat; for in the day that you eat from it, you shall surely die.*[1]

It was inconceivable for the sages that there could be a period in human history without law. Unlike eighteenth-century political contract theorists, who posited a natural order prior to the establishing of a binding political contract, Jewish scholars of the Talmudic period believed that nomos entered the world with the creation of mankind. God made the world in six days as a preparation for human beings. According to tradition, God spoke to the newly formed primordial man within just a few hours of Adam's creation.[2] These earliest words included a legal injunction. *And the Lord God commanded man, saying from every tree of the garden you shall surely eat; but of the Tree of the Knowledge of Good and Evil you shall not eat.*[3] It was the first law, presumably, because it contains a commanding figure, the command itself, and a sanction as a consequence of violation, *on that day you shall surely die*. Adam was, in fact, alone when he received the original divine statute.

This chapter looks at this raw, formative encounter between human beings and law. Adam was untrained in legal analysis. Nevertheless, commentators asserted this first command contained three expectations—for obedience to norms; the requirement to transmit legal rules to others; and, lastly, the mastery of the art of statutory interpretation. These expectations relied upon the rational faculty. Like all other law, the command not to eat of the Tree of Knowledge of Good and Evil was contingent upon human agency. Only through following this triptych would the law be actualized, and become more than simply a voice echoing in the Garden. In this sense, the command not to eat of the Tree of Knowledge of Good and Evil was not just a unique dictate—which concerns one person, a single fruit-bearing tree—imposed in the solitude of a newly created world. It prompted the initial response of mankind to legal norms, and served as a model to define the requirements of later generations, Jew and gentile alike, towards statutes.

By introducing law into nature, a relationship was established between human beings and God, not simply between individuals themselves. Only with the coming of the Noahide code did norms emerge which would regulate social relations. Traditional Jewish sources derived the seven Noahide commandments through a virtuoso unpacking of our same verse.[4] As we shall see, each word in the verse is seen as hinting at a discrete Noahide statute. To the triptych of obedience, transmission, and interpretation, exegetes added a fourth requirement for law. Legal codes should be dynamic, capable of expansion. But these same commentators described the Noahide code as inert law, insufficiently mutable, and therefore compared it unfavorably to later developments in Jewish law. Even though, in the course of time, Jewish law incorporated the basic statutes of the Noahide law, its creative extrapolation of the statutes was presented as a marked departure from non-Jewish conservative approaches to law making. The Noahide code thus was seen as the law of the other—both the precursor and the counter-point to Jewish law.

For commentators, then, the law of Adam was about an initial encounter with law. Adam, it was claimed, experienced the introduction of the abstract concept of law; Noah, his descendant, marked the creation of a first code. In many ways, these understandings of the first grappling with law focuses on failures as much as it does success. Adam allowed his desire to eat from the fruit of the Tree of Knowledge of Good and Evil to disorient his intuitive legal analytic skills; Noah's code is quickly breached since it does not create hedges around its core statutes; and, following the chronicle of formative legal encounters, the builders of the Tower of Babel seek to establish a unified and strictly enforced law in order to forestall the kind of transgressions which led to the divine punishment of the Flood and, ironically as a result, elicit a second catastrophe. But this is not just a narrative of missed opportunities. It should not be forgotten that law was seen as introduced into the collective memory of mankind through these encounters. Abraham, as these exegetical traditions suggest, had his own law before the law. He will ultimately come to view his law against an already existing tableau of legalism.

Procreation and the Law

Was the prohibition of the Tree of Knowledge of Good and Evil truly the first commandment? To be sure, God had previously told Adam and Eve to *be fruitful and multiply, and to fill the earth.*[5] Before discussing what many commentators considered the first commandment, the prohibition against eating the fruit of the Tree of Knowledge of Good and Evil, it is necessary to examine why procreation was *not* the first commandment even though it is mentioned towards the beginning of the Biblical narrative. The brief unpacking of this legal exegetical puzzle tells us something about why Jewish commentators wanted to claim that law was introduced into the world with the proscription of the fruit of the Tree; how the *nomos* of Adam is ultimately linked to Jewish law as a whole; and the methods used within the law before the law to determine the scope of pre-Sinai law.

Medieval commentators saw reproduction as a commandment. But it was generally argued that God's statement to Adam was *not* its source. Rashi, for example, interprets the first divine statement about reproduction as a blessing vesting generative power with human beings, and claims only the later address to Noah, *And you, be you fruitful and multiply*, has the normative weight of command.[6] The Talmud also cites the later procreative directive addressed to Noah as the source for the commandment, but it adds a significant detail: "And there is the commandment of procreation, which was uttered to the Noahides—as it is written [Gen. 9:7] *be fertile, then increase*, and which was repeated at Sinai [as it is written Deut. 5:27], *go say to them, return to your tents* [to resume the conjugal relations suspended prior to the giving of the Torah] so it was given to Israel and not the Noahides."[7]

How do we explain this perplexing Talmudic passage? Why should the command to procreate—founded upon a biological capacity common to mankind—need to wait for Sinai to become binding law? The question here is not whether non-Jews have reproductive rights. At issue for the Jewish exegetes was what constitutes a divine command with normative weight. When does the *legal obligation* to reproduce attach? It made sense to dismiss the utterance to Adam as non-normative since it is listed among the blessings, *and God blessed them* (the verse begins). Just as fish are blessed with procreative power, following Rashi's reading, so are human beings. Procreation represents a continuation of the natural order. Law, conversely, is what stands in opposition to nature, defining boundaries to curb natural or innate impulses.[8] According to this reading, Adam was not obligated to be fruitful and multiply.

The address to Noah to *be fruitful and multiply, and fill the earth* makes more sense as a command since it is linked to two legal restrictions, not to eat the limb of a living animal and not to murder, in surrounding verses.[9] Reproduction is a positive command of generating limbs and blood as opposed to the negative commandments forbidding consumption of the limb of a living animal and bloodshed. In other words, procreation is the affirmative commandment which parallels these negative commandments regarding the foreshortening of life. Noah's procreative impulse, unlike Adam's, is embedded in a legal code.

The rabbis rejected the forthright divine statements to Adam as lacking binding legal authority. While the permissive charge to Noah, on the other hand, had a legal dimension, it was superseded by the revelation at Sinai. In a sense, then, the natural world of creation (Adam) and re-creation (Noah) was pushed aside by a full-formed legal cultural creation (in the time of Moses) of revelatory law.[10] But what text situates the command for procreation within the framework of revelation? Here the exegesis is truly imaginative. It draws upon a laconic description of the Jews at Mount Sinai, a passage not clearly expressing the imperative itself. Upon receiving the law in its entirety, the Israelites were subsequently told to *return to their tents.*[11]

Here we see the power of commentators in uncovering law through even the barest of textual clues. There is no *specific* command to procreate; no parsing of whom this norm binds. The Israelites had performed three days of sexual abstinence prior to revelation. *Return to their tents* quite simply meant the revocation of the prohibition banning intimacy. This revocation is unnecessary since the prohibition was time limited, and would have concluded after three days with or without an additional instruction. With its brusque and euphemistic language, the phrase must hold additional significance. Exegetes suggest that within this private setting conjugal relations will resume under different circumstances. As one contemporary commentator points out, couples which cohabited under the Noahide laws prior to Sinai, were—with the command to *return to your tents*—reconstituted as married under Jewish law and permitted to procreate within a sanctified union.[12]

All the normative elements are present as Moses communicates the prohibition, and the subsequent permission, for relations at Sinai: the superior to command—an imminent God; a sharply defined law—*do not draw near a woman;* and the nearby rule with sanction—*whoever touches the mountain shall be put to death.*[13] The Talmud sees this as the source of the commandment precisely because it differs from the generative blessing to Adam. While Adam simply follows nature, procreating like the fish, reproduction has a different meaning after Sinai. The purpose of abstinence during the revelatory moment is to ensure the people remain in a holy state. But once the actual giving of the Torah has taken place, the law *must* be passed down. *You shall teach it to your children.*[14] Revelation is connected to the generative insofar as Jews are told to embark upon a process of transmitting a legal tradition from generation to generation. Reproduction has a largely legal purpose. Following this interpretation, then, the first command after the creation of the world was not an affirmative one of procreation. Instead, a charge to engage in sexual relations, with its generative implications, was kept in abeyance, and emerged as the first commandment performed by the Jews after the revelation at Sinai.

The First Commandment

Let us return, then, to what was truly seen as the first law given to man in the Biblical text: the command not to eat of the Tree of Knowledge of Good and Evil. Unlike the generalized blessing of procreation—all human beings are identified with reproduction—this initial divine command is surprisingly less universal. It is directed solely to Adam as an individual. Here is a model for how God will approach other figures. His first words to Abraham are *Go out of your land*; he encounters Moses at the burning bush where he is ordered to take off his shoes.[15] These commands to Abraham and Moses are commands of the moment, where the scope of the imperative is limited to a certain time and place, and without consequence for the promulgation of established law. Abraham must gather his possessions and leave for the land of Israel; Moses must reach down and slip off his shoe as he stands on hallowed ground; but we need do neither. The command to Adam may have been interpreted in much the same way: *he* (not his descendants) must not eat of the Tree of Knowledge of Good and Evil, and the imperative is limited in time and place. However, the Talmud sees the command quite differently. Through divine communication introducing law, man for the first time encounters restrictions on his behavior and must respond to a binding obligation.

Quite strikingly, Adam greets the first law with silence. The response of recognition—the seeing of law as mirroring human concerns—demands an utterance on Adam's part. But there is no equivalent of the *here I am* (*hineni*), of other Biblical figures or even the *we shall do and we shall listen* with which the Israelites meet the revelation at Sinai.[16] Newly created man may have been disoriented. As has been suggested, law is interjected into the Biblical narrative at liminal moments such as the post-diluvial covenant with Noah; or after Jacob is maimed by an angel and receives the precept of not eating a sinew; or, most notably, at Sinai where a liberated people awaits entry into their promised land.

No episode of "promise and jeopardy" exists more notable than creation itself.[17] Perhaps this is the reason the command begins with a permissive prefatory phrase: *from every* [*kol*] *tree of the garden you may surely eat*. The word every or all, *kol* in Hebrew, echos the earlier blessing of providing food for mankind. *See, I give you every* [*kol*] *seed-bearing plant that is upon the earth, and every* [*kol*] *tree that has seed-bearing fruit; they shall be yours for food*. Nature—*all* of nature—is to be subjugated to man; but man, in turn, must obey the divine decree.[18] The offering of provisions is a blessing; the command requiring the limiting of that consumption by not eating of the Tree of Knowledge of Good and Evil is a negative commandment.

Primordial Emergence of the Idea of Law: Obedience, Transmission, and Interpretation

From the very beginning, the twin creations of law and man were intertwined. *And the Lord God commanded to man*. Making an individual the recipient of God's command summons law into life itself, compelling humankind to accommodate legalism in three important ways: through obedience, transmission, and interpretation. First, obedience establishes Adam (like God himself) as a norm-bearing figure. As with so many subjects, Nachmanides and Maimonides differ as to the nature of this obedience. For Nachmanides, perfectly following law implies the absence of human will. Primordial man did "whatever was proper for him to do naturally, just as the heavens and their host, faithful workers . . . who do not alter from their prescribed course."[19] Adam no more expressed desire than did a celestial body. But Nachmanides is not suggesting here the abrogation of reason. It is simply that reason becomes completely *nomian*, a neutral compass designed to follow with absolute fealty to divine will.

To the contrary, Maimonides sees the rational mind as a deliberative instrument. Its purpose is to allow the assertion of will—but ultimately the choosing should be for the good. *God made man in His own image and likeness*, where the *likeness*, according to Maimonides, refers to the ability to distinguish between good and evil. It was this moral discrimination, recognized as legal capacity, which made Adam worthy of command "for commandments are not given to beasts and beings devoid of intellect."[20] In other words, Maimonides adds an important coda to the long tradition of defining humankind as a reasoning species: man's ultimate perfection comes from being in God's likeness—capable not merely of obedience to a divine injunction because of his ability to blindly submit to a superior, but because of his *legal* knowledge of good and evil even prior to eating the fruit of the tree with the same name.

Transmission was also a consequence of the first command. If Adam was in the *likeness* of God (*pace* Maimonides) through legal capacity for obedience, secondly, he also engaged in a sublime act of *imitatio dei* by communicating the divine injunction. Here, again, we should consider our earlier discussion of the procreative commandment. To the exegetical mind, God was first imitated through Adam's identification as a law giver rather than (as is the case with reproduction) a biological creator. Receiving God's initial injunction—*and the Lord God commanded man, saying from every tree of the garden you may surely eat,* the word *saying*, suggests Adam was also implicitly told to transmit this statute to others. The wording *saying* is unnecessary, and therefore was interpreted as requiring him to warn his wife. From this surplusage of a single extra word, the Rabbis discerned an obligation to disseminate the seven Noahide laws. These statutes, as we shall see, are grounded upon the same verse. The duty of legal transmission extended beyond Adam's sole direct command to the legal framework of the Noahide code, and by extension to the entirety of law—and such transmission was not just the telling of a single other individual about the consequences of breaching God's command; but would span across the generations.[21] Adam would come to resemble God through transmitting His command.

Indeed, while this was derived from the text, it was quite logical to assume that the first command implied the duty of transmission. For what would become of a legal system if its injunctions remained unknown? The duty to warn was so strongly engraved in the first command that it is one of the few details we know of the relationship between Adam and Eve.[22] Surprisingly, since following custom is so often posited as the counterpoint to reason, Nachmanides assumes a central role for the rational mind in communicating the law and establishing a chain of tradition. The seven Noahide commandments were classified as "rational commands." Therefore, their transmission across the generations depended upon a rational awareness of creation. The idea of God as the creator establishes both divine authority to legislate and a sense of human obligation. Just as Abraham's passing on his legal norms was founded on knowledge of his prophetic connection to God so was Noahide law rooted in creation. In both cases of law giving, the transmission of the source of authority serves as the foundation for law. "The literal reading of scripture [states that] these are rational commandments and every individual who recognizes his creator must be careful about them, as it is written of Abraham [who commanded his children] *to keep the way of God, to do righteousness and justice* (Gen. 18:19) even though [there was no more defined command]."[23]

The imperative to transmit law, however, was made intrinsic to *all* law—not simply to the specific prohibition against eating from the Tree of Knowledge of Good and Evil. After all, the violation of the prohibition and the subsequent sanction of exile would render the first commandment null and void. But the narrative of edict-violation-punishment would itself be transmitted as part of the dissemination of the law itself. Take, for example, the narrative of legal transmission in the apocryphal book of Jubilees, where a dying Noah instructs his children in the law. "And in the twenty-eight[h] jubilee, Noah began to instruct his grandsons in the precepts and commandments, and in all the statutes that he knew; and he exhorted his sons to do what is right, to cover the shame of their flesh, to bless their creator, to honor father and mother, to love each his neighbor, and to keep themselves from fornication and uncleanness and all iniquity. For it was because of [wrongs], . . . Noah told them, the Flood came on the earth."[24]

Jubilees clearly represents an early tradition of the law before the law. There has been some debate about when the work was composed, but strong evidence suggests that it was written in the middle of the second century, B.C.E. Jubilees has been called "rewritten Bible," an attempt to retell the Biblical narrative with numerous alterations; but, equally so, it is a revised legal code, compiling bits and pieces of pre-

Sinai norms.[25] It may very well be addressing, as Elias Bickerman has suggested, Hellenistic claims that there was once a golden age when universal norms prevailed, and that Mosaic revelation led to a separation of Jews from non-Jews. In contrast, Jubilees insists that *halacha* is rooted in particular legal traditions from the very beginning of human history.[26] Intriguingly, the very idea of rediscovering archaic law suggests impaired memory. Jubilees is a work of retrieval.[27] It traces the various laws passed down from Adam (keep themselves from fornication appears to be similar to the Noahide injunction against sexual impropriety); the transgressions of Adam's and Noah's generations (cover the shame of their flesh); and the collective narrative of wrongdoing and punishment (the Flood). Noah's last words are remarkably like the Jewish custom of the ethical will, whereby norms are transmitted across the generations.

Covering the flesh as a sign of fealty to Noahide law is especially intriguing. By concealing their private parts, Adam and Eve conceded that they had committed a wrong in the primordial garden. The covering therefore was an emblem of the meting out of justice much as are the scales and sword of the figure of Justice in our own times. Through marking the transgression of a commandment in this fashion, Adam and Eve—who left no other symbols—established the covering as a tangible representation of the law itself. Moreover, garments distinguished them from animals who are not bound by norms.[28] Clothing in this case has multiple meanings—as an admission of guilt; as a moniker for the duty of legal transmission—the faulty transmission of law between Adam and Eve has been reconfigured as a transmission across the generations; as a distinguishing feature of human beings—the norm bearing creature; and as an insignia of submission to norms. When Noah's sons exposed their father, it was evidence of shameless behavior. But it also may have meant more—an undoing of the sign of fealty, a threat to rupture the transgenerational transmission of legal norms.

The covering of the genitals linked the procreative organ of biologic transmission, the locus of the command to be fruitful and multiply, with the cultural imperative of legal transmission. It served as a token of adherence to Noahide law much as circumcision of the same generative organ would later become a hallmark of the transmission of Jewish law. In a telling midrash, Japheth, who represents the Greeks, and Shem, mythic ancestor of the Israelites, were rewarded for covering the exposed Noah with a garment. The descendants of Japheth were granted the *pallium*, a cloak associated with philosophers, and presumably reflecting an adherence to norms associated with reason; upon Israel was conferred the *tallit*, a cloak with ritual fringes serving as a mnemonic device for all the six hundred and thirteen commandments of the Torah.[29]

Obedience and transmission are not the only markers of Adam's normative capabilities. In a remarkable passage, a mid-nineteenth-century commentator, Meir Loeb ben Jehiel Michael, known as Malbim, adds an *interpretive* legal capacity to the list. Malbim's Adam is assumed to be capable of deriving one law from another, extrapolating in the mode of Jewish legal reasoning to understand a legal norm. Here, we must take another look at the first legal injunction established for mankind, this time with a more exact translation from the Hebrew: *From the tree of the knowledge of good and evil, from it you shall not eat*. In the Hebrew, then, there is a troubling double use of the word *from*, one of which is seemingly superfluous. According to Malbim, Adam interpreted the repetition to mean that he was prohibited only eating *from* the tree's branches—that is, when the fruit remains attached. Since Eve removed the fruit from the tree, Adam wrongly believed, the action could be parsed into two separate actions—plucking and eating, where both together are necessary *sine qua non* prerequisites for establishing a violation. In Adam's flawed legal analysis, therefore, eating was not forbidden if Eve had already separated the fruit from its branches.[30]

Such an approach presumes Adam might analyze the command with the skill of a well-trained yeshiva student. While this seems a peculiar burden to place upon a newly created individual, the Talmud presumes that Adam was endowed with extraordinary capacities. He appreciated legal dialectics and—like Moses in the more well-known version of the tale—was shown Rabbi Akiva's mastery of the Torah.[31] Malbim states Adam should have interpreted the ambiguity strictly. In other words, though Malbim does not use the classic phrase, Adam should have followed the *halachic* rule of deciding an ambiguous law in the written Torah strictly—as opposed to rabbinic enactments which may be interpreted leniently.

No doubt Malbim's comment may be situated within the context of his contentious struggle with the Reform movement.[32] Lenient interpretation for the sake of fulfilling mere human desire represents a moral failure. Adam, who dealt with legal uncertainty, becomes, with the Malbim's polemic thrust, a proxy for the Reform innovators of his own day. The very indeterminacy of the law should have prompted Adam towards *strict* obedience to the divine injunction. Instead, as Malbim implies, Adam chose a self-serving interpretation so as to indulge in eating the fruit. By doing so, he treated lightly the first command established by his creator. What is the significance of arguing that the fall of man from Eden is brought about by a failure of legal analysis? Clearly, man is meant not merely to obey or even to transmit law. Adam, and his descendants, are charged with being fully norm-bearing beings who must construct law through extrapolation of received norms and who must use law as an instrument to set bounds over their own desire.

From Adam to Noah

As mentioned earlier, this one sentence—*And the Lord God commanded man, saying from every tree of the garden you may surely eat; but from the tree of good and evil you shall not eat*—did not only refer to a specific injunction for the moment, but was interpreted as encompassing a broader legal regulation of social relationships. It was said to contain the entire body of the Noahide law which non-Jews were charged with following.[33] The Noahide commandments were addressed to all human beings, Jew and non-Jew alike, who are descendants of Adam and, ultimately, Noah. It is the beginning of a formal legal system meant to govern a civil society. According to the classic rabbinic formulation, these are seven commandments. Six prohibitions relate to idolatry, blasphemy, sexual offenses (such as pederasty, sexual relations with animals, adultery, and incest), consuming flesh cut from the limb of a living animal; bloodshed and theft. In addition, there is a single positive commandment to establish courts of law.[34] Other lists of commandments vary slightly in those enumerated.[35] The link between Adam and Noah is strengthened by the syntactic similarity between Adam's command beginning with what is allowed (to eat from any tree in the garden), and only afterwards adding the exception of not eating from the Tree of Knowledge of Good and Evil, and the permission granted Noah to eat any living creature, but forbidding the limb of a living creature.[36]

To derive these seven laws from our single verse requires a demanding feat of textual acrobatics. In part, it is founded on the interpretive principle mandating economy of language since God had already informed man that he may eat from all vegetation, *behold I have given to you all herbage yielding seed that is on the surface of the earth, and every tree that has seed bearing fruit; it shall be yours for food*, as a coda to the blessing to be fruitful and multiply.[37] There was no reason to repeat permission to eat of the *other* trees in the garden. Yet the verse forbidding the eating from the Tree of Knowledge of Good and Evil includes a prefatory clause reiterating leave to do so, *And the Lord God commanded man, saying from every tree of the garden you may surely eat; but from the tree of good and evil you shall not eat; for in the day that you eat from it, you shall surely die.*[38] No doubt, the command not to eat of the Tree of Knowledge of Good and Evil could have omitted the first half of the verse, *And the Lord God commanded man, saying from every tree of the garden you may surely eat*, and therefore this surplusage must tell the reader something beyond its straightforward meaning.

Rabbinic exegetes therefore found within each word of this prefatory phrase the legal authority for the Noahide code.[39] The first word in the Hebrew verse, *and he commanded* (*vayiẓav*), was connected with a later passage in Genesis where Abraham was *commanded* (*yiẓave*) to engage in justice, Abraham *commands* (*yiẓave*) *his children and his household after him that they keep the way of the Lord, doing charity and justice.*[40] This was interpreted as one of the Noahide commandments—to establish courts of law. Abraham's commanding others implies enforcement. For how can there be a command without a demand for obedience? How might law exist without a tribunal?

The second word, God's name or *the Lord*, is interpreted as referring to a second Noahide commandment, the prohibition against blasphemy. Here the proof text is from Leviticus, *and one who pronounces blasphemously the name of the Lord shall be put to death.*[41] By drawing a connection between the use of the tetragrammaton in both passages, rabbinic exegetes saw this one word as establishing sanctions against blasphemy. The word *elohim*, another name of God, is the source of the third Noahide commandment, the injunction concerning idolatry. It makes an allusion to the passage in the decalogue, *you shall have no other gods* (*elohim*) *before Me.*[42] Like the Sinai code, Noahide law requires the recognition of God's unique position in the world.

The fourth Noahide law is derived from the word in the verse *adam* or man. This is seen as echoing the resonant verse in *Genesis* addressed to Noah, *whoever sheds the blood of man* (*dam ha-adam*), by man shall his blood be shed.[43] Again, we have the case of a later criminal statute being seen as embedded within the precise language of our verse. The Noahide commandment against sexual immorality is derived from the fifth word *l'emor* or *saying*. This interpretation is somewhat more difficult to make than the rest. The rabbis found the same word, *saying*, in a passage from Jeremiah *saying if a man sends away his wife*.[44] Presumably, the most compelling reason for banishing the spouse is sexual immorality. The phrase as a whole suggests that there must be a framework for property law. Through granting permission, *from every tree of the garden you may surely eat*, it implies that certain property is available for use; while taking other property—such as from the Tree of Knowledge of Good and Evil—may be considered stealing. Therefore, the Noahide injunction against theft derives from this section of the verse in its entirety. Finally, the Noahide law against eating the limb of a living animal also came from an extended phrase—*you may surely eat*. The English translation of surely comes from the doubling of the Hebrew term, *akhol tokhel*, and implies, of course, that one may only eat what is permissible. Therefore, there must be a restriction on eating all the forms of food which are edible. The rabbinic answer is that the limb of a living animal is the example of what might be consumed, but remains forbidden solely through the power of legal fiat.

There are other interpretative moves to derive the seven Noahide commandments from this verse. For example there is a controversy regarding the prooftext for the requirement to establish a court of justice. R. Johanan, as suggested above, sees this first word of *command* (*vayiẓav*) as establishing courts of justice.[45] Another view deduces adjudication from the word *elohim* or God. The latter approach draws upon an alternative meaning for *elohim* as judges, such as in the verse in Exodus, *the judges (elohim) you shall not curse*.[46] This is a profound debate. Is the source of the law instituting courts, the command or He who commands? Or, to phrase it another way, is it the very presence of the legal charge itself or the presence of a supreme being to whom we are accountable, which imposes upon us the obligation to sustain law through the authority of tribunals?

What is so significant about this virtuoso exegetical performance is that Noahide law must be established to deal with potential or impending corruption of the very gifts granted by God to Adam. God's image in which man is created may be debased through idolatry or bloodshed; speech, associated with the naming of animals in creation, tarnished by blasphemy; procreative impulses—which were blessed by God—might devolve into sexual immorality; consuming food corrupted through acts of cruelty such as eating the limb of an animal; and the task of guarding the Garden turned into the mockery of theft. In contrast to Paul's association of Eden with a pre-legal past, it is the very act of creation which prompts the almost immediate genesis of legalism. Creation brings law in its wake. Within only a few hours of emerging from dust, according to the midrash, mankind experienced not only the burden of receiving the first law—to set metes and bounds for his own capacities—but also the expectation that Adam, bestowed with an interpretive gift, would be able to unpack the meaning of law as well.

Here lies another major disagreement with Paul. Legal interpretation was present at the very birth of law. Perhaps there was no choice. The very ambiguity of legal language demands interpretation. More importantly, mankind was not only vested with desire—which might lead to the overstepping of boundaries—but with the compass of reason to set limits. On one hand, the intellectual faculty with which God has endowed man, his penultimate creation, makes him most in the *likeness of God*, and establishes the legal capacity to receive the first command. On the other hand, reason, is a trickster figure. As Malbim's reading of Adam's misconstrued interpretation of the first command implies, untrained reason may be used as an instrument to rationalize breaches of the law, and lead to a distortion of the law itself.

Malbim's Adam failed his first test: could he master legal interpretation, and not simple mechanical obedience? But the rabbis stepped into the breach. Commentators demonstrated how various general aspects of law—obedience, transmission, and interpretation—might be derived from the circumstances of the first command. More importantly, they showed how to create a specific substantive law through interpretation. Hanging their exegesis upon a mere verse or two, they exercised such stunning interpretive analysis of the injunction concerning eating the fruit of the Tree of Knowledge of Good and Evil so that an entire system of law, the Noahide commandments, might be spun out of their legal imagination. New binding law was created which would curb desire and guide mankind's dominion over nature. This was more than clever law-thinking. It was a redemptive act itself.

The Law of the Other

Since law is meant to assure "the permanence of this species," Maimonides wrote, God bestowed upon mankind "the faculty of ruling."[47] The purpose of legal norms is to make man into a ruler.[48] But what does this mean? Adam had difficulty ruling his own desire. As the Malbim's exegesis describes, Adam failed to interpret a command in an otherwise static world. Imagine, then, the difficulty for his descendants in applying law to nature in new circumstances. How shall we rule the unruly newly emerging impulses, both erotic and violent, that burst forth when mankind is cast out of the Garden of Eden? What sorts of judgments must be applied in the case of Cain's first homicide? And how should courts of law be devised when we know so little of divine will?

In other words, commentators grappled with the next step beyond Adam's triptych of obedience, transmission, and interpretation—the very expansion of law into a complex systematic jurisprudence. Mankind became a ruler through domesticating the divine decree in the course of a series of complex negotiations with both general and detailed legal principles, often layering one upon another. Such internalizing of norms was a crucial feature of early attempts to systematize and institutionalize an archaic legal system. Sometimes it is the most unprepossessing particulars of law which prove most important for this task. Abstract principles emerge from debates over concrete cases. Law's purposes must be plumbed through comparing how like cases are alike, and distinguishing those which differ, in order to embark upon elaboration. Moreover, legal codes define not simply what can be derived from them, but—recognizing their own limitations—what cannot. All these contradictory thrusts are part of the first stage towards the enlargement of law which came with how Jewish exegetes understood the introduction of the Noahide code.

For legal exegetes, the seven Noahide statutes represented a counterpoint to the codification at Sinai. As a parallel, though vestigial system, it had a complex, often conflicting set of roles. First, it created a minimum threshold for rule of law which would permit the social intercourse between different peoples. It formed the basis of international law, of a rabbinic *ius gentium*. Certain legal principles, such as the rejection of bloodshed and the establishment of courts, were too important to the social order to be independent of an over-arching set of norms. Any viable society must have a fundamental legal framework which overlaps with core moral precepts. It was a form of archaic law, secondly, presaging Sinai and later appropriated by *halacha*. In this conception, Noahide law serves as part of the legal heritage of archaic Jewish law. The Patriarchs, as we shall see, were said to observe the Noahide code. Indeed, rabbinic sources classified the Patriarchs as among the sons of Noah in terms of their legal obligations.[49] An analogy might be made to Norman legal principles within Anglo-American law or, alternatively, Roman law for the civil law system. These legal systems are incorporated and ultimately preempted by what are considered more advanced forms of law.

Thirdly, it is the doctrinal counterpoint to Jewish law. As the law of the *other* against which the character of *halacha* might be measured, it is the rejected step-child of Jewish law. But truly in all three ways, then, the Noahide code is the mirror of *halacha*. What was the relationship between the Noahide *nomos* and Jewish law? How might it be elaborated in much the same way as *halacha* itself expanded over time? Seeing the Noahide code as a counter-model, the rabbis employed the same yardstick they would use to explore Jewish law. The question was whether the Noahide code might be considered what I call portmanteau law, which might be unpacked to determine if as a legal framework it had the interpretive flexibility necessary for expansion through traditional tools of legal analysis.

What of the alternative argument that mankind after its original exile from Eden took to ruling through adopting the norms of nature as general principles of justice? The Maimonidean nod to the "permanence of the species" was said to suggest natural law, a universal, enduring basis for this complex systematic jurisprudence. All human beings, so the argument goes, seek virtue—and there must be some valid and discernable rules to which they all adhere. According to Aristotle, natural law (*physikon dikaion*) and conventional law (*nomikon dikaion*) represent, respectively, immutable universal principles and mutable particulars.[50] In the words of Cicero, who provides the *locus classicus* for natural law's significance, "true law is right reason in agreement with nature; it is of universal application, unchanging and everlasting. . . . We cannot be freed from its obligations by senate or people, and we need not look outside ourselves for an expounder or interpreter of it. And there will not be different laws at Rome and at Athens, or different laws now and in the future, but one eternal and unchangeable law will be valid for all nations and all times, and there will be one master and rule, that is God [*omnium deus*] over us all, for he is the author of this law, its promulgator, and its enforcing judge."[51]

Did Jewish law manifest a similar longing for the universal? Was there a desire for an all-inclusive set of norms which would embrace Rome and Athens, and Jerusalem as well? A number of scholars, most notably David Novak, recently have revived the idea that the Noahide laws may serve as the paradigm for a parallel system of Jewish law governed by natural law. I address this debate reluctantly because it has attracted sophisticated arguments on either side, and these cannot be fully discussed here. Even Nachmanides referred to the seven Noahide laws as an obscure subject.[52] It is nevertheless important to consider two important reasons why this natural law argument fails. First, we must take up the question of the psychological posture of those who have called for seeing the Noahide code as the Jewish prototype of universal natural law. Many of these arguments rely upon the claim that there is an intrinsic need for *halacha* to address universal concerns through broad, cross-cultural principles. However, as will be shown, this demand itself has fluctuated over time and relies upon weak textual sources. We, secondly, must understand how Jewish exegetes *did* respond to the Noahide code as the law of the *other*, and—out of disappointment with the stunted character of Noahide jurisprudence—read this parallel legal system through the common law fabric of Jewish law.[53] Considered through the lenses of the Jewish exegetical legal imagination, Noahide law was seen as particular, rather than universal. Noahide law was unable to encompass the *idea* of law—the ability to marshal interpretation as a means of expanding legal rules—and to develop into a full-fledged legal system.

Why did Jewish exegetes not embrace the concept of a Jewish natural law, and why have moderns been so drawn to it? For, it turns out, the attraction to immutable legal principles is historically contingent. A.P. D'Entrèves has made an astute observation: natural law is as much a psychological stance as it is a jurisprudential theory.[54] Natural law theory is attractive because it encompasses the yearning for a supreme rational law which is immutable, absolute, and universally binding. It is the dream of a common legal language. Ironically, however, this very impulse for a timeless legalism has waxed and waned with historical circumstances. Such historical shifting of fortunes alone should warn us of the contingency of seemingly immutable legal principles with various legal cultures.

Christian interest in natural law and the Noahide code, for example, emerged during the seventeenth century when Europe was engulfed in religious wars. Debating the meaning of the Biblical text, and whether its interpretation should follow Catholic or Protestant exegetical strategies, led to the search for an extra-textual legal authority which would be common among all men. In brief, law conforming to universal reason would replace denominational readings of divine law. English Protestant jurist John Selden originated the identification of Noahide precepts with Natural Law. Written in 1640, his treatise entitled *De Jure Naturali et Gentium Juxta Disciplinam Ebraeorum* assumes that Jewish law, like Roman law, was divided between the *ius civile,* governing citizens, and the *ius gentium,* which might be applied to individuals of any nation. But the date of Selden's treatise, the beginning of the English Civil War, speaks more to the impetus behind Selden's assertion of the significance of the Noahide laws. In a social landscape deeply divided between various sects, in a country torn apart by wars of religion, the notion that there exists a universal legal truth accessible through reason had enormous appeal.[55]

For modern Jews, too, an elective affinity towards natural law emerged as the result of particular historical experiences. Natural law resolves the enlightenment problem of Jewish law as exclusionary. This problem was raised as early as the introduction of R. Aaron Halevi to his *Sefer ha-Ḥinukh*: "If it [the Torah] is meant for the perfection of human beings, why was it given to only one people from among the nations of the world, not to all?"[56] But particularism became an even more pivotal concern for moderns, such as Moses Mendelssohn and Spinoza, who saw fealty to Jewish law as an impediment to full civil equality. If revelation is so important, why should it be written in an obscure language, and vested in an obscure Near Eastern tribe? The answer to the parochialism of *halacha* is natural law.[57] Most certainly, the identification of Noahide law with natural law emerges from a psychological stance towards universalism.

These are its evident attractions. But so much remains unclear. There has been a great deal of debate over how natural law rules are determined. Must they be derived from logic or will divine edict also suffice? Should utility trump moral duty? Look at the *Sifra*, for example, which states that some of the Noahide prohibitions would have been derived from logic in any event, even if the Torah had not commanded—theft, sexual offenses, idolatry, blasphemy, and bloodshed; but not the limb of a living animal or courts of justice.[58] At times the natural law of the Noahides is described, like that of Aquinas, as being dependent upon divine edict; at other times determined by human reason.[59] Moreover, the difficulty of establishing universal principles which every reasonable person may adopt; the failures of those universal principles in the twentieth century to prevent its unique calamities, such as World War and genocide, has engendered skepticism. Most importantly, however, the case for designating the Noahide prescriptions as natural law is not well rooted in Jewish tradition. There is little sustainable evidence of rabbinic discussions of natural law.[60]

In fact, proponents of the natural law-Noahide law relationship have had to contend with a troubling passage from Maimonides' code where he argues that non-Jews must accept its rules as binding based upon belief in revelation, not reason.[61] The accuracy of this passage has been a matter of debate. It has been suggested that a scribal error in one character altered the meaning to the opposite of Maimonides's original intent. Nevertheless, the very fact that so much has to be made out of a single letter in the Maimonidean corpus should tell us something about the problem of envisioning in Novak's terms, Noahide law and *halacha* as creating two parallel legal systems "where neither is reduced to the other."[62] Novak's arguments rely upon the *need* for a system of natural law in Judaism for such reasons as the necessity of Jewish moral dialogue with non-Jews and for the dignity of all mankind. This raises the familiar is/ought problem which bedevils so much of the discussion about law-making in general.

As far as the *ought* is concerned, the Rabbis had little expectation that the Noahide code could become the subject of systematic elaboration, and expanded into a well-ordered code of law like the *Shulḥan Arukh.* Never perceived of as a full-bodied parallel system, there was no sense of loss about its stunted evolution. In fact, such limitations fit neatly with the idea of the Noahide code as a predecessor. To a certain extent, as we shall see, the rabbis and later Jewish legal scholars amplified the Noahide code through applying Jewish legal hermeneutic tools to its basic commandments. The Noahide code assumed a variety of roles as rabbinic analysis was brought to bear on its fundamental statutes. It was a training ground for a much more well developed system of *halacha*; a precursor whose rules must be understood like any other earlier strata of precedent; and a poor cousin which might benefit from Jewish legal analysis. Despite the potential conflict between these multiple perceived roles, one thing is certain. The Noahide code was not seen as a natural law parallel to Jewish law.[63]

How, then, did the exegetical imagination conceive of Noahide law? The midrash calls the Noahide statutes "unformed commandments" (*miẓvot galmiot*) which must be worked.[64] The Hebrew root of the word *galmiot* is the same as for the *golem*, the legendary anthropoid created out of clay and animated through the magic arts.[65] Similarly, the Noahide code seems inert, lifeless, waiting to be formed into a full form. In short, it is mute law. For Israel, God would later explain the purpose behind the law, make distinctions between the pure and the impure, and clarify the punishment and reward. Law—at least full-bodied law—implies expansion.

This is the classic anthropological trope of the raw and the cooked. The developed legal culture of Jewish law would fashion the raw elements of a Noahide nascent legal system into a refined legal culture.[66] Noahide law is a creature of the exegetical legal imagination. It did not in its ancient incarnation constitute a legal system in its own right. Rather, it needed to be elaborated, internalized as norms for each individual, and transmitted in order for it to become a fully constituted legal system. True, Noahide law might have become a system—through either elaborating each general category into a large number of particulars or, alternatively, by identifying the underlying abstract principles behind the seven statutes.[67] But, in the eyes of Jewish commentators, it did not.

Just as Adam failed to embody interpretive rules so were the generations from Adam to Noah to the birth of Abraham unable to fashion a coherent code from such a laconic set of rules. The real failure was the inability to internalize legal norms in such a way as to make law generative. Most striking to modern observers, is that absent any sweeping calls for justice or service towards the divine, the Noahide code lacked "positive religious or moral content."[68] Yet what has made Jewish law so creative for traditional exegetes has not been the abstract or the absolute. Instead, it has been the most detailed aspects of ritual law which have been active areas of analysis. So often dealing with everyday life—the nitty gritty of pots and pans; cultic sacrifices; and Sabbath observance—these have shaped a powerful, self-disciplining normative consciousness.[69]

Most legal construction takes place around what H.L.A. Hart has called primary and secondary rules. Primary rules are rules of obligation, requiring individuals to either engage in an action or abstain from one. The Noahide commandments themselves fit into this category. Secondary rules grow hedge-like around primary rules and "specify the ways in which the primary rules may be conclusively ascertained, introduced, eliminated, varied, and the fact of their violation conclusively determined."[70] This generative quality thus could have emerged in three ways: (1) through the primary rules within the Noahide code itself being enlarged; (2) establishing secondary rules, a detailed underbrush around the injunctions; or (3) creating a powerful sense of normative obligation within each individual.

Let us begin with the question why the Noahide code did not grow over time. According to the dominant tradition, the fundamental seven Noahide statutes expanded only once. While Adam consumed only a vegetarian diet, Noah was granted permission to partake of animal flesh as well. Adam's commandment not to eat of the Tree of Knowledge of Good and Evil, we recall, was related to the license to eat of any other tree. In a similar fashion, the enlargement of Noah's diet was marked by a new injunction as a precept was added against eating the limb of a living creature. This minimal expansion from six to seven statutes hints at the potential of Nohaide legalism to develop more basic laws.[71] Another statute was altered after the Flood as well. The commandment against bloodshed was not changed in its substance as it was reiterated to Noah; but this time the directive included a rationale: *whoever sheds a man's blood, his blood will be shed by man, for God made man in His image.*[72] Such a declaration of aims suggests that the ambit of statute might be expanded to reflect the intent of the law giver. Indeed, the fact that man was created in God's image has been the cornerstone for all sorts of dignitary legislation in Jewish law. Why could not the reason behind the law suffice as the basis for future legislation concerning a broad array of dignitary torts actionable under the Noahide code where, borrowing a phrase from R. Akiva, "God's image is impaired"? Or, as has been suggested in the Talmud, why could it not serve as the justification for establishing legal liability when a person is deprived of his or her reproductive ability?[73]

For a further example, consider the writings of eleventh-century Babylonian scholar, Samuel ben Hofni Gaon, who assumes thirty Noahide laws.[74] From Adam's response to God after committing a wrong, *I heard Your voice in the Garden, and I was afraid*, with voice seen as the equivalent of awareness of his creator, he derives knowing God as the first commandment.[75] Elaboration was part of Jewish law from the very beginning. "How could Moses [at Sinai] have possibly learned the entire Torah, whose measure is called *greater than the earth* (Job 11:19)? Moses was taught only the general principles," and derived the rest from them.[76] The Noahide code, too, could have done the same—deriving from hermeneutic impulses a vast written code and an even more capacious set of oral legal elaborations to supplement the written statutes. This imagined flowering of Noahide law, of course, looks a great deal like the romantic vision of Jewish law described by Cover: "Law would develop within small communities of mutually committed individuals who cared about the text, about what each made of the text, and about one another and the common life they shared. . . . [This is] the underlying reality of the jurisgenerative process in the way in which real communities do create law and do give meaning to law through their narratives and precepts, through their somewhat distinct *nomos*."[77]

The Noahide code therefore was law *in potentia*. New law might have emerged as the legal system encounters new facts. However, any well-formed legal system must also encourage *existing* statutes to be surrounded with a dense underbrush of legal definitions, procedural norms, and standards for determining violations. Here it is important to note, with some irony, that rabbinic Jews, who had more than enough law of their own, chose to ask such traditional normative questions about the Noahide statutes. The *locus classicus* for these secondary rules is the eighth chapter of the *Tosefta Avodah Zarah*. There, for example, the rabbis sought to establish the threshold minimum requirement (*shiur)* for the prohibition of eating the limb of a living animal in a case when the entire creature, in this case a bird, is less than the traditional cognizable *halachic* measure, an olive's bulk. One position suggests that no violation has occurred when less than this threshold amount of the animal's flesh is consumed. But a dissenting view argues that if liability attaches with a single limb, then, it follows logically that the entire bird should meet the threshold.[78] Clearly, this debate in the *Tosefta* is between whether Jewish secondary principles or only those derived from reason should be dispositive for the Noahide code. The *Tosefta* also raises classic *halachic* conundrums such as what happens if a limb is partly severed and begins to heal.[79] In a comprehensive legal system, such as *halacha*, such contradictions are sought out in order to identify the precise scope of legal responsibility.

Most notably, however, the Noahides failed to internalize law. Internalization really speaks to a kind of elaboration of law as well. For as the oral law reminds us, not all legal norms are formal, and established in either tautly constructed codes or defining rules. There must be an expansion of norms out of text and into the very flesh of human beings. After the downfall of Adam, his descendants could have learned about how to establish hedges to circumscribe human impulsive behavior. This is suggested, commentators note, in the descriptive phrase *a tiller of the ground* (*ish ha-adama*; literally, *a person of the earth*) which refers to

Noah in the Biblical tale relating his drunken state after the flood. The phrase, however, also includes word play hinting at Adam, a human being formed out of the earth. Through recalling Adam's fragility and his inability to conform to legal norms, the rabbis claim, Noah should have taken special care to drink moderately. The lesson which should have been learned was quite simple. If Adam's failure took place within the ambit of ordinary desire, how much more might intoxication result in the loosening of inhibitions and the violation of divine legislation.[80]

A telling set of differences between Noahide law and Jewish law, moreover, highlights the third problem, the failure to create a norm-bearing consciousness. For example, Nachmanides describes how under Jewish law, an individual may not decline service as a judge as long as he is safe from threats, but one may refuse to judge a case when there might be adverse repercussions. Under Noahide law a judge may decline under any circumstances. As Nachmanides explains the difference in this rule: "With respect to Jewish laws, if [after having heard both parties] you know perfectly well what the proper legal decision should be, you are not permitted to withdraw from the case without rendering a decision, and if you know that it is not perfectly clear to you, you may withdraw from the case without rendering a decision. But with respect to their [Noahide] laws, even though you know the law perfectly well you may withdraw from it." For Israel "there is the extra admonishment—*you shall not be afraid of the face of any man*" (Deut. 1:17), meaning you shall not gather in your words before any man.[81] To recuse oneself would be to replace an internalized fear of God, and the law, with fear of the external coercion of fellow human beings.

Clearly, there is a different expectation for the heirs of Sinai than for those inheriting the Noahide code. Through its sense of awe, revelation has created a deep commitment to the law itself—even if actualizing it requires self-sacrifice. What distinguishes Jews who are obligated to perform six hundred and thirteen commandments and those who follow the seven Noahide commandments? It is not simply a matter of the number of precepts or whether the underbrush of legal reasoning is equally dense. Most importantly, the core question is whether the law is internalized to create a norm-bearing figure. Again, in order to address this issue it is important to return to the disputed passage from Maimonides' *Mishneh Torah* quoted earlier. The two alternative readings are: "if he [the non-Jew] performs them [the Noahide commandments] because of the determinations of reason this [person] is not a resident alien and he is not of the pious of the nations *nor* [*velo*] of their wise men"; or, perhaps, the text might read "*but* [*ela*] of their wise men."[82] In the most generous of readings (*but of their wise men*) Maimonides posits two ways of knowing divine law, through accepting revelation or, as a lesser form, philosophical knowledge uncovered through the application of reason; but for both he requires *affirmative* knowledge of the law-giver above and beyond simple mechanical adherence to the Noahide code. Compare this to his *negative* requirement for observing Jews. According to Maimonides, "one who acknowledges idolatry rejects the entire Torah [irrespective of other religious practice] . . . and this is the fundamental principle of all the commandments."[83] In other words, Sinaitic revelation creates a presumption that observance of Jewish law commandments means internalizing the underlying meaning of law as divine legislation while following Noahide commandments does not.

A similar idea is embodied in Maimonides' decision that a Noahide who is forced to transgress is not punished for the wrongdoing even when there is no clear and present danger. "A Noahide who is coerced to transgress one of the [Noahide] commandments is permitted to do so—even if he is forced to commit idolatry—because he is not obligated to sanctify the name."[84] Jews, on the other hand, must be willing to die rather than commit one of three wrongs: idolatry, sexual wrongdoing, or bloodshed.[85] From such examples it is clear that less is expected when compliance emerges from external sanctions and courts rather than from the internalization of norms.

We should discuss one more intriguing case where Jewish law differs from the Noahide code. After an extensive purification process described in Deuteronomy, a female captive is sexually permitted to Israelites; nevertheless, she would be forbidden to Noahides in similar circumstances under the prohibition against theft, which includes kidnaping within its ambit.[86] The presumption, not explicitly stated, is that a Jewish soldier has an exemption from the prohibition against claiming a captive woman because they are serving in a war sanctioned by law. This difference between the two legal systems should cast more doubt upon the idea of Noahide law as natural law—how could the Noahide laws be universal, immutable, and determined by reason if in the case of the female captive her fate was contingent upon the religious status of the parties involved?

Not only has the idea of the Noahide code as a repository for natural law *in potentia* failed to materialize, but it has also inhabited a conceptual hinterland in Jewish thought every bit as particular as Jewish law itself. Indeed, commentators have focused upon the fact that the Noahide code is a Jewish law for strangers much as the Roman *ius gentium* governed aliens within the Empire. In his philosophical work *Rosh Emunah*, sixteenth-century Spanish commentator Isaac Abravanel, for example, described the Noahide laws as "certainly not teachings which perfect the human soul. They were enacted solely to preserve human society according to the nature of the times in which they were set down. They are at the level of conventional law."[87] Abravanel is following the classification system of Joseph Albo who defined conventional law as necessary to preserving political society, but incapable of imparting full knowledge of the good.[88]

What was the psychological stance of most Jewish commentators? It was to recognize the need for a unifying set of norms to sustain harmony in a fragile world prone to corruption; to prevent humankind from tearing itself apart.[89] The fact is that just as the Noahide laws were a prerequisite to living as a resident alien in the Land of Israel so was it incumbent for all those who reside on earth and must, therefore, interact with each other. Perhaps this limited and functional definition of law made sense since man had proved to be the most dangerous of all creatures. After Adam's disobedience of the first law came the first homicide. In Noah's own generation, *the earth was filled with violence*, and a different psychological stance was required towards the Noahide code.[90] The natural law vision of a legal system derived purely from human reason (the *what should be*) had to be modified by the Hobbesian realization (the *what is in actuality*) that the impulse towards disobedience is as innate as the desire for virtue.[91] Mankind had shown itself to be lawless, selfish, and in need of strong coercion and punishment—in summary, to require as the central feature of the Noahide code, the establishing of courts of law. Perhaps Noahide law could have been a parallel system of law; instead, it became a dead-end, whose law only becomes binding when it is affirmed during the Sinaitic revelation—Noahide law was a truncated code, a presaging of a far richer Jewish law.

A Janus-Faced Code

To understand the Noahide commandments as a Janus-faced code, pointed simultaneously backwards towards creation and forwards towards the revelation at Sinai, we must closely read two texts. These alternative versions from the *Mekhilta* and the *Sifre* proffer different explanations for what is identified as a failure of compliance, and will be quoted at length with divergent readings identified. We shall begin with the *Mekhilta*:

> R. Simon ben Eleazer says: If the sons of Noah could not endure the seven commandments which were enjoined upon them, how much less could they have endured all the commandments in the Torah! To give a parable. A king had appointed two administrators [*apitrophin*]. One was appointed over a store of straw and the other was appointed over a treasure of silver and gold. The one who was appointed over the store of straw was held in suspicion. But he used to complain about the fact that they had not appointed him over the treasure of silver and gold. The people then said to him: *Reka* [you good for nothing]! If you were under suspicion in connection with the store of straw, how could they trust you with the store of silver and gold! Behold it is a matter of reasoning by the method of *kal vaḥomer* [*a fortiori*]: If the sons of Noah could not endure the seven commandments enjoined upon them, how much less could they have endured all the commandments in the Torah.[92]

Now let us look at the version in the *Sifre*:

> They [nations of the world] were not even able to observe the seven commandments that the children of Noah had accepted upon themselves, and they cast them off. When the Holy One, blessed be He, saw that, He surrendered them to Israel. A parable: A man took his ass and his dog to the threshing floor and loaded the ass with a *letek* (of grain) and the dog with three *se'ah*. The ass went along (easily), but the dog began to pant, so the man took off a *se'ah* and put it on the ass, and so too with the second and third *se'ah*. So also Israel accepted the Torah, with all of its explanations and details, as well as the seven commandments which the children of Noah had not been able to observe and had cast off [*parkum*]. Therefore, it is said, *And he said: The Lord came from Sinai and shines forth from Seir to them.*[93]

There are numerous differences between these two accounts: (1) the protagonists—according to the *Mekhilta*, these are administrators of royal store houses; according to *Sifre,* they are a dog (the Noahides) and a donkey (the Jews); (2) the action of abandoning the Noahide code—according to *Mekhilta*, the administrators were guilty of mishandling the store; according to the *Sifre*, the Noahides *cast off* their commandments;

(3) the result of the action—according to the *Mekhilta*, the descendants of Noah are unable to receive additional commandments; according to the *Sifre*, they are forced to transfer the Noahide commandments from non-Jews to Jews. How do we explain these textual variations?

The *Mekhilta*, I would argue, sees the failure of the collective *construction* of the Noahide code as resulting in a cul-de-sac in the evolution of law. As a legal system *in potentia*, Noahide law should have emerged as a full-fledged code in its own right. But the store house of straw—the material used to make bricks in the poignant account of the Exodus—was poorly governed, and no building emerges. What precisely was the breach of the [Noahide] administrator's fiduciary duty to the king? He was held to be under suspicion. This term is often used in cases of misappropriation, and the implication was that the straw was being used for the benefit of the administrator himself. In other words, the law of the Noahides was functioning to establish a reasonable social order, but was not used to further the purposes of following the dictates of divine law. The failure of the Noahides in the *Sifre*, on the other hand, was one of individual *compliance*. Non-Jews could not follow the injunctions against sexual impropriety, bloodshed, and others of the seven commandments. The panting dog lacks the natural capacity to follow law while the steady (and obedient?) donkey can better bear allegiance to legal rules. Instead of being simply under suspicion for failure to use the Noahide code to construct a new law, the non-Jews have cast off [*parkum*] the law. The verb used here is similar to the one employed for removing a yoke for a domestic animal. It is active, unambiguous, and founded upon the intent to be relieved of the rules which bind.

The disparity between the failure of a collective system of legal *construction* (*Mekhilta*) and individual non-Jewish *compliance* with the Noahide code (*Sifre)* represents a significant divergence about the ultimate meaning of the Noahide laws. The *Mekhilta* suggests a prospective law, a legal system which might have been, if only the royal administrator would have properly utilized the store of (albeit less desirable) commandments. This is the depiction of the Noahide code as a stunted, almost primitive version of the law in contrast to the Torah. It is straw rather than silver and gold. Nevertheless, it retains an independent existence just as the materials of one storehouse are not transferred to the other. The *Sifre* posits an alternative meaning. Here the commandments of the Noahide code are just as valid, but simply less numerous. At the core is a problem of *compliance*. While the *Mekhilta* suggests the Noahide code remains in place (though less significant), the *Sifre* sees it as supplanted by the giving of the Torah at Mount Sinai. Whatever remains of the Noahide laws exists as part of the Written Law. The difference, in sum, is between a truncated law looking *forward* to Sinai (*Mekhilta*) and a superseded law seen through a *backwards* glance from Sinai (*Sifre*).

The notion of supplanting Noahide law, and delivering its commandments to Israel, is expressed in the dramatic conclusion of the *Sifre* selection with the verse, *The Lord came from Sinai and shines forth from Seir to them.*[94] Mount Seir, the traditional inheritance of the descendants of Esau, was conceived as another possible site of revelation—much like Sinai.[95] In short, all the glory of Sinai was conjured up for the *potential*—but lost—giving of the written law also upon Mount Seir. Similarly, Jubilees describes the day of the command to Noah not to eat the blood of a living animal as a holiday established by Noah in order to renew the covenant. Over time, however, this feast day became corrupted until his descendants did precisely the opposite, and ate blood on the anniversary of the command.[96] The date of the feast day was the holiday of *Shavuot*. According to Jubilees, *Shavuot* derives its name from the Hebrew word "oaths" for Noah and his sons swore an oath that they would not eat of the blood of a living animal. The Jewish holiday of *Shavuot*, which marks the receiving of the Torah at Sinai, was therefore established first on this particular date as a consequence of an earlier giving of the law to Noah.

This is a remarkable gesture to the law before the law. Noah's anniversary of receiving the law became the date of the revelation at Sinai. It points to the recognition of loss as *halacha* from Moses at Sinai supplants an earlier system of law under the tutelage of non-Jews as well as Jews. It also suggests how this dispossession was encapsulated in later Jewish law giving, making Jewish law the sum of all earlier laws. If we return to the close reading of the *Mekhilta* at the beginning of our study, we can see how Jubilees conceived of the readings for the fifth day. The *Mekhilta* describes how Moses sprinkled half the blood on the alter and half on the people when the Jews were bound by a new covenant. "They [the people as they heard the reading] said we accept all these upon ourselves. He [Moses] took the blood and sprinkled it on the people, as it is said: *And Moses took the blood and sprinkled it on the people* (Exod. 24:8). He said to them: Now you are bound, held, and tied; tomorrow, come and receive all the commandments." The ritual of the fifth day had two of the same customary elements of a covenant—blood and the taking of an oath. Nevertheless, there was one addition to the Sinai covenant:

the readings. Jewish law encompassed all that came before it. Sometimes this was done overtly. As we have seen, the readings of Judah ha-Nasi included narratives of the law before the law; sometimes it was done through incorporating and transfiguring symbolic relics from the past law giving.

For the rabbinic exegetical mind, the incorporating of earlier elements of law giving fit neatly with the promise made to the descendants of Jacob: *Two nations are in your womb* [Jacob and Esau]*; two peoples from your insides shall be separated; the might shall pass from one regime to the other, and the elder shall serve the younger.*[97] If Jacob would be politically subjugated by Esau, the Jewish people by Rome, and later Christendom, then, at least, they would carve out a cultural sphere where Jewish law would overshadow, and supplant, the law of others. Law giving meant the affirmation of Jacob/Israel's right to the birthright for God says *Israel is My son, My first born.*[98] This fits within the pattern of second-son successions in the Bible. Just as the younger son, Jacob, displaces the older son, Esau, so the more ancient code, Noahide law, was replaced by Jewish law.

But it was not a simple displacement. As in traditional Jewish primogeniture, the Jews receive a double portion at Sinai—both the original Noahide code and the Sinai code.[99] What was an exercise of exegetical imagination became the legal rule in *halacha*: any normative commandment which was given to Noahides and not repeated at Sinai is obligatory upon Israel alone, and *not upon* Noahides. It is implied that the Jews were heirs to both sets of law. However, those commandments which were given to Noahides and repeated at Sinai are intended for both Noahides as well as for Israel.[100] The Noahide laws are a classic case of the legal doctrine of preemption—where a code still exists, but another, more robust set of laws take precedence over it.

Supplanting law, of course, is a dangerous business. In ancient Athens, for example, a brief (*graphē*) had to be brought by a person seeking to replace an old law with a new one. If this proposal could be shown to undermine a fundamental value, this individual might be prosecuted in turn through the *graphē paranomōn*.[101] The irony here, of course, is that Jewish law itself would be seen by Christianity as superseded. While such a suggestion may be speculative, it does not seem unreasonable to conjecture that the notion of a succession of laws may have been a tradition invented by the Jews themselves vis-a-vis Noahide laws and adopted by early Christians. According to Paul, law was "our custodian [*paidagôgus*] until Christ came."[102] Paul uses the Greek word *paidagôgus* which means a household retainer charged with the responsibility of the moral education of a child. Paul would draw upon the idea of a moral law—embodied in both the Noahide commandments and the revelation at Sinai—which may serve as the tutor to *all* humankind until they might be justified by faith.[103] Christianity, however, would ultimately render both codes, Noahide and rabbinic, irrelevant as the gospel would create a universal norm, a "law written in their hearts, their conscience also bearing witness."[104]

I Am a Stranger on Earth, Hide Not Your Commandments from Me[105]

The narrative of law endowing man with ruling authority begins with the introduction of a first commandment to Adam to curb his natural impulses; continues with the failure of the descendants of Noah to realize law in nature through establishing a robust Noahide regime; and ends with the erection of the Tower of Babel, the dispersion of its builders, and the division of mankind into so many languages that it could no longer realize the dream of a single universal law. Let us pause briefly to look at the story of the Tower of Babel as a jurisprudential narrative. For here, unlike with Adam, we shift from a discussion of an individual to society; and, unlike our exploration of the Noahide code, we see legal rules actualized. It is the first instance of the Bible describing the legal governance of civil society.

No doubt the generation of the Dispersion, as the builders of the Tower are known in rabbinic literature, were scarred by the experience of the Flood. According to the Talmud, the builders sought to ascend to the heavens in order to strike at it with axes so "its water will flow." Samuel Edels, the early seventeenth-century exegete known as the Maharsha, explains that this was to allow the water to drain out so God will not use it to destroy the world again.[106] Perhaps the very height of the Tower suggested a means to escape the water which might flood their valley if another inundation was to occur. What must it be like to live in a world so fragile? While many commentators see hubris as the purpose behind building the Tower of Babel, and the establishing of a society dedicated to this purpose, an alternative interpretive trope reads the narrative as a response to feelings of vulnerability in the face of possible divine wrath.

Ironically, the Tower of Babel narrative epitomizes the model of universal law based upon the common principle of banding together for survival. Reading the narrative this way might explain its first verse. *All the earth had one single language [safah eḥat], and the same expressions [devarim eḥadim].*[107] The multiple phrases used to describe shared speech suggests more was shared than simply language. It points to the overarching need for conformity.[108] Absent the generation of the Dispersion was the divine voice which is heard by Adam in the Garden after his transgression; the voice which Abraham listens to obediently, and which echoes within him as he wanders the world.[109] Nor, as we have seen, did the generation of the Dispersion seek to inculcate the Noahide laws—and foster the evolution of legal pluralism with a shared set of norms. God as law giver remains hidden—even in regards to inherited norms. The idea that each individual would judge himself and others—an internalized law where self-discipline replaced external surveillance—would have to wait and take root later in the time of the Patriarchs.

In contrast, the generation of the Dispersion was portrayed as imagining an artificial unity, where in lieu of plural internal voices stood a singular, controlled speech. The nineteenth-century commentator Naftali Ẓvi Yehuda Berlin, known as Neẓiv, envisioned the Tower as a kind of panopticon. From its heights, the builders might monitor the behavior of all those on earth.[110] Human beings would not be allowed to become—as they had in the time of Noah—*the way of all flesh corrupted on the earth*, and risk incurring a second Flood.[111] Perhaps this concern with survival might be seen as reflecting the core natural law norm of self-defense. After all, the generation of the Dispersion sought to compel regulation in a way that echoed the Maimonidean notion of ensuring the permanence of the species by establishing the dominion of human law. They were so sure of their universal law, founded almost certainly upon their conception of reason, that they insisted upon its unity. No dissent would be brooked.[112]

In this jurisprudential narrative, law constitutes the primary form of social control. It was used to enforce a unitary set of norms. As a consequence, the divine punishment corresponded to the wrong, and the world would be turned upside down. A once common language would be splintered, speech would be confounded; the Tower itself, representing a geographic focal point, would be replaced with a dispersion. *Therefore was the name of it called Babel; because the Lord did there confound the language of all the earth; and from there did the Lord scatter them upon the face of the earth.*[113] God did not repeat the punishment of the Flood, leveling mass destruction, since this punishment corresponded to a corruption of *all* moral values.[114] Instead, Nachmanides points out how the transgression of the generation of the Dispersion "was comparable to that of Adam." It resulted from the misuse of the gift of law. For both Adam and the architects of the Tower, the punishment was therefore similar—exile.[115] Nachmanides portrays the sin of the Tower of Babel as a poignant failure rooted in the human condition, an idea echoed in the phrase used to refer to the protagonists. *And the Lord came down to see the city and the tower which man (benei Adam) had made.*[116] The divine gaze sees mankind as the children of Adam (*benei Adam*) who, like Adam, chose to use the gifts of intelligence, speech, and dominion over the material world to transgress.

The punishment therefore flows from the wrong. Just as Adam was exiled from the garden so was the generation of the Dispersion exiled from speech.[117] This may be an even more severe failing in the case of the generation of the Dispersion, a true "original sin." For establishing a disciplining mechanism in lieu of cultivating proper adherence to the Noahide law results ultimately in the alienation of individuals from each other for all future generations.[118] The dream of a common legal idiom founded upon reason, and fashioned from words, became still more remote. Even the site where the tower once stood—so the Talmud claims—now produces forgetfulness.[119] But there were positive consequences as well. According to Menachem Nachum of Chernobyl, an eighteenth-century Hasidic commentator, though the languages were scattered, there "remained in each a fragment of the Holy Language, letters of the law."[120] These fragments were to be uplifted, and—in the form of one distinct legal tradition of a people more scattered than the rest—would be unified again.

Notes

1. Gen. 2:16.

2. According to the *Midrash Tanḥuma,* the entire drama of the creation of man; the command; the act of disobedience; and the punishment all took place within a day. In the first hour God conceived of the plan of creation. By the sixth hour, God had created out of dust a lifeless form; and by the seventh hour, had breathed life into it. In the ninth hour, Adam was given the com-

mandment. Only one hour later, in the tenth hour, he committed the wrong of tasting the fruit. Tanḥuma [Buber], *Bereshit.*; B. San. 38b.; Exod. R.32:1, Adam was tried for only three hours before death was decreed. *See* PRK 23, 1, where the day for Adam's command and its violation is identified as Rosh Ha-Shana. Compare this Jewish focus on law with the well-known description of a ante-nomian Golden Age at the beginning of Ovid's Metamorphosis: "The age was formed of gold; in those first days; No law or force was needed; Men did right; Freely without duress they kept their word; No punishment or fear of it; No threats inscribed on brazen tablets; No jostling crowds beseeching mercy from a lofty judge; For without law or judge all men were safe." Ovid, *Metamorphosis*, Book I.

3. Gen. 2:16.

4. B. San., 56b.

5. Gen. 1:28.

6. Rashi, Gen. 9:7. See, also, Nachmanides, Gen. 9:7. It may be that the commandment to procreate at this point was for this particular moment alone (*lefi sha'ah* or *sh'ein nohagot le-dorot*).

7. B. San. 59b. Jeremy Cohen, *"Be Fertile, and Increase, Fill the Earth and Master It": The Ancient and Medieval Career of a Biblical Text* (Ithaca: Cornell University Press, 1989), 148-49. See also, B. Beẓ. 5b, Rashi loc. cit. which asks if the period of abstinence has a defined period of three days, why must there be additional permission granted to return to the tents?

8. In the words of Pascal, *la coutume est une seconde nature qui détruit la première*. Custom is a second nature which destroys the first [nature]. Pascal, *Pensées*, no. 454.2. Maimonides states something similar when he says: "What is natural is left according to nature, but measures are taken against excess." Moses Maimonides, *The Guide of the Perplexed*, trans. Shlomo Pines, 2 vols. (Chicago: University of Chicago Press, 1963), III: 49, 611 (hereafter *Guide*). Rabbenu Baḥyya, Gen. 1:27, believes that God, who sought to distinguish man from other creatures, thought of reproduction as directed towards divine service. The purpose of procreation was "not as the wicked believe, in order to settle the world, and to eat and to drink like animals."

9. Gen. 9:4-6. Cf. Rashi, Gen. 9:7: "According to the midrash [this precept is situated after the injunction not to murder] in order to compare one who abstains from reproduction to one who sheds blood."

10. According to R. David Kimhi (Radak), the repetition of the call to be fruitful and multiply can be explained by seeing it as marking a new creation after the Flood. Radak, Gen. 9:1.

11. Deut. 5:27. B. Bez. 5b. Apparently, the rabbis believed a similar set of events took place at the time of the Flood. During their stay in the ark, Noah and his family were forbidden to engage in sexual intimacy. God's directive to Noah, *Go forth from the ark, you and your wife* (Gen. 8:16) was said to imply a close to this period of abstinence and permission to resume ordinary marital

relations. Tanhuma [Buber] *Noach* 11. This is remarkably similar to the implied permission to resume sexual intercourse given to the Israelites at Sinai. Some feminist thinkers interpret the command for sexual abstinence as emblematic of gender exclusion at Sinai, and indeed throughout the process of legal reception and legal rule making. *See* Judith Plaskow, *Standing at Sinai: Judaism from a Feminist Perspective* (San Francisco: Harper & Row Publishers, 1990), 25-52.

12. Moshe Sternbuch, *Ta'am ve-Da'at*, Deut. 5:27. The rabbis saw the shift from the Noahide code to Post-Sinai *halacha* as affecting marital status in other ways as well. According to an interpretation of the *Sifra* on Lev. 24:10, prior to Sinai the son of a gentile father and Jewish mother would not be a *mamzer*, but might convert to become a member of the community. If he had been born after the revelation, the laws of *mamzerut* would apply and neither conversion nor any other mechanism would permit him to marry a Jewish woman. Shaye J.D. Cohen, *The Beginnings of Jewishness: Boundaries, Varieties, Uncertainties* (Berkeley: University of California Press, 1999), 317-18.

13. Exod. 19:12.

14. Deut. 6:6.

15. Gen. 12:1; Exod. 3:5.

16. André Neher, *The Exile of the Word: From the Silence of the Bible to the Silence of Auschwitz*, trans. David Meisel (Philadelphia: Jewish Publication Society, 1981), 96-97.

17. Nanette Stahl, *Law and Liminality in the Bible*. (Sheffield: Sheffield Academic Press, 1995, 12-16.

18. Stahl, *Law and Liminality*, 27-36. Most commentators interpret the first part of the verse as permission to eat from any fruit, and only the second part restricting the consumption of the Tree of Knowledge of Good and Evil as comprising a command. Rabbenu Baḥyya and R. David Kimchi (Radak) (Gen. 2:16), however, see both as having the normative weight of command. Radak bases this upon the doubling of the Hebrew, *you shall surely eat* (*akhol tokhel*). Humankind is *ordered* to sustain itself through permissible foods.

19. Gen. 2:9., Nachmanides *loc. cit*. For an example of the opposing position, see Seforno, 2:17, where he suggests that the Tree of the Knowledge (with the punishment of death for eating its fruit) and the Tree of Life are placed near each other as, he implies, an exemplar of human free will. Seforno quotes Deut. 30:19, *life and death I have set before you*.

20. Maimonides, *Guide*, I: 2, 23-26. Ibn Ezra also assumes intelligence as prerequisite to receiving a command, *see* Gen. 2:16-17. *In Our image* (*be-ẓalmenu*) may be distinguished from *likeness* (*ki-demutenu*), insofar as likeness suggests resemblance where there is a set of shared attributes, rather than a shadow-like correspondence (the Hebrew root of the word *image* is shadow). In this case, the shared attribute is the ability to rule through being norm-bearing. *See*, for example, the commentary of S.D. Luzzatto, Gen. 1:26, where

Luzzatto sees the fundamental corresponding attribute as dominion over the forces of nature.

21. R. Moshe Alsheikh, Gen. 2:16.

22. B. San. 38b. According to tradition, Adam married Eve in the seventh hour, and in the ninth hour God commanded him not to eat the fruit. During the tenth hour, the command was violated; the eleventh hour marked his judgment; and in the twelfth hour he was expelled from the Garden.

23. Moses ben Nachman, *Torat ha-Shem Temimah* in *Kitvei Rabbenu Moshe ben Naḥman*, ed. Chayim Dov Chevel (Jerusalem: Mossad Harav Kook, 1984), 163-64.

24. Jubilees 7:20-21. *The Apocryphal Old Testament*, ed. H.F.D. Sparks (Oxford: Oxford University Press, 1984), 33. Interestingly, the description in Jubilees also includes Noah urging his children to observe the Jewish agricultural law: "For three years the fruit of everything that can be eaten must not be gathered; and in the fourth year its fruit shall be reckoned holy, and they shall offer first-fruits, acceptable before the Most High God, who created heaven and earth and all things. Let them offer it sprinkled with the first of the wine and the oil as first-fruits on the alter of the Lord, who receives it. And in the fifth year let the land lie fallow, so that you let it lie fallow in righteousness and honesty; and you will be righteous, and all of your orchards will be ritually pure." Jubilees 7:36-37.

25. On Jubilees, generally, *see* Matthias Albani, Jörg Frey, Armin Lange, *Studies in the Book of Jubilees* (Tübingen: Mohr Siebeck, 1997), 3-24, J.C. VanderKam, *The Book of Jubilees*, 2 vols. (Leuven: Peeters, 1989); J.T.A.G. M. Van Ruiten, *Primaeval History Interpreted: The Rewriting of Gen. 1-11 in the Book of Jubilees* (Leiden: Brill, 2000); Ida Fröhlich, *Time and Times and Half a Time: Historical Consciousness in the Jewish Literature of the Persian and Hellenistic Eras* (Sheffield: Sheffield Academic Press, 1996), 91-105. James Kugel states that the author(s) of the Book of Jubilees "understood Genesis to be a crypto-halakhic work." James Kugel, *The Ladder of Jacob: Ancient Interpretations of the Biblical Story of Jacob and his Children* (Princeton: Princeton University Press, 2006), 1.

26. Elias Bickerman, *The God of the Maccabees* (Leiden: Brill, 1979), 83-88.

27. Joseph P. Schultz, "Two Views of the Patriarchs: Noahides and Pre-Sinai Israelites," in Michael A. Fishbane and Paul R. Flohr, *Texts and Responses: Studies Presented to Nahum N. Glazer on the Occasion of his Seventieth Birthday by his Students* (Leiden: Brill, 1975), 43-60. Theodore Albeck, *Das Buch der Jubiläen und die Halacha* (Berlin, 1930), 34-36, suggests the similarity between the teaching in Jubilees and the provisions of the Noahide code.

28. Seforno, Gen. 3:21 states that God Himself clothed Adam and Eve in order that they not mistakenly believe that they had learned this distinguishing art from tasting the Tree of Knowledge of Good and Evil.

29. Gen. R. 36:6. The garment as an emblem of legal transmission might be seen in Num. R 4:8, where Adam's garments were left as a legacy to Seth, passed on to Methuselah, and, ultimately, inherited by Noah. These robes, truly priestly attire, were worn by Noah when he officiated at sacrifices. Instead of leaving these garments to his firstborn, Noah bequeathed them to Shem since the Patriarchs would issue from him. According to Jubilees 3:31, it is prescribed that "all those who know the judgment of the law, that they should cover their shame." The author of Jubilees implicitly criticizes Jewish participation in Greek athletics which requires exposure of the athlete's physique.

30. Meir Loeb ben Jehiel Michael (hereafter Malbim), Gen. 2:16. Malbim bases his analysis upon Adam's response to God when confronted about his wrong: *the woman whom You gave to be with me—she gave me of the tree, and I ate* (Gen. 3:12). Presumably, according to Malbim, this defense suggests that Eve's act of plucking and Adam's act of eating could be parsed. I would suggest that Malbim's comment may be part of a polemic against *halachic* analysis in his own time. For a different approach to the significance of the double *from (mimenu)*, compare Abraham Ibn Ezra, who claims it means consume not even the smallest amount. Also, Isaac ben Moses Arama, a well-known fifteenth-century Spanish preacher, states that Adam might have benefitted in other ways from the tree, through its scent or touch, without eating its fruit, *Akedat Yiẓḥak*, I: 77. The most common interpretive failure ascribed to Adam and Eve comes from Eve's stating the injunction comprises *you shall neither eat of it nor touch it* (Gen. 3:2), when, in fact, it is only consuming the fruit which is prohibited. *See*, for example, *The Fathers According to R. Nathan*, ed. Judah Goldin (New Haven: Yale University Press, 1955), 8, which attributes the additional prohibition to a hedge Adam placed around his words when he transmitted the law to Eve. According to R. Moshe Sternbuch, a contemporary commentator, this reflects an inability to distinguish between the legal categories of *isur* (what is actually forbidden) and *ḥumra* (extra stringencies often added to lessen the likelihood of violating the prohibited act). *See* Moshe Sternbuch, *Ta'am ve-Da'at*, in Gen. 2:16.

31. B. San. 38b.

32. On Malbim's life and commentary project, *see* H. Rosenblum, *Ha-Malbim: Parshanut, Filosofiah, mada, u-Mistorin be-Kitvei HaRav Meir Leibush Malbim* (Jerusalem: Mossad HaRav Kook, 1988).

33. It may very well be, as Judah Ha-Levi suggested in the *Kuzari*, that this verse is simply an *asmakhta*, a mnemonic device in order to remember an oral tradition concerning the list of Noahide commandments. Yehuda Halevi, *Sefer ha-Kuzari*, III: 73, 149. Rabbenu Baḥyya also refers to it as a mnemonic, Gen. 2:16. For a version of this derivation of the Noahide code, see: PRK 12:1.

34. *See* T. A.Z. 8:4; B. San. 56a. Nahum Rakover, *Law and the Noahides: Law as a Universal Value* (Jerusalem: Library of Jewish Law, 1998). The scope of these injunctions is open to some debate. For example, in the *Tosefta*,

R. Meir states that prohibited sexual relations consists of any case where a Jewish court imposes a capital sentence. The sages add that there are other forbidden relations which are judged in accordance with the laws governing the nations. In the Talmud, other possible prohibitions are raised: *consuming* blood from an animal; sterilization of an animal; performing sorcery; and planting mixed species together or mating different species together [*kilayim*]. B San. 56b.

35. Of these seven laws, only two, the injunctions against consuming the limb of a live animal and against bloodshed are mentioned in the Bible itself (Gen. 9:4-6). Maimonides, MT XIV, v 9:1 lists the commandments, and states that from the "entire import of Torah" Adam was required to observe six precepts (for the additional seventh commanded directly to Noah, see below). According to the Talmud in B. Ḥul. 92a, there are thirty commandments, though Rashi expresses his puzzlement as to their nature. Aaron Lichtenstein, "Noahide Law from the Genizah: The Thirty Laws of Samuel ben Hophni Gaon," *Hebrew Studies* 28 (1987): 113-16. A number of these statutes may be seen as an expansion of the standard seven Noahide statutes, such as an injunction against suicide in addition to the bar against bloodshed. Others, for example the commandment requiring formal marriage with a dowry, cannot be easily identified as falling within the categories of any of the seven Noahide commandments. *Perush Shmuel ben Hofni Gaon*, ed. A. Greenbaum (Jerusalem: Mosad Harav Kook, 1979, 52-58 (Gen. 34:12).

36. R. Levi ben Gershom, (hereafter Ralbag), Gen. 9:4, suggests that the prohibition against eating the limb of a living creature, which was transmitted first to Adam, was later explicitly repeated to Noah because he was now granted permission to consume animal flesh.

37. Gen. 1:29.

38. Gen. 2:16.

39. B. San. 56b. For a slight variation in deriving these laws, *see* Rabbenu Bahyya, Gen. 2:17.

40. Gen. 18:19.

41. Lev. 24:16.

42. Exod. 20:3.

43. Gen. 9:6.

44. Jeremiah 3:1.

45. B. San. 56b. R. Johanan connects the Hebrew word in this passage for command, *vayiẓav*, with the passage in Gen. 18:16 where Abraham is commanded to do justice (*yeẓaveh*).

46. Exod. 22:27.

47. Maimonides, *Guide,* II, 40 3, 82. David Novak, *The Image of the Non-Jew in Judaism: An Historical and Constructive Study of the Noahide Laws* (Queenston, Ontario: Edwin Mellon Press, 1983), 290-94.

48. Malbim observes that the making of man in God's image [*be-ẓelem elohim*] entails making man a ruler in his microcosm—capable of altering nature—just as God may do so for the entire world. Malbim, Gen. 1:27.

49. B. Ḥul. 100b.

50. Aristotle, *Nicomachaean Ethics*, trans. Terence Irwin (Indianapolis: Hackett Publishing Company, 1985), 133-36.

51. Cicero, *De Res Publica*, XXII, 211.

52. Moses ben Naḥman, *Torat ha-Shem Temimah* in *Kitvei Rabbenu Moshe ben Naḥman*, ed. Ḥayim Dov Chevel. (Jerusalem: Mossad Harav Kook, 1984), 163-64.

53. Jewish law also establishes the sense of the legal other through asymmetrical rules which treat non-Jews differently in certain discrete legal situations. *See* Steven D. Fraade, "Navigating the Anomalous: Non-Jews at the Intersection of Early Rabbinic Law and Narrative," in *The Other in Jewish Thought and History" Constructions of Jewish Culture and Identity*, eds. Laurence J. Silberstein and Robert L. Cohen (New York: New York University Press, 1994), 145-65.

54. A.P. D'Entrèves, *Natural Law: An Introduction to Legal Philosophy*. (London: Hutchinson's University Library, 1951), 12-13.

55. On Selden and his relationship to seventeenth-century Hebraism, *see* Adam Sutcliffe, *Judaism and Enlightenment* (Cambridge: Cambridge University Press, 2003), 46-49. Rosenblatt, Jason. *Renaissance England's Chief Rabbi: John Selden* (Oxford: Oxford University Press, 2006).

56. Aaron Halevi, *Sefer ha-Ḥinukh* (Jerusalem: Eshkol, 1977/8), introduction (Citations to *Sefer ha-Ḥinukh* are otherwise according to the number of the Commandment). Responding to this question, the *Sefer ha-Ḥinukh* claims that all moves towards perfection engender the selection of a chosen portion, and he draws the analogy between the special status of Levites among Jews—he himself was a Levite—and the role of Jews among the nations. Interestingly, the seven Noahide laws are considered part of this process by establishing a distinction between humankind and all other living creatures.

57. Mendelssohn seeks to resolve the problem by distinguishing between national legislation revealed at Sinai and non-legal universal religious truths which were not. Moses Mendelssohn, *Jerusalem or On Religious Power and Judaism*, transl. Allan Arkush (Hanover: Brandeis University Press, 1983), 97-100. Mendelssohn, especially, was troubled by the problem of Jewish legal particularism. See his impassioned letter to Jacob Emden: "These things are more difficult for me than flinty rock. Should all the dwellers on earth, from the East to the West, other than ourselves . . . be an object of condemnation to all human beings if they do not believe in the Torah, which was given as an inheritance only to the Congregation of Jacob?" Quoted in Steven S. Schwartzchild, "Do Noachites Have to Believe in Revelation? A Passage in Dispute Between Maimonides, Spinoza, Mendelssohn, and Hermann Cohen: A

Contribution to a Jewish View of Natural Law," in *Pursuit of the Ideal: Jewish Writings of Steven Schwarzschild*, ed. Menachem Kellner (Albany: State University of New York Press, 1990), 36.

58. Sifra, 9, 10. Also, B. Eruv. 100b, "If the Torah had not been given we could have learned modesty from the cat, aversion to robbery from the ant, chastity from the dove, and sexual mores from the rooster."

59. Anthony J. Kisska, *Aquinas's Theory of Natural Law: An Analytic Reconstruction* (Oxford: Clarendon Press, 1996), 84-89. Of course, divine commands must be in accord with the reason.

60. J. David Bleich, "Judaism and Natural Law," *The Jewish Law Annual* 7 (1988): 5-42. In fact, the notion that there might be a separate system of natural law in Jewish law founded upon Noahide law does not appear in rabbinic sources, but in the New Testament. Paul borrows from classical sources the idea of "precepts carried out by the light of nature." Romans 2:14. The Apostolic Decree (Acts 15:20, 28) appears to include a version of three of the Noahide prohibitions: idolatry, consuming the flesh of an animal (in this case one which has been smothered), and sexual violations.

61. Maimonides, MT XIV, v 8:11: Any person [non-Jew] who accepts the Seven Commandments and observes them scrupulously is one of the pious of the nations of the world and he possesses a share in the world to come. But this is [only] if he accepts them and performs them because God commanded them in the Torah and made known to us through Moses, our teacher, that their observance had been enjoined previously upon the descendants of Noah. However, if he performs them because of the determinations of reason [*hekhra ha-da'at*] this [person] is not a *ger toshav* [resident alien] and he is not of the pious of the nations nor of their wise men. Maimonides' statement denies a legal system predicated upon reason. Some have suggested that this text contains a scribal error, and that "nor of their wise men" [*velo meḥakhamekhem*] should read "but of their scholars" [*ela meḥakhamekhem*]. *Encyclopedia Talmudit*, VI, 290, note 11 for these readings. Abraham Isaac Kook *Iggerot Reiyah*, I, no. 89. The manuscript of the MT in the Bodleian Library reads "but [*ela*] of their scholars." Schwartzchild, "Do Noachites Have to Believe in Revelation?," 29-59. *See*, also, Katz, *Exclusiveness and Tolerance*, 175ff. Bleich, Judaism and Natural Law, 9.

62. Novak. *The Image of the Non-Jew*. Novak addresses in detail the relationship between Jewish and Noahide law, discussing whether Noahide legalism is transcended by *halacha* or whether Jewish law must be seen as moving towards a greater universalism. Novak's argument continues a line of argumentation from Elijah Benamozegh calling for the establishment of a "*loi universelle*." See, Elijah Benamozegh, *Israël et l'Humanité: Etude sur le problème de la religion universelle et sa solution* (Paris: Ernest Leroux, 1914), 458-528.

63. Exod. R. 30:9 compares the slow enlargement of commandments to the Noahide code to a monarch slowly adding of one dish after another. First,

Adam is granted six commandments; Noah's code consists of seven statutes when he is also commanded not to eat the limb of a living animal; Abraham is granted an eighth injunction concerning circumcision; and Jacob is enjoined with a ninth commandment not to eat the sinew of the thigh. However, for Israel—the son of the monarch—he sets the entire table.

64. Exod. R. 30:9.

65. *Golem* may be used to refer to the amorphous phase of an embryo. Moshe Idel, *Golem: Jewish Magical and Mystical Traditions on the Artificial Anthropoid* (Albany: State University of New York Press, 1990), 36-37.

66. Claude Lévi-Strauss, *The Raw and the Cooked*, trans. John and Doreen Weightman (New York: Harper & Row, 1970), 335-37.

67. See Aaron of Barcelona, *Sefer ha-Ḥinukh* 424 (Deut. 5:18), where he identifies Noahide laws as general categories containing particulars. Aaron Lichtenstein, Rosh Yeshiva of Yeshivat Gush Etzion has sought to do precisely this by comparing the seven Noahide laws with the 613 commandments traditionally enumerated for Jewish law, and determining how many of the Jewish commandments might fall under each Noahide precept. He identifies, for example, sixteen Jewish commandments classified as theft; ten Jewish commandments as sexual prohibitions; and nineteen requiring the establishment of courts of justice. Aaron Lichtenstein, *The Seven Laws of Noah* (New York: Berman Books, 1981), 89-103.

68. Gerald J. Blidstein, "Rabbinic Judaism and General Culture: Normative Discussion and Attitudes," in *Judaism's Encounter with Other Cultures: Rejection or Integration* (Jerusalem: Jason Aronson, 1997), 28.

69. *See* Yeshayahu Leibowitz, *Judaism, Human Values, and the Jewish State*, ed. Eliezer Goldman (Cambridge: Harvard University Press, 1992), 3-29.

70. H.L.A. Hart, *The Concept of Law* (Oxford: Oxford University Press, 1961), 77-96; Melvin Aaron Eisenberg, *The Nature of the Common Law* (Cambridge: Harvard University Press, 1988), 146-51. The absence of procedural rules is also notable. More robust conceptions of natural law, as Lon Fuller has suggested, require as a precondition various procedural norms concerning the making and interpreting of law. Lon Fuller, *The Morality of Law* (New Haven: Yale University Press, 1969).

71. In Jewish tradition, Noah's right to eat flesh is seen as an expansion of Adam's original vegetarian diet since *And God said* [to Adam], *Behold I have given you every herb yielding, which is upon the face of all the earth, and every tree, in which is the fruit of a tree yielding seed—to you it shall be for food* (Gen. 1:29). As a consequence, the seventh Noahide injunction against eating the limb of a living animal now became applicable. Maimonides, MT XIV, v 9:1. On Adam receiving six commandments, *see* PRK 12:1. This explains why the code is called Noahide, rather than being attributed to Adam, since it is only under Noah that it comes to its full seven-injunction form. Another explanation might be that Noah is the most recent progenitor common to all humanity.

72. Gen. 9:6.

73. *See* Lev. R. 34, 3 where Hillel cites this verse as requiring hygiene. See R. Akiva's statement in T. Yev. 8:7 where preventing reproduction is equated with spilling blood. B. Yev. 63b.

74. Samuel ben Hofni, *Treatise on the Commandments* in David E. Sklare, *Samuel ben Hofni Gaon and his Cultural World: Texts and Studies* (Leiden: E.J. Brill, 1996), 213. *Perush Shmuel ben Ḥofni Gaon*, ed. A. Greenbaum (Jerusalem: Mosad Ha-Rav Kook, 1979, 52-58 (Gen. 34:12). The reference to thirty Noahide laws, *see* B. Ḥul. 92a-b. In his introduction to the Talmud, R. Nissim Gaon (found at the beginning of Tractate *Berakhot* in the Vilna edition), envisions just such an enlargement, claiming there were as many as thirty Noahide commandments added prior to the revelation at Sinai. Rakover, *Law of the Noahides*, 13, n. 15.

75. Gen. 3:10; Sklare, *Samuel ben Ḥofni Gaon*, 214.

76. Tanḥuma 16.

77. Cover, *Nomos and Narrative*, 139.

78. T. A.Z. 8:6. Also, B. Ḥul. 102a on the standard of an olive's bulk for violating the prohibition against consuming the limb of a living creature.

79. *Ibid.*

80. B. San. 70a. *And Noah, the tiller of ground, planted a vineyard* (Gen. 9:20). On Noah's being debased due to his failure to learn the lesson of Adam, see the comment of Rashi loc. cit.

81. Nachmanides, Gen. 34:13. *See* B. San. 6b. This follows the comment of Johanan ben Zakkai on his deathbed: "May it be God's will that the fear of God be as real for you as the fear of a human being." B. Ber. 28b.

82. Maimonides, MT XIV, v, 8:11.

83. Maimonides, MT I, iv, 2:4. See also Maimonides, *Guide of the Perplexed,* III, 29.

84. Maimonides, MT XIV, v, 10:2.

85. B. San. 74a specifying idol worship, illicit sexual relations, and murder as the grounds upon which the one should suffer death rather than be compelled to commit a transgression.

86. *Sifre Devarim, piska* 76; T. A.Z. 8:5. It appears from the Tosefta that while sexual access to the captive woman remains prohibited to the Noahide under the category of theft, even among Jews it was permitted only to the generation that conquered the land.

87. Isaac Abravanel, *Rosh Emunah* [Konigsberg ed.] (Jerusalem: 1996/97), 16. Isaac Abravanel, *Principles of Faith*, trans. Menachem Marc Kellner (London: Littman Library, 1982), 123.

88. Joseph Albo, *Sefer Ha-Ikkarim, Book of Principles*, trans. Isaac Husik (Philadelphia: Jewish Publication Society, 1929), I: 81.

89. As it says in Lev. R., 9:3 *derech ereẓ*, or the customary way of life, preceded the giving of the Torah for twenty-six generations from Adam to

Sinai. The source for this idea is the passage, *to guard the way* [*derekh*] *to the Tree of Life* (Gen. 3:34), which describes the guarding of the Garden when Adam and Eve are cast into exile. In this image, the Tree of Life refers to the Torah. The sanctions emerging from the punishment of Adam serve to guard mankind until the coming of the Torah.

90. Gen. 6:11.

91. Thomas Hobbes, *Leviathan*, ed. Richard Tuck (Cambridge: Cambridge University Press, 1991), 37-46; R.S. White, *Natural Law in English Renaissance Literature* (Cambridge: Cambridge University Press, 1996), 12-16, 243-51.

92. Mek. 2:235-36. My commentary on the *Mekhilta* text and its parallel in the *Sifre* owes much to an excellent study, Steven D. Fraade, *From Tradition to Commentary: Torah and its Interpretation in the Midrash Sifre to Deuteronomy* (Albany: State University of New York Press, 1991), 33-35.

93. *Sifre Devarim, piska* 343 (Hammer); Finkelstein, 396-7. Two *leket* is the equivalent of 30 *se'ah.*

94. Deut. 33:2.

95. Mount Seir is derived from word hairy, see Gen. 25:24. In the Mek., 2:5 God offers to give the Torah on Mount Seir (traditional home of the descendants of Esau) and Mount Paran (traditional home of the descendants of Ishmael), but both reject the burden of additional commandments.

96. R.H. Charles, *The Book of Jubilees or the Little Genesis* (London: Adam and Charles Black, 1902, 6: 17-19; James L. Kugel, *The Bible as It Was* (Cambridge: Harvard University Press, 1997), 412-14. Indeed, three events were said to take place during this day—the acceptance of the Noahide code; Abraham renewed the festival through the Covenant Between the Pieces (Jubilees 14:19-20); and the Sinai Covenant. It is suggested that the sprinkling of blood during the Sinai Covenant may be linked to the covenant made by Noah and his sons on that same day "not to eat any blood that was in any fleshy." Jubilees 6, 10.

97. Gen. 25:23.

98. Exod. 4:22.

99. As part of a polemic against those having argued for the superseding of Jewish law from Sinai, R. Saadia Gaon denies that Mount Seir and Mount Sinai are two separate mountains; but considers them different parts of one mountain which point in different directions. Clearly, he is responding to debates concerning the shift in tense in the verse so Mount Seir may be interpreted by non-Jews as coming after Sinai. Saadia Gaon, *Emunot ve-De'ot*, ed. Joseph Kafach (Jerusalem: Makhon Mishnat Ha-Rambam, 1994/5), 137-38.

100. B. San. 59a. See for this evocation of supplanting: *And Edom shall be dispossed, and Seir's enemies shall inherit her, yea, Israel shall triumph* (Num. 24:18).

101. J.M. Kelly, *A Short History of Western Legal Theory* (Oxford: Oxford University Press, 1992), 11.

102. Galatians 3:24. See J. Louis Martyn, *Galatians: A New Translation with Introduction and Commentary* [*Anchor Bible*] (New York: Doubleday1998), 352-70.

103. Alan F. Segal. *Paul the Convert: The Apostolate and Apostasy of Saul the Pharisee* (New Haven: Yale University Press, 1990), 195-201.

104. Romans 2:15.

105. Psalms 119:19.

106. B. San. 109a.

107. Gen. 11:1. On the contrary, Samuel David Luzzatto (Shadal), *loc.cit.*, suggests these two phrases are simply synonyms.

108. Sternbuch, *Ta'am ve-Da'at*, Gen. 11:5. *Eliyahu Zuta* 190, suggests that God at first intended to give humanity seventy languages, one for each of the peoples of the world; but he changed his mind and instead directed them to speak one language.

109. Gen. 3:19; Gen. 22:18, *because you* [Abraham] *listened to my voice* after the binding of Isaac, Abraham was rewarded with receiving further law.

110. Naftali Ẓevi Yehudah Berlin (Neẓiv), *Ha-Amek Ha-Davar*, Gen. 11:1-9. Jeremy Bentham, *The Panopticon Writings*, ed. Miran Božіvič (London: Verso, 1995), 29-96.

111. Gen. 6:12.

112. Gen. 11:1-9. *See,* Neẓiv loc. cit.

113. Gen. 11:9.

114. Tanḥuma [Buber], *Noah*, 2.

115. Nachmanides, Gen. 11:2. Bezalel Safran, "Rabbi Azriel and Nachmanides: Two Views of the Fall of Man," in Isadore Twersky, *Rabbi Moses Nachmanides (Ramban): Explorations in his Religious and Literary Virtuosity* (Cambridge: Harvard University Press, 1983), 75-106.

116. Gen. 11:5.

117. Such an approach would make sense to Nachmanides who treats punishment and expulsion as the centerpiece of the creation narrative—rather than the manifestation of the physical world itself—because this is a paradigm for the Jewish relationship with the land of Israel. If the Jews properly fulfill the commandments, they may remain in the land of Israel. Otherwise, like Adam, they shall be expelled. Nachmanides' comment is one of a number of responses to the problem of why a legal code begins with a description of the creation of the natural world.

118. The connection between the division of language and original sin, see: Gershom Scholem letter to Werner Kraft, 3 August 1917, Anthony David Skinner, *Gershom Scholem: A Life in Letters 1914-1982* (Cambridge: Harvard University Press, 2002), 50-52.

119. B. San. 109a.

120. Menaḥem, Naḥum of Chernobyl, *Meor 'Enayim* (Square: Meor ha-Torah, 1993/4), 27. The correspondence of the post-Babel dispersion and the

election of Israel is also implied Rashi's understanding of the verse: *He set the borders of the peoples; for the number of the children of Israel* (Deut. 32:8). For Rashi, this suggests the correspondence between the seventy languages of the nations and the seventy souls (descendants of Jacob) who went down to Egypt.

Chapter Three

Did the Patriarchs Know the Torah?

Inasmuch as Abraham obeyed Me and kept My charge; My commandments; My laws; and My teachings.[1]

Abraham serves as the paradigm for the internalization of law precisely because he became norm-bearing without possessing a written code founded upon revelation. Simeon ben Halafta observes, this means undertaking a surplus of duties and obligations beyond those of the other descendants of Adam: "If you have [earned the] merit of upholding the words of Torah, you will be referred to [in the same way] as Abraham, Isaac, and Jacob, who upheld the Torah and were called *men* [*ishim,* meaning *distinguished men*]. If not, you will be called not *men*, but *mankind* [*bnei Adam*], like Adam, who did not uphold the Torah and was banished from the Garden of Eden."[2] *Bnei Adam*, as we recall, was the language applied both in the narrative of Adam's interpretive failure and after the collapse of the Tower of Babel.

To be sure, Abraham's emergence may be seen as a response to God's disappointment with Adam and Noah. A midrash compares Abraham's fealty to the law as comparable to the obedience of a devoted wife. "*Grace is deceitful and beauty is vain; but a woman that fears the Lord, she shall be praised* (Prov. 31:30). *Grace is deceitful*—Noah's grace proved deceitful, *Noah found grace in the eyes of the Lord* (Gen. 6:8). *And beauty is vain.* Adam's beauty [the perfect form of primordial man] proved vain."[3] Abraham's inward fealty to Torah forms the completion of the passage: because he is God's betrothed who *fears the Lord.*

In the eyes of commentators, Abraham's status rests upon being the first to become aware of God's unitary nature—and to respond by obeying a unitary law; to withstand ten tests whereby he places what is most dear to him (*take your son, your only son, Isaac, whom you love, and go to the land of Moriah, and offer him there as a burnt offering*) at risk; to commune with God through frequent prophetic moments and established covenants.[4] It may be possible to view Abraham's unparalleled obedience to God in submitting his son as a burnt offering as the ultimate stage in the fulfillment of the obligation to obey divine law—with all other deference to the commandments flowing from this act of self-sacrifice.

From another perspective, however, becoming a norm-bearing being is a long and arduous process. No sudden transformations take place on the roads to either Mount Moriah or Damascus. According to this view, the binding of Isaac marks a preliminary stage towards the development of legal consciousness; where its obedience must be augmented over time by internalizing law. Through a series of encounters—establishing of a chain of tradition; through mastering legal interpretation in the course of judging others and oneself; and expanding law by using categories to classify different sorts of legal doctrine—emerges a figure who commentators see as redeeming Adam's failure. Abraham, unlike Adam, will become the archetype for the legalist Patriarch envisioned by the rabbis.

For Abraham, this was accomplished alone as an individual absent a community to reinforce norms. As the contemporary Talmudist Joseph B. Soloveitchik poignantly remarks, with the appearance of Abraham "loneliness entered our world."[5] Despite the promise that Abraham will some day become the father of a people, much of the beginning of the Abraham narrative accentuates his loneliness by recounting his desperate search for an heir. It tells of his successive rejections of various aspirants for this role: a collateral relative, Lot who, as we shall see in our discussion of the Sodom narrative, fails to master the ethos of judging; Ishmael, the son of his handmaid, has deep-seated character flaws which are uncovered by Abraham's wife, Sarah; and, as an adoptive heir, the steward of his house, Eliezer who cannot seem to surmount his servile status—as Abraham laments, *I shall die childless and the one in charge of my household is Eliezer of Damascus.*[6] Finally, just as it appears his line will be preserved through a miraculously born son, Abraham must endanger the transmission of the law in the haunting tale of the binding of Isaac.

Did the Patriarchs know the Torah prior to revelation? This question poses all sorts of difficulties for the exegetical legal imagination. For if Abraham, Isaac, and Jacob had acquired this knowledge, how do we explain their many lapses in compliance with traditional Jewish law? Nachmanides does not flinch from listing these contradictions in his discussion of pre-Sinaitic revelation.[7] "The question presents itself: If it be the case [that the laws of the Torah were observed by our ancestors before the Torah was given on Sinai], how did Jacob erect a pillar [although this is specifically forbidden as idolatrous according to Deuteronomy 16:22, *do not erect a pillar (mazevah) which God hates*][8] and marry two sisters in their lifetime, and, in the opinion of our Rabbis, four sisters.[9] Also, Amram [Moses's father] married his aunt,[10] and Moses our teacher erected twelve pillars.[11] How was it possible that they should be permissive in matters of Torah which Abraham their ancestor had prohibited on himself, and for which God appointed him rewards, when he [Abraham] was wont to *command his children and his household afer him*."[12] Even the meal Abraham served to the angels violated prohibitions governing kosher food. *He* [Abraham] *took curds, milk, and the prepared calf meat, and placed these before them*."[13]

The response to these contradictions would make any common law lawyer proud. When Jacob or Moses built their pillars, such an action was not prohibited. According to Nachmanides, the ban on erecting a pillar only came about later, in the period of the conquest when the Canaanites made it the object of idolatry. Prior to this time, so the argument goes, the pillar (for pouring out libations) and the alter (for sacrificing burnt offerings) were both legitimate means of serving God.[14] Jacob might marry two sisters because such unions were only banned in the land of Israel, and the marriage took place in Aram Naharyim.[15] Shmuel Edels, the early seventeenth-century commentator known as Maharsha, suggests that Rachel and Leah had not yet converted, and, therefore may be considered as having no blood relationship to each other under Jewish law.[16] If Abraham provided milk and meat to his guests, he served the milk first so as to permit its consumption under kosher rules. Or, as another commentary suggested, Abraham provided meat which came from the unborn fetus of a cow (*ben pekuah*) and was therefore under the oral law not considered meat at all.[17]

This is not to say Abraham or the other Patriarchs were perfect. Abraham, for example, was chided for falsely identifying his wife as his sister, thereby tempting a local king to commit adultery, and for arming his disciples.[18] On the other hand, if the Patriarchs did not follow the dictates of *halacha*, there would be a terrible rupture between the patriarchal generations and those who came after Sinai. How could we idealize Abraham, Isaac, and Jacob as servants of God, and at the same time valorize a *halacha* designed as an ideal instrument of divine service, if, in fact they did not keep kosher or guard the Sabbath?[19] How might we model ourselves after the core characteristics of their personalities (Abraham representing kindness; Isaac awe, and Jacob embodying the study of Torah), if these personalities did not include adherence to the fundamentals of Jewish law? As a result, numerous comments in the midrash suggest the Patriarchs observed *halacha*. Abraham wrote a bill of divorce for Hagar; Isaac set aside the second tithe; Jacob observed the law of the Sabbath boundaries which limited how far one might walk on the day of rest.[20]

But this anachronism had its limits. Commentators still felt uncomfortable with the contradiction between the Patriarchs as faithful to the law and their obvious breaches. One way to address this old and nagging dilemma was to suggest Abraham did not know the entire law. An alternative approach was to determine that Abraham had full knowledge of the Torah but to see these laws as not fully binding. We shall examine how the exegetical imagination employed both sets of arguments.

Law and the Problem of Succession

Abraham inherited the legal landscape described in the last chapter. However, even though Abraham was portrayed by commentators as resolving certain of the conundrums of the ante-Patriarchal world other issues remained. If Adam stumbled over the task of legal interpretation, Noah failed in expanding the law; and the generation of the Tower of Babel erred in demanding obedience without recognizing personal autonomy, Abraham corrected these blemishes. Abraham internalized the law until he became law bearing. Like a respected magistrate, he might be trusted with legal discretion. Nevertheless, Abraham had difficulties with the question of transmission. How can the internal voice be imparted to others?

The pivotal question framing the Patriarchal narrative, and providing the surrounding context for our verse, is the problem of succession. Who will be vested with the mantle of Abraham? With the birthright comes envy. Isaac and Ishmael set the stage for other stories of contention. Isaac's twin children, Jacob and Esau, pose competing claims of succession which dominate much of the remainder of the Book of Genesis. The struggle between them, Jacob's exile and return, and the consequences of this tangled legacy of family jealousies frame the Biblical themes through the remainder of the Jacob cycle. Abraham's transmission of norms seems fragile. In order to ensure Abraham's legal legacy continues, Isaac must alter traditional rules of inheritance.

Nothing better illustrates the dangers posed in the course of legal transmission than the beginning of the Jacob cycle and the tale of the sale of the birthright. After a difficult conception, two twins are born to Abraham's son, Isaac and his wife, Rebecca. These siblings are envisioned in rabbinic literature as having opposite temperaments from the very beginning of their lives. Esau's character seems unformed, linking him to the unformed commandments which are binding upon all the descendants of mankind. But his reddish color hints at Esau's proclivity towards bloodshed, and suggests that he inevitably will breach this particular Noahide injunction. Prior to his birth, traditional sources tell us, Jacob struggles to exit the womb when Rebecca passes near a place where the law is studied.[21] Encased with the womb, he is not drawn by the sight of the written law. Rather, it is the unceasing sound of the *lex non scripta* which proves so enticing.

Jacob will become the *dweller in tents*—seen as the house of study—and prefigures the future unfolding of the oral law. The rabbinic reading juxtaposes two types of law. Esau's legal framework looks backwards towards Noahide law; Jacob's forward to an evolving oral law which would come to fruition with the Talmudic academies. Both brothers contend for Abraham's legacy, and there is a special moment of danger as the birthright becomes contested. From the barter of lentil soup for the birthright, a well-known midrash derives the fact that Abraham has just passed away. Lentils are a traditional Jewish sign of mourning since they are smooth (have no mouth) and therefore serve as a reminder of the individual rendered mute through loss.[22] At this moment, Essau reveals his identity. He sees the red color of the pottage with its subliminal suggestion of blood, missing the cultural symbolism of the lentil. Claude Levi Strauss' raw trumps the cooked.

Perhaps Abraham's death would not be so traumatic if the legacy of law was not a matter of personal succession. To *be fruitful and multiply* was a blessing for Adam, we saw earlier, without legal weight. Adam was blessed with the power of reproduction, and this blessing, *be fruitful and multiply, and fill the land*, was repeated for Noah upon leaving the ark—what really might be thought of as a second creation.[23] The original blessing of Adam was passed down from generation to generation until the time of the Tower of Babel when this blessing—according to Baḥyya ben Asher—was suspended. Abraham renewed the blessing through constituting it as the birthright granted to the favored son.[24] But procreation is now identified as a form of legal transmission. With the preface to the Covenant Between the Pieces, Abraham learns the critical link between procreation and inheritance. Abraham steps into the night sky at God's request, *gaze at the heavens and count the stars, if you are able to count them, and He said to him, so shall your offspring be.*[25]

Abraham, however, is not content with knowing that he will have numerous descendants. He wants to know who precisely will be his heir. The land, and similarly the law, must be passed down. No matter what divine promises might exist, it was Abraham's role to determine the legal framework of this cultural transmission. Procreation was not simply a biological process. Producing offspring was charged with expectations because it played a critical role in establishing a chain of legal tradition—and one which has been most difficult as it has been fraught with barren women, adulterous potentates, and a God which may at any moment demand the sacrifice of an heir apparent.[26]

Quite famously, Franz Rosenzweig calls the Jews a blood community or *Blutgemeinschaft*. Other communities have to take extraordinary measures to pass values to the next generation; but "the blood community does not have to resort to such measures. It does not have to hire the services of the spirit; the natural propagation of the body guarantees it eternity."[27] Just the opposite is true. Birth is fraught with a sense of rupture as an unformed being comes into existence, a being with claims to legal and emotional ties despite all the uncertainties about the child's future promise. Blood therefore does not resolve the problem of community. It creates dilemmas. Is the biologic heir truly the cultural heir? How do we engage in legal transmission when the first child turns out to be unworthy? In many ways, the tension between blood and culture revolves around, and ultimately must be resolved, through law.

To make the correct choice between the brothers, Isaac must rupture the traditional custom of primogeniture, and ratify the awarding of the birthright to the younger son. This requires, of course, the rejection of Esau's straightforward claims based upon being the first of the twins to exit the womb, and the understanding that legal transmission relies upon election of a presumptive heir and not *per se* biological rules. It is not easy to do away with the ordinary law of primogeniture. In traditional *halacha*, the first-born's right of inheritance is reflected in the granting of a double portion.[28] The sale of a birthright or, indeed, any prospective inheritance has no validity under Jewish law.[29] Such an abrogating of customary rules, so the younger will rule the elder, as Rebecca is told prior to the birth of the siblings, does not come easily.

A midrash, for example, proffers an apologetic explanation that Jacob was, in fact, the first born since he came from the first drop of semen, and it was simply that the first drop comes out of the womb last. Even this requires a rewriting of the legal rule to favor the first to be conceived rather than the first to emerge at birth. When all is said and done, however, the transfer of the birthright relies upon its dubious sale by Esau and the exacting of Isaac's blessing through chicanery. Even though Jacob's deceitful procurement of the birthright follows the divine plan, it has tremendous cost. From this juncture onwards, the succession is fraught with ever mounting danger as Jacob is forced into exile and the sons born to Jacob ultimately descend into internecine struggle. This is a family which threatens—to borrow a Biblical phrase—to *devour its own inhabitants*.[30]

Why must the birthright belong to Jacob? Here, again, we see the theme of interpretation versus obedience dramatized. Rebecca and Jacob, and ultimately Isaac who ratifies the identification of Jacob as his spiritual heir, rely upon their interpretation of succession based upon merit, rather than simply obeying a system reflecting birth order. Moreover, Jacob represents legal interpretation. He is the figure who internalizes law, dwelling in tents (studies in yeshiva, according to its traditional meaning) and "became expert in Scripture, Mishnah, midrash, *halacha*, and *aggadah*."[31] Jacob manifests his appropriation of norms through subtle decisions about his own moral conduct and through transmitting knowledge of the law to children. Esau, on the other hand, was portrayed by midrash as outwardly obedient. He was a "cunning hunter" [*ish yodea ẓayid*], one who hunts with words, and who would capture the affection of Isaac by asking his father whether salt or straw require tithes without any real concern about strict observance of the commandments.[32]

These two examples of piety—which might be labeled internal and external—are not accidental. Both Jacob and Esau draw upon motifs concerning Abraham's commitment to *halacha*. In the model of Abraham, as we shall see shortly, Jacob learns *all* of torah. Moreover, Jacob embodies the core command to Abraham for legal transmission, *I* [God] *have known him* [Abraham] *in order that he may command his children and his household after him*.[33] Esau, too, seemingly followed Abraham's conduct through his concern with tithes. Abraham forged an alliance with Melchizedek and other local rulers to liberate Lot, his captive nephew. At the conclusion of the war, Abraham delivered a tenth (*ma'aser*) to Melchizedek, and the midrash has interpreted Abraham as observing the giving of tithes.[34] By raising the tithing of straw or salt as an outward posture of religious behavior, as tradition relates, Esau may be seen as suggesting that he, too, could be a warrior-Patriarch.[35]

The drama lies with Isaac, blind and long in his father's shadow, who must now decipher these two competing claims. Which one will be the heir in the model of Abraham? The transmitter of an inchoate law or the follower of the customary norms of the warrior-Patriarch?

The more immediate narrative strand, concerned with the question of whether Isaac should descend to Egypt, also deals with the abrogation of a prior standard of behavior and, in its own way, the issue of succession. According to the verse just prior to the promise to Isaac, there is a famine, much like the one in Abraham's day, which threatens to compel Isaac to journey to Egypt in search of food. God reassures Isaac, telling him to remain in the Land of Israel, and promising to assign the land to Abraham's descendants and multiply their number. The famine introduces a challenge. Should Isaac descend to Egypt or remain in Israel? The choice, Egypt versus the Land of Israel parallels the decision about the selection of Esau versus Jacob (who shall be renamed Israel). The uncomplicated response is to do precisely as his father has done (*ma'aseh avot siman le-banim*). Abraham also faced a famine; the challenge of exile in Egypt; the lechery of rulers who desired his wife; and the hardship of travel. Much could be learned from Abraham's custom, commentators tell us, of patronizing the same inns upon his return from Egypt as he did during the original journey.[36] Literal emulation would have been a natural course. Even Isaac's facial features, Rashi reminds us, were formed as almost an exact replica of his father's.[37] Isaac might have descended to Egypt with the expectation of experiencing, and surmounting, similar trials to those of Abraham.

Nevertheless, Isaac does not follow Abraham's behavior as a norm. Indeed, Isaac's action foreshadows the future command to the Israelites after the Exodus, *as you have seen Egypt, you shall not see them ever again.*[38] He, alone among the Patriarchs, refuses to go down to Egypt. Just as Isaac ruptures traditional rules of primogeniture in order to pursue a true transmission of values, he must *not* follow the customary conduct of Abraham in regards to leaving the Land, and instead his behavior gestures towards a prospective discomfort with Egypt. The dilemma of succession—or transmission of law—is resolved in these verses through Isaac making judgments within a complex *nomian* landscape where simple obedience to rules is not enough. Indeed, these twin decisions mark the move towards *internalizing* legal norms. Transmission means thinking about the meaning behind law as well as the rules themselves. If succession depends upon becoming norm-bearing, then this might explain why this narrative is the context for our verse, *Inasmuch as Abraham obeyed Me and kept My charge; My commandments; My laws; and My teachings.*[39] Isaac must learn how to follow law like Abraham precisely through not becoming wedded to a one-dimensional understanding of law; but, as the plural terms for law in this passage suggest, he must probe the different ways law may be observed.

Towards an Ethos of Judging

Transmission therefore means ascertaining how to respond creatively to the legal challenges posed from the outside—even when this means altering inherited norms. Abraham learned much the same lesson as an apprentice to God as magistrate. Man was created in the image of God the judge. At least this is the interpretation suggested by the medieval commentator Ḥezekiah ben Manoah, better known as Ḥizḳuni, in his reading of the Noahide commandment *whosoever sheds the blood of man, by man shall his blood be shed for in the image of God He made man.*[40] The ordinary way of understanding the verse is to see the latter section as a justification for the prohibition against homicide. To destroy a human being is to deface the divine likeness. However, Hizḳuni turns the verse on its head. It is not the victim whom he describes as being cast in the image of God, it is the magistrate conducting the subsequent trial. God is described as the *judge of all the earth.*[41] Since *in the image of God He made man* the earthly magistrate will serve as a proxy for divine judgment.[42]

No one, until Abraham, has yet engaged so fully in the art judging as *imitatio dei*. Adam fails through lacking a compass for his legal analysis, substituting desire for objective law; Noah, faced with a corrupt generation, remains oddly mute in the face of God's judgment; his descendants do not persevere in unpacking the many sorts of potential law—what might be called the portmanteau law—inherent in the Noahide code through bringing legal analysis to bear in cases of first impression; the generation of the Dispersion substitutes external supervision for the discipline of judging. Judging implies the crafting of temperament. It is more than mere dispute resolution, more than adjudication. It requires deliberative reasoning. Like cases must be treated alike; persuasive authority must be marshaled with care to reflect how facts differ on the ground. Both must reflect the adjudicating self.

Let us turn, then, to the judgment of Sodom, and Abraham's depiction of the judges as an ideal type. Abraham begins by pointing out to God that judges must consult with others, and, according to midrash, cites the example of Romulus and Remus, two law givers who acted in concert. It seems that the midrash is insisting that procedure, not substantive law, must adhere to a fundamental threshold of justice. Drawing again upon comparative law examples, Abraham also cites the multi-stage Roman appellate system. How, Abraham asks, can there be a judgment without the deliberation of another judge elicited through appeal?[43] God at least must be held to the same standard as Roman law. Presumably this human measure of procedural fairness—true for Rome as well as Jerusalem—determines the validity of legal decision making, and even divine judgment.

Common law judging—and Abraham's judging fits neatly into the common law model—means pragmatic, contextual, discretionary legalism, whereby pervasive legal prescriptions are modified over time as they come into contact with the challenges of different situations. There are less hard and fast rules, and more a sense of law as a way of thinking. Such a judicial apprenticeship nurtures a personality which can master all these complexities through an oral tutelage—what Walter Benjamin calls "artisan communication."[44] Abraham must transmit this *idea* of law—ever so legal and ever so flexible—to his descendants. How might this be done? The expression for law, *mishpat*, shares the same etymological roots as the Hebrew word *judge*. Abraham must internalize the law until he establishes deliberative habits of mind, weighing it with righteousness, so as to become a judge—and, then, to impart this judicial temperament to his descendants.

What does it mean to cultivate the personality of judging? Identifying the concept of law with judging would remain in the realm of abstraction, like castles in Spain, if it were not for the fact that the introduction of the word for law in scripture, *mishpat*, was immediately followed by its explication in the narrative of the destruction of Sodom and Gomorrah. In the course of this tale, the Hebrew root for the word law or judgment (*sh-p-t*) will repeatedly appear, and Abraham will be transformed into a judge-like figure. Perhaps the need to train Abraham and his descendants was the reason God consulted Abraham about his decision to destroy Sodom. Certainly, the text seems to suggest reading the Sodom narrative within the framework of legal transmission: *shall I conceal from Abraham that thing which I am about to do. . . . For I know him, in order that he shall command his children and his household after him to keep the way of God, to do justice* [*ẓedaka*] *and law* [*mishpat*].[45] God seems to be providing reasons for informing Abraham. The first is that he knows him—and here Rashi comments that *I know him* suggests kinship. In other words, God's relationship to Abraham is marked by legal cultural transmission to descendants, paralleling Abraham's relationship to Isaac.[46]

However, the second reason is more intriguing. Abraham must know how to judge in order to transmit this quality to his children—and not just how to render decisions; but how to act like a judge who discerns the delicate balance between justice and law. As a consequence, God confers with Abraham just as a judge in a capital case must look into the matter with great care.[47] God asks *shall I conceal (hamekase) from Abraham* what He will do to Sodom. A concealed judge is mentioned in the Book of Job where Job complains *the earth is delivered into the hand of the wicked; He covers (yeakase) the face of the judges*.[48] While the classic figure of Justice judging with her eyes blindfolded represents neutral treatment of litigants, the Hebrew image of the veiled judge is overtly negative. Job is not privy to God's plans because he must learn to submit to life's sorrows without understanding. Abraham, on the other hand, is told about the future destruction so as to explain the workings of divine justice. Why the difference?

There are a number of places where the midrash suggests that God conferred with Abraham about Sodom because Abraham had already been thinking about abstract questions of justice as a result of the narrative of the Flood. "R. Levi discussed the question: Why did the Holy One, blessed be He, reveal His decision concerning Sodom and Gemorrah to Abraham? He did so because Abraham had previously reflected upon the episode of the Flood and had said to himself: It is impossible that there were not twenty righteous men or perhaps even ten righteous men in that generation for whose sake the Holy One, blessed be he, might have abrogated his decision."[49] A second midrash states even more starkly the legal precedential connection between the Flood and the destruction of Sodom. Abraham questioned God for bringing a flood of fire to Sodom after his promise not to bring a flood of water to earth. Was this not, the midrash asks, a material breach of a prior contractual promise?[50] Both of these exegetical comments suggest that the narrative of the Flood was perhaps the most persuasive precedent used by Abraham in understanding divine collective punishment. The Flood, then, is a *leitmotif* for the Sodom narrative. It suggests that God's own justice is not defined in absolute terms, but must also be measured in equitable terms against standards of prior judgments.

The idea of collective punishment, however, poses all sorts of problems for a coherent conception of justice. Here, again, we see Abraham confronting this difficulty while considering the persona of the judge. How can God *sweep away the righteous with the wicked*? *How shall the judge of all the world, not do justice*?[51] While the narrative of the judgment of Sodom is often misrepresented as Abraham's challenge of the substantive justice of God's decision, various sources suggest that Abraham is really promoting procedural justice.[52] Abraham is not suggesting a higher law which trumps God's own sense of justice. As the binding of Isaac demonstrates, it would have been inconceivable to suggest any role for man other than submission in the face of divine command. This is even more true when God has so clearly made manifest His will. Moreover, personal visions of justice are often flawed. Varying conceptions of the good create contingency, and it is difficult to achieve uniformity on the equity of substantive legal issues. What Abraham demands, however, is an adherence to procedural norms. The tribunal must consist of the correct number of judges; it must be founded upon persuasive precedent from the earlier instance of the Flood; and it must include an articulation of God's legal reasoning. This latter is a legitimate claim since God himself has chosen to reveal his intention to destroy the cities—*shall I conceal from Abraham what I am about to do*?[53] According to Rashi, Abraham's pressing for transparency is manifested in the *ḥataf pataḥ*, the quivering dot located in the first letter (*heh*) of the Hebrew word *the judge*.[54] Abraham insists upon a window into the process of judging.

Just because Abraham *should* know how to judge does not mean that God *must* reveal how He engages in *mishpat emet*, true justice. But procedural justice is often explicitly dialogic, requiring adversarial relationships or, at the least, conversation in order to work out the legal issues.[55] By marshaling precedent of how divine justice has operated in the past, Abraham creates—as we have described for traditional law—a dialogue between one instance of the imposition of punishment and another. Abraham gropes at trying to reconcile two competing cases—the Flood of water and the flood of fire intended for Sodom. In one particular instance, Rashi claims, Abraham derived his numbers for those to be saved from the precedent of the deluge. Mindful of the fact that in the generation of the Flood there were eight righteous individuals, Noah and his family, and they failed to save the world, Abraham initially petitions for preventing the destruction if it proves that fifty righteous people should be found. The calculation is predicated on the idea of ten righteous individuals. Since there were five cities, and there would be ten righteous per city, he suggests the number of fifty righteous individuals. Abraham does not depart from this threshold. Instead, he simply continues the tally with a smaller number of cities. This is the reason he ultimately will halt his pleading after God agrees to save Sodom if in the city alone there were ten righteous people.[56]

An important aspect of judging appears from this narrative. Adjudication is deeply contextual and reflects experiential knowledge. God seems to have accepted the fact that in order to teach Abraham the craft of judging, Abraham must be apprenticed like any law clerk and be brought into the process. Both Abraham and God fall silent at the end as Abraham exhausts his legal arguments. Abraham did not simply succumb to the divine sanction against Sodom—as well he might. Silence also was the prevailing response of Noah to the Flood. Nor was Abraham's posture the absolute obedience of the Binding of Isaac. Here, where there was no self-interest beyond the preservation of Lot and his kin, Abraham assumed the posture of judging. The response to what Robert Cover called the moral-formal dilemma—the struggle between the troubling moral issues of the destruction which Abraham first recognized when considering the Flood and the formal demand for compliance Abraham accepted at the time of the Binding of Isaac—was not helplessness.[57]

Instead, Abraham's response was to fully assume the principled interpretive posture of judges. He would be deliberative in the weighing of the punishment, muster precedent, exercise self-restraint, and, above all, anguish over his judgment within the ambit of established law and justice. Abraham was ever mindful of the practical implications of the legal decision. This was training in judging through experience. Abraham did not argue with God over the number of righteous individuals to be spared simply from compassion. He is, perhaps in light of the *akedah*, described in the Prayer Book as a figure who vanquished his merciful character. In contrast to Noah, who *did as God commanded him* and approached the ark without comment, Abraham embodies the full complexity of the idea of law—which may be both accepted and contested; a source of obedience and of struggle; and whose narrow contours must be tempered with an interpretive search for justice.[58]

Lot, too, had in mind an historical paradigm as he contemplated the idea of justice. Lot saw in Sodom an Eden, for it was *full of water before God destroyed Sodom and Gemorrah—like the Garden of God.*[59] According to Elijah Mizrachi, this meant that like Eden it was full of trees.[60] In other words, the Flood did not serve as precedent for Lot. Rather, it was the idealized antediluvian legal landscape of a lost primordial world. The trees recall Adam's transgression and punishment. Perhaps Lot hoped to reconstruct a civil society founded upon material ease, hoping God's earlier judgment to cast out humankind from the Garden might be undone. With the wealth of Sodom, individuals might be freed from the divine curse of a hardscrabble pursuit of sustenance. An earthly, civil magistrate in Sodom—and here Lot envisions himself in this role—would have the power to set the place right again. However, the kind of judge Lot chooses to be is a *doppelgänger* of the model of Abraham as just magistrate. While Abraham assumes the mantle of judging in order to be reconfigured in the likeness of God, Lot becomes a judge in shallow imitation of Abraham according to commentators. He does not seem to fathom the deliberative reasoning needed to apply rules justly. Lot seems inadequate to the task of redeeming even the least of Sodom's citizens let alone the idea of a fallen Eden.

Lot sits within the gates of the city, the traditional place of judging, and thus the midrash identifies him as one of the five judges of Sodom.[61] Yet Sodom is a legal world turned upside down. With another of the judges named Immense Deceit (*Rav Shaker*), it is not surprising that the fundamental principles of rule of law are annulled.[62] Theft is an established norm and, as the midrash explains, hospitality is forbidden. Anyone who invites a foreigner to a wedding feast is taxed.[63] The rabbis have constructed a robust portrait of this inversion. The owner of one ox must graze the oxen of other citizens for one day, while someone who does not own an ox is obligated to graze the animals of others for two days. There is a legal principle involved—perhaps the presumption that those who do not have an animal have more time available for their upkeep—but this makes the rule all the more troubling for it is contrary to fundamental notions of fairness. Similarly, the people of Sodom were said to misappropriate one onion or one garlic from vegetable sellers without payment since such a small theft was below the minium amount which constitutes theft and was therefore not legally cognizable.

Even family life is not sacred. According to rabbinic sources, a pregnant married woman who miscarried due to an assailant would be delivered to the assailant so the wrongdoer might make her pregnant again.[64] The husband presumably would not lose the prerogative of a child's future labor. Rights of persons are trumped by property rights. Legal principles are clearly evident at the core of Sodom society: sumptuary laws; proportionality between theft and punishment; setting a minimum threshold value required for recovery; an individual guilty of tort liability should make the injured party whole again. But this is a parody of law. Making someone whole, for example in the case of the injured pregnant woman, means diminishing her psychologically with another instance of coerced sexual intercourse. Notwithstanding the thinking behind these norms, the result is an indisputable perversion of justice.

Lot erects a distinction between his public, externalized role and his private life. As a local magistrate, Lot must have enforced Sodom's corrupt laws. When a decision was to their liking, the midrash tells us, the townspeople would promote him; when his decision displeased them, the citizens of Sodom would say, this fellow came to sojourn and would act as judge.[65] Nowhere is he seen challenging their authority. What is to be done, Lot may have asked, the law on the books is the law? Nevertheless, as a private citizen he sought to emulate Abraham and invite guests. Lot sits at the city gate for another reason besides judging. He hopes to welcome sojourners just as Abraham peers out of his tent at the surrounding roads; Lot *greatly urges them* to stay with him; and he provides—much as Abraham did for the visitors who heralded Sarah giving birth—the washing of feet, a feast, and even, again like Abraham (similarly, prompting the midrash to see the time of the occurrence as Passover) serves unleavened bread.[66]

But the comparison between Abraham and Lot is superficial. When the people of Sodom realize the guests' presence, and demand that he hand them over so they may sodomize these strangers, Lot exhibits poor judgment. He offers his own daughters to be violated in their stead. The men of Sodom respond, *this one came to dwell with us, and now he has come to act like a judge?*[67] Such a remark might be made of Abraham. Abraham, too, was only a sojourner in the land; he, too, in the narrative seeks to judge. It is Abraham, however, who demands God explicate his judicial reasoning, and calls for mingling justice with law; and it is Lot who—in an official capacity—makes a mockery of judgment by insisting upon a *per se* adherence to legal norms. Lot's judging is a jester-like mirroring of Abraham's, making him a literary foil to his kinsman.

In the end, God will *overturn the cities* just as they have inverted the meaning of law.[68] The entire story of Sodom's destruction might be seen as an exemplar for judging—both well-crafted judging and the mockery of judging. In this sense, the destruction of Sodom stands like the Exodus as a pedagogical narrative. It would allow Abraham to *command his children and his household after him to keep the way of God, to do justice* [*ẓedakah*] *and law* [*mishpat*] through the unpacking of a particular case.[69] Abraham's archetypal legal endeavor would not be code-making; but judging. To be sure, the denouement of the story highlights the difference between Abraham's complex, multifaceted law—with its demand for deliberative reasoning—and Lot's naive acceptance of rules. After the destruction of Sodom and the fleeing of Lot's family to the mountains, his daughters are convinced that they are the sole survivors of the human race. Perhaps also drawing the analogy between the two destructions—of water and of fire, and convinced the devastation is as widespread as it was in the time of the deluge, they seek to fulfill the command given Noah after the Flood to *be fruitful and multiply*.[70] Fearing their father is the sole remaining male alive, Lot's daughters make him intoxicated in order to initiate sexual relations with him. *The first born said to the younger one, our father is old and there is no other man in the earth to come to us in the manner of all the earth. Come let us make our father drink wine, and we will lie with him that we may preserve the seed of our father*.[71]

There are numerous ironies here. In keeping with Lot's mistaken association of Sodom as Eden, Lot himself is wrongly presumed to be the new progenitor of mankind. The first-born, literally the one with the birthright, chooses the father, not the other way around.[72] The judge who made legal decisions within a disfigured legal culture becomes the object of a decision with legal consequence—the invoking of an exemption to the Noahide injunction against incest. The father who was willing to have his daughters ravished does, in fact, turn out to be violated by them. Finally, Lot, the relative of Abraham who perhaps hoped for the similar honor of becoming the progenitor of nations, would be disgraced through having a people descended from him named Moab, meaning from the father, which forever hints at the incestuous act at the root of the founding narrative.[73]

Nevertheless, it is the play on the tale of Noah which remains most striking. Like Noah, Lot becomes intoxicated in the aftermath of the desolation; his nakedness is uncovered by his children, and, most ironically of all, sexual depravity—which contributed to the ruin of both Noah's world and Sodom—becomes shockingly realized in an act of multiple incest. Lot's literalist understanding of law has reaped a transmission of this unthinking legalism to his daughters, and as a consequence replicates the cycle of destruction and failure from the time of Noah.

By contrast, Abraham was able to transmit the notion of a double-minded law, a law which interpreters envisioned as following the approach of wise and troublesome judges which embraces both the larger equitable purposes of law (*ẓedakah*) and the rules themselves (*mishpat*). Uniting such opposites is not a task which takes place solely within the shadow of a sublime moment like the Binding of Isaac. Just prior to addressing God in the matter of Sodom, Abraham escorts his guests on their way. This accompanying represents *ẓedakah.*[74] But, after all, it was also Abraham who left his father and the land of his birth—a first conquering of his attribute of mercy—and walked towards the Land of Israel as an act of pure obedience or *mishpat*. Rashi comments that within the charge *he will command* [*yeẓave*] his *children and his household after him, and they shall keep the way of God to do righteousness and judgment*, the Hebrew word *command* is written in the imperfect form of the verb, implying that this is an oft-repeated action. In other words, Abraham's transmission took place within everyday life through both acts of *ẓedakah* and acts of *mishpat*; through both study and his role as an exemplar of divine law. Perhaps this is why the Renaissance commentator Seforno sees the last statement in Abraham's appeal to God, *and Abraham returned to his place* as Abraham returning to his home.[75] Abraham will transmit the law within the ambit of his domestic sphere.

In many ways, the Sodom narrative is not simply a story about legal tutelage—through Abraham's participation in the adjudication process and his confronting the counter-paradigm of topsy-turvy justice. It is also a succession narrative. Indeed, the problem of succession, the transmission of law to a next generation, dominates Abraham's life. Ishmael, the son of his handmaid, forfeits his place as heir because he has made a mockery of the law through his uncontrollable urges. According to a well-known midrash, Ishmael's *making sport*, included shooting arrows in Isaac's direction.[76] Isaac—whose potential sacrifice would cause so much pain might be killed through an idle game. Although a faithful servant, Eliezer cannot become the heir because as a subordinate he remains unable to establish his own independent faculties of judging.

The Sodom story explains why Lot, perhaps the best possible candidate as heir, cannot be the focus of legal transmission. Son of Abraham's deceased brother, he might be both kin and—following a model common in the ancient world—adopted successor. To be sure, Lot has lived with Abraham, and should have learned his ways. Unlike Ishmael, Lot has learned to curb his appetites; unlike Eliezer, he is a substantial figure with a finely honed sense of duty towards the community where he dwells. He seems keenly aware of Abraham's role as magistrate. Nevertheless, as we have seen, Lot suffers from a failure of legal imagination. He, too, cannot serve as a successor. Abraham must wait for a yet unborn heir—this is why he must return home—and soon he will face the ultimate test of his own obedience in the Binding of Isaac.

But it is the Hebrew word at the beginning of Abraham's speech in the adjudication of Sodom which provides a potent sign that the problem of legal transmission will be with the Patriarchs for some time, *and he approached* [*va-yigash*].[77] This verb has a troubled history. It will play a central role in the deception of Isaac as Jacob, disguised in goat skin, pursues the birthright when Isaac evokes the verb *and approach* [*gesha na*] and Jacob approaches [*va-yigash*].[78] Perhaps Isaac wishes to know whether the person before him is truly his (and Abraham's heir) by the closeness of the approach. But Jacob, following Rebecca's orders, does not rely upon the insight of the blind Isaac. Rebecca conjures up the compelling words *listen to my voice*, precisely the phrase which serves as a prelude to the Binding of Isaac.[79] Rebecca signals the language of command. Since the birthright must be transmitted to the worthy son, there exists in this instance a moment of necessity where ordinary morality must be shunted aside. Indeed, this particular drawing close is entangled with duplicity, initiating a series of subterfuges.

What follows is Jacob's flight to the home of his kinsman, Laban; the chicanery of Laban in substituting Rachel for Leah on Jacob's wedding night; and Jacob's ensuing marriage to the handmaidens of his wives as they jostle for reproductive supremacy. As a result of the initial deception, then, comes, the sibling rivalry which rends the domestic fabric of Jacob's home. Joseph, as the favored son of Rachel, the favored wife, was sold into slavery. Like his father, Jacob would be tricked as he was falsely told of Joseph's death. For all the twists and turns in the plot, the dramatic resolution of the conflict over the birthright takes us full circle.

It occurs when Judah defends his brother Benjamin, Rachel's other son, against the false accusations leveled by Joseph. Here the verb reappears, *and Judah approached* [*va-yigash*] *him.*[80] If we had any doubts about the link between Abraham's approach [*va-yigash*] to God in the matter of the destruction of Sodom and Judah's approach [*va-yigash*], Rashi quickly dispels them. He suggests Abraham and Judah both came forward to contest and to importune at the same time. Most assuredly, then, Judah proves himself to be Abraham's descendant as he challenges a source of legitimate legal authority. To the absolute obedience of listening to God's voice required to accompany a child to the sacrificial altar or to deceive a husband/father in the uncompromising pursuit of the birthright, must ultimately come an adherence to equitable justice [*ẓedakah*] and formal law [*mishpat*], and the unadulterated courage to approach authority in the tradition of approaching as an adversary in judgment as expressed through *va-yigash*.

The Four-Fold Meaning of Law

The most puzzling aspect of our prooftext, however, remains the multiple phrases referring to law: *My charge* [*mishmarti*]*; My commandments* [*miẓvotai*]*; My statutes* [*ḥukotai*]*; and My teachings* [*torotai*]. What do they all mean? Why must there be so many terms? At the most straightforward level, these clearly indicate the comprehensive nature of the law. There are other places in the Five Books of Moses where there are similar lists, such as *These are the statutes* [*ḥukim*] *and the ordinances* [*mishpatim*] and *laws* [*torot*] which *the Lord made between Him and the children of Israel in Mount Sinai by the hand of Moses*.[81] Or, alternatively, *these are the statutes* [*ḥukim*] *and ordinances* [*mishpatim*]*, which you shall guard to do in the land which the Lord, the God of your fathers, has given you to possess.*[82] But in both of these cases there is a full body of law to observe—the entire weight of Jewish law after the revelation at Sinai or the many commandments pertaining to the land. Here, Abraham might only have been obligated to observe a limited number of laws. Our text, nevertheless, is burdened by four phrases referring to law. Each of them is different. If we assume, as we generally do, that divine speech is never needlessly redundant, then we need to account for what truly must be terms of art referring to different bodies of law.

The four-fold use of these terms for law is even more striking when we consider that there has been few previous references to law as a noun. God *commands* Adam and Noah. We saw how the exegetical imagination had to labor so hard to unpack the first command to Adam in order to discern the idea of law within this verb, and even the claims that command implies the giving of a rudimentary code of law. In the narrative of how Adam was enjoined from eating from the Tree of Knowledge of Good and Evil, there was no specific word for law. Adam must grasp the requirements of obedience, interpretation, and transmission from the act of being commanded for the first time. It is only in the context of Abraham teaching his children where law becomes a noun, *Because he commands his children that they observe righteousness* [*ẓedakah*] *and law* [*mishpat*], *in order that God might then bring upon Abraham that which He had spoken of him.*[83] Abraham, the surrogate of a divine magistrate, commands; however, the subject of the command is open-ended—not simply a specified act such as not eating of a certain tree or even dedicating a child as a burnt offering—but the transmission of a robust expression of law in all its guises.

The problem of parsing the surplusage of the four-fold language of law was already identified in the time of the Talmud. "Rab said: Abraham, our father, kept the whole Torah, as it is said: *Because Abraham hearkened to my voice*. R. Shimi bar Hiyya said to Rab: Perhaps this refers to the seven laws [of Noah]? Surely there was also that of circumcision. Then say that it refers to the seven laws and circumcision [and not to the Torah in its entirety]. If that were so, why does scripture say, *My commandments and My Laws*? Raba or R. Ashi said: Abraham, our father, kept even *eruv tavshilin* [a minor rabbinic ordinance], as it is said: *my torahs*, one being the written Torah, the other the oral Torah."[84] Clearly, the Talmudic text is trying to grapple with each of these terms as a separate category. *My voice* reflects the Noahide law since this referred to the voice of command passed down from an earlier time.

More strikingly, circumcision is embodied in the term *My statutes* (*ḥukotai*). This may be derived from the word *ḥok* which also means engraved. Just as statutes are engraved in stone, the covenant is engraved in the circumcised flesh.[85] The minimalist position, Noahide laws and the specific command of circumcision, suggest Abraham as a link in legal transmission. He received a legal tradition extending from Adam to Noah and through the generation of the dispersion. His own reproductive organ becomes engraved like a tablet of the law to symbolize his transmission of the covenant. The midrash tells how Abraham, unsure of the precise place to be circumcised, was informed that it was the organ where he will be "fruitful and multiply."[86] There exists, as we have discussed earlier, a strong link between transmission of legal knowledge as cultural reproduction and the commandment to have children.

If for Jews, then, circumcision served as indicia of Abraham's fealty to law, for Justin Martyr, following the tradition of Paul, it would ultimately become the mark of his descendants' false adherence to legalism. As Justin writes, circumcision was "given to you as a distinguishing mark, to set you off from other nations and from us Christians. The purpose of this was that you and only you might suffer the afflictions that are now justly yours; that only your land be desolate, and your cities ruined by fire; and that the fruits of your land be eaten by strangers before your very eyes; and that not one of you be permitted to enter your city of Jerusalem. Your circumcision of the flesh is the only mark by which you can certainly be distinguished by other men."[87] Like the mark of Cain, removal of the foreskin allowed Jews, whose misguided law brings down punishment, to be identified and persecuted. For both Jew and Gentile, then, Abraham's circumcision represented much more than simply the following of a single commandment. It speaks to the broader command of legal transmission itself.

Nevertheless, the minimalist position, which attributes to Abraham the observance of the Noahide laws and circumcision, leaves other terms unaccounted for—*My commandments and My laws*—which are those implying a larger set of laws. Two commentators in sharp disagreement, Rashi and Seforno, pose competing arguments for deciphering the four-fold set of legal terms. Rashi interprets these four designations for law as follows: *My charge*—these are the precautionary measures (such as those rabbinical decrees concerning second degree incest or additional requirements to rest on the Sabbath); *My commandments*—these are matters which even if not written in the Torah would have been worthy of command (such as robbery or homicide); *My statutes*—those injunctions where there are no clear foundation upon reason (such as the prohibition against eating pork or wearing garments made of a mixture of wool and linen); and *my teachings*—these are both written and oral law.[88] Seforno, on the other hand, divides these four-fold terms into two categories. *My charge*—acts of kindness in the model of Abraham; *My commandments, My laws and My teachings*—the laws established as part of the Noahide code.[89]

These two positions, so strikingly different, have a long lineage. Both already appear in the Babylonian Talmud, and there the controversy remains unresolved.[90] In the Talmud, Shimi bar Hiyya claims

Abraham only fulfilled the Noahide code, and, as is also suggested in the midst of the debate, circumcision. Rava, like Rashi, claims that Abraham fulfilled both the written and the oral law. This approach is clearly anachronistic. It suggests that Abraham embodies the law in its full rabbinic manifestation with fences around the law; social legislation and ritual law; and much later oral law interpretation. As discussed, Rashi partly grounds this capacious view of Abraham's knowledge upon the phrase *my teachings* [*torati*] which in the plural might be said to imply two *torah(s)*, written and oral. To the contrary, Seforno only attributes to Abraham those statutes seen as pre-Sinai: injunctions enunciated under the Noahide code; a non-binding set of altruistic norms; and, as expressed in the phrase *listened to My voice*, specific commands, like circumcision, directed to Abraham in particular. While Abraham may have been particularly careful in his performance of the Noahide commandments—one midrash suggests he feared that in the course of battle he may have violated the prohibition against bloodshed—nevertheless, following Seforno's view, Abraham remains very much bound by the dictates of his particular time and circumstances.[91]

Rashi's position resolves the difficulty of how to envision Abraham as a full-fledged servant of God prior to the revelation at Sinai. Abraham knew all the Torah, past and future. Nevertheless, claiming Abraham followed both the written law and later traditions creates as many problems as it resolves. It raises the issue of how pre-Sinaitic legal practice contradicts the norms of *halacha*—those examples unpacked by Nachmanides in the ways we have seen. Seforno's explanation evades this pitfall. Nevertheless, Seforno's approach means portraying Abraham as not terribly different from his contemporaries except in his obedience to divine command and his well-developed character. After cleaving to God, Abraham has little to show in the way of *halacha*. For Seforno, there seems to be another path consisting of good deeds where the religious vigor of the patriarchs might be directed, rather than law. How can Seforno's rendering of Abraham as a faithful servant of God absent *halacha* be reconciled with the notion of Jewish law as the *sunum bonum*? Why should the flourishing of Jewish legal culture need to wait for the revelatory moment at Sinai? Moreover, Seforno fails to properly account for the use of four terms of art for law for Abraham's binding legal world, instead conflating these into little more than the bare scaffolding of the Noahide code.

As he so often does, Nachmanides astutely breaks open the debate. He returns to Rashi's taxonomy of law, unpacking each term of art. However, Nachmanides shows that each word for law might be conceived in a particularly pre-Sinaitic fashion—through pointing forward to a full manifestation of *halacha*: *My charge*—refers to second degree marriages which were forbidden under the Noahide code; *My commandments*—refers to robbery and murder which directly correspond to two of the Noahide commandments, and which Nachmanides calls "precepts which, had they not been written in the Torah, were requisite to have been written"; *My statutes*—refers to the law against eating the limb of a living animal and breeding mixed species—laws with "no apparent rationale"; and *My teachings*—refers to civil statutes which govern society and the prohibition against idolatry.

In other words, Abraham has been taught the Noahide code. But Abraham's approach to this pre-existing law allows him to see the possibilities inherent within it—possibilities that might lead to a creation of a new law in the future. Included within the lesser form of Noahide incest, for example, are all sorts of rules about how to devise precautionary statutes such as the ban on second degree marriages. The pre-Sinai law without a rationale, eating the limb of a living animal, has built-in the possibility of future difficult to explain post-Sinai laws such as the prohibition against mixed species. Injunctions against robbery and murder suggest social laws may be established for reasons of governance when the Jews become a people.[92] No longer is the Noahide code an inert, unexpansive body of statutes. Abraham has breathed life into this earlier law before the law through appropriating its categories.

Nachmanides suggests Abraham has a genius for classification. According to Nachmanides, Abraham finds in the Noahide code the *typologies* of the *halacha*, the different kinds of laws into which it may be classified: *charge* refers to "precautionary decrees" such as those later instituted by the rabbis to prevent the violation of underlying laws; *commandments* refers to universal norms, including limitations on violence; *statutes* [*ḥukim*], as it commonly does in rabbinic legal analysis, refers to those laws which are unique to the Jewish people. It seems that Abraham is involved in the project of classifying and systematizing law as well as explaining its rationales. Baḥyya ben Asher who so often addresses issues posed in Nachminides commentary, sees the verse dividing the entirety of the six hundred and thirteen commandments into three categories. It is intriguing that this classification depends upon how the person observing them, such as Abraham, perceives their rationality. Social laws regulate the behavior between members of society and therefore follow the rule of reason; testimonies, often religious norms, make sense once one accepts the traditional place of God within the culture; and, finally, there is the *ḥok* which cannot be understood by the rational faculty.[93]

The traditional rabbinic category of the *ḥok*, the statute which cannot be legitimized through reason and must be accepted as the decree of God as ruler, is represented by the Noahide proscription of the limb of a living creature. For, after all, why should any restriction be placed upon what might be consumed? Nachmanides clearly sees this prohibition as a precursor to the later Jewish religious norms of refraining from eating the flesh of swine. From this compliance with laws independent of reason, however, may come various religious requirements. According to Nachmanides, Abraham learned God's teaching so as to understand the *Grundnorm* behind each Noahide rule. Through interpretation, he enlarged the Noahide system on his own so as to approximate a miniature of the law as given at Sinai. Just as Rashi derived the idea that Abraham was aware of two legal traditions, the oral and written law, from the plural form of the noun (*torotai*); so does Nachmanides pair laws between individuals, and laws between the individual and God. Nachmanides implies Abraham was taught to *read* the Noahide code differently. Discerning the abstraction behind the seven commandments will permit the emergence of a robust legal code. In other words, Abraham—as Nachmanides depicts him—has the insight to abstract and expand the Noahide statutes, seeing it as the basis for an entire legal world in a way that never became clear to the Noahides themselves.

Nachmanides neatly resolves the dilemma of Abraham's awareness of *halacha*. Abraham knows the law fully, and understands the depth of the Torah. Experiencing its profundity through elaborating upon Noahide law—such as through tithing—and through being "occupied with its study, the reason for the commandments and its secrets, he follows Torah in its entirety as one who is not commanded but nevertheless observes it."[94] This striking statement has to be read within the context of the medieval debate over the importance of discerning the rationale behind commandments (*ta'amei ha-miẓvot*).[95] The project of *ta'amei ha-miẓvot* became an important one for medieval Jewish philosophers seeking to demonstrate the perfection of the law.

Maimonides identifies a number of statutes not based upon rational reasons (*ḥukim*) such as the prohibition against wearing a garment with mixed fibers of wool and linen (*sha'atnez*) or burning the red heifer—as historical artifacts. These are reactions to once existing forms of idolatry. Recollection of the specific idolatrous practices may have disappeared as these are relegated to the distant past, but the Jewish legal responses produce traces which still survive. Nachmanides, on the other hand, largely avoids such historical arguments, which might underscore the irrelevance of the law in contemporary settings rather than establish justifications for observance. According to Nachmanides, Abraham "learned the entire Torah through divine instruction and occupied himself with its study and the reason for its commandments and its secrets, and he observed it in its entirety as one who is not commanded but nevertheless observes it."[96]

If Abraham had to delve into the reasons behind these puzzling commandments, which seemingly have no clear rationale, then they cannot be a means of responding to idolatry in Abraham's time as Maimonides suggests. Instead, there must be some more hidden purpose—perhaps philosophical or mystical—grounding *ḥukim* and indeed behind all commandments. Such an interpretive posture is centered not upon observance as much as it is focused upon understanding law's purpose. The debate between Maimonides and Nachmanides reflects a difference of opinion over the nature of law. For Maimonides, law is functional. Since norms emerge through the needs of society, searching for their rationale legitimizes the legal system to later generations.

Nachmanides sees law as a set of autonomous and absolute principles which will some day be made manifest after the settling of the land of Israel. Therefore, Nachmanides turns to what is behind the outward performance of the law. If the Patriarchs kept the Torah, then it was with the focus on the ideas behind the actual laws rather than straight-forward obedience. Nachmanides's approach evokes an even more striking anachronism than the rabbinic idea that Abraham knew both the written and oral law. According to Nachmanides, Abraham is also engaged in the medieval exegetical enterprise of *ta'amei ha-miẓvot*.

What does it mean to follow Nachmanides's approach in locating foundational abstract principles of law within the details of legal practice? Take, as a hypothetical example, Jacob, who as we shall see shortly was said to have kept the Sabbath boundaries.[97] The Sabbath boundaries might be seen as a symbol of the Sabbath. They mark the existence of the Sabbath through setting metes and bounds much as lighting candles sets the boundaries in time. Eventually, these boundaries will have practical legal significance when the Jews again enter the land of Israel and need to know the extent they are allowed to travel from one place to another. However, even for the Patriarchs, the Sabbath represents the abstract principle of attesting to God's role as the creator of the world. Following Nachmanides approach, moreover, it may well be that what seems a peculiarly Jewish anachronism—the Patriarchs marking the Sabbath boundaries—therefore corresponds to the Noahide prohibition of recognizing any other divinity as the creator. The Sabbath might be considered an affirmative version of the negative Noahide commandment against idolatry.[98]

Nachmanides sees the primary import of the commandments as providing an opportunity to engage in the enterprise of discovering their hidden designs. An even more daring version of this approach is assumed by Ḥayyim of Volozhin, the preeminent Lithuanian yeshiva head in the early nineteenth century. In his major work, *Nefesh Ha-Ḥayyim*, Ḥayyim of Volozhin valorizes Torah study as the penultimate task for the religious Jew. Not surprisingly, then, he identifies Abraham's relationship to law as one of learning—observance in the time of the Patriarchs was consequently left to their discretion. "In accordance with the root of their soul," each Patriarch would follow the law after determining *himself* whether its particular application would be beneficial or not.[99]

The Patriarchs might violate the letter of the law in order to bring about a realization of God's purpose. Such a law is hortatory, not binding. Sinai would do more than create a new obligatory law so that no individual might follow his or her will contrary to the straight-forward demands of the Torah. It also would sweep away an archaic customary law with its reliance on the elective decisions of remarkable individuals. Both the Patriarchs and the law are treated differently in the *Nefesh Ha-Ḥayyim*. In this tradition of the law before Sinai, Abraham is not simply the obedient servant. He is the *gavra rabba*, the idealized legal scholar vested with commanding authority whose presence must be treated with the same honor as a scroll of the law.[100] Moreover, the law is idealized for the knowledge it embodies. To study statutes, not simply to obey their directives, realizes the apotheosis of the law.

Setting Boundaries

Perhaps the most often repeated commonplace about Abraham's observance is the one mentioned at the conclusion of the Talmudic passage quoted above: Abraham fulfilled all the Torah—even *eruv tavshilin*.[101]

The *eruv tavshilin* is a legal device employed to circumvent the usual prohibition against preparing food on a holiday for the next day. Certain foods, usually bread and one cooked dish, are set aside as a Sabbath meal prior to the holiday. Anything added to this cooked on the holiday is simply considered as supplemental to this preexisting meal, and is therefore not prohibited. The statement of Abraham observing *eruv tavshilin* must surely be seen as *Sondersprache*—extraordinary speech creating a startling image.[102] For the *eruv tavshilin* is an unabashedly anachronistic choice.

Of rabbinic origin, and not mentioned at all in the written law, the *eruv tavshilin* only serves as a legal device if the rabbinic prohibition against cooking food on a holiday is followed. Abraham, of course, presumably predates this prohibition becoming standard *halacha* by many centuries. Unlike the oral law dictates Rashi mentions, such as second degree incest, it does not serve as a fence to protect against the transgression of a mandate from the written law. The *eruv tavshilin* is an entirely new enactment, a decree of sorts, completely separate from any *lex scripta* source.[103] In other words, it is an oral law addition to the core of the oral law itself. But this is precisely what the exegetical imagination wanted to invoke. "R. Samuel bar Naḥmani said, R. Jonathan said: Abraham, our father, kept *eruv tavshilin* since it says two torahs—these must include oral law."[104] In other words, *eruv tavshilin* identifies the maximalist position: Abraham fulfilled *all* the Torah.

There is a textual variant where the *eruv tavshilin* is joined with the *eruv ḥaẓerot*. In some texts, such as *Midrash Tehillim*, both forms are cited.[105] The *eruv ḥaẓerot*, the joining of courtyards, is another legal device. Ordinarily, the carrying of an object, no matter how small, is forbidden on the Sabbath in property that is rented or owned by more than one unrelated person. By placing food in a common place prior to the Sabbath with the understanding that this shared meal creates a single household, however, it is permissible to carry between the domains of different individuals. Both of these two devices reflect a larger law—the command to remember the Sabbath.[106] The *eruv ḥaẓerot* consolidates together space much as the *eruv tavshilin* joins time. But why did Abraham need either of these contrivances? Were the rabbis suggesting he celebrated historical events for future generations such as the Passover (marking the Exodus) or Shavuot (commemorating the giving of the Torah) or Sukkot (recalling the journey through the Wilderness)? After all, were not all three festivals commemorative? With whom did Abraham share a courtyard—if he, as a tent dweller, could have even envisioned living in such a fixed abode? These two devices, the *eruv tavshilin* and the *eruv chatzerot*, only make sense within the framework of established religious communities following the entry into the Land of Israel.

Perhaps it was difficult to imagine the fundamental loneliness of law outside of society. The *Midrash Tanḥuma* addresses this dilemma. "R. Aḥa said in the name of R. Alexandri, and R. Samuel bar Naḥmani in the name of R. Jonathan, even *eruvin tavshilin* was observed in Abraham's house. . . . He was meticulous with all the commandments [in the oral and written] Torah[s]. Said the Holy One: you are meticulous with my commandments, and [yet] you dwell among idolaters? Go out."[107] The first words God speaks to Abraham in the written *Torah*, the command *Go out from your land; from the place where you were born; from your father's house*, only comes *after* Abraham has performed the oral law—and even *eruv tavshilin*. These legal devices are not accidental choices for the exegetical imagination. "The *eruv* was instituted," the midrash tells us, only to foster the ways of peace [*mipnei darkhei shalom*]."[108]

Looking backwards in time, it was contrasted to the Tower of Babel where architecture led to the division of humankind.[109] The Tower of Babel dissolved separate dominions into an authoritarian whole. It established one sovereign voice. When this authority was broken, and the Tower reduced to rubble, the resulting divisions would lead to a shattering into multiple languages, different linguistic domains, and ultimately to internecine conflict. But the *eruv* does just the opposite. By allowing separate households to exist under the umbrella of a common domain absent compulsion, it thus accommodates the carrying of objects across individual property lines—and, as a consequence, comes social peace. It permits both the private autonomous sphere of the household and the public sphere of the neighborhood community.

This rabbinic characterization points to the ways that a detailed ritual law might be rendered abstract. The *eruv* was no longer a series of boundary markers used to institute a legal fiction; but the representation of peace itself. In the twentieth century, Abraham Isaac Kook would also take a turn towards legal abstraction when addressing what for him was the puzzling anachronistic character of the rabbinic assertion that Abraham observed the *eruv tavshilin*. This statement, Kook declared, must be read figuratively. Abraham could not only distinguish between the sacred and the profane or between the pure and the impure. He even had the capacity to make finer distinctions between one form of the sacred and another—between the holiday and the Sabbath. According to Kook, Abraham could peer within a commandment, seeing the "intention within," and see the finer points of its spiritual nature.[110]

But the *eruv* of courtyards reflects another notion—one which we will discuss later. Metes and bounds are metaphors for law. Being norm bearing means setting limits, erecting boundaries for behavior—and, ultimately, upon property. In this way, too, it is the basis for civil society. The image of the *eruv* as a proxy for property rules is meaningful in light of the promise made to Abraham that he would inherit the Land. The Land of Israel would be divided among households and tribes. Like the imagined courtyards of Abraham, there would be both private areas—where individuals would inherit stakes from the time of the conquest—and common holdings on the Land as well. Abraham's *eruv* anticipated these divisions—the very fabric of the promise of the land—and allowed them to be internalized well before the command to enter the Land of Israel. Here, again, we follow the identification of the law concerning the Land—as we saw in our discussion of the readings for the fifth day—as the paradigm for the law as a whole. As a reward for his scrupulous observance of these minor rules establishing perimeters, one commentator suggests, Abraham would be granted the Land.[111] In all sorts of ways, then, these set boundaries were linked to a *future* settled society in the land which God has promised.[112] Abraham's knowledge of this minor legal mechanism, therefore, was a hint of the future interpretive community which would some day emerge within the parameters of a settled people on their own land.

The Case of the Puzzling "Inasmuch"

Even if we understand the four-fold terms for law at the heartland of this verse, *Inasmuch as Abraham listened to My voice and kept My charge; My commandments; My laws; and My teachings*, its overall grammatical structure remains puzzling.[113] It reads like an introduction to a second clause; but one which no longer exists. What does the word *inasmuch* [*ekev*] mean? The usual English rendering of *ekev* is *inasmuch, as a consequence,* or *therefore*. It is used as a conjunction. However, there is also a legal meaning to the word. This expression evokes exchange or reciprocity. *Targum Onkelos*, the ancient Aramaic translation of the Bible, translates *ekev* as an exchange.

The *Targum*'s use of the word exchange, *ḥalaf*, suggests the Talmudic form of acquisition, *kinyan ḥalifin*, or barter. It is effected through the handing to the purchaser of an object as a symbolic substitute for what is being delivered.[114] Acquisition of a cow, for example, might take place through handing an individual another form of livestock or even a completely different object. The obligation takes place the moment one form of chattel changes hands.[115] Yet the idea of *inasmuch* with exchange marks only the beginning of the enquiry. What precisely is being exchanged? Moreover, why do we need an exchange at this juncture? This verse and its focus on exchange, relates to the *performance* of the covenant, on Abraham's part. Indeed, it will be argued, the essence of fulfilling the covenant consists not simply of obedience, but also interpretation, insofar as Abraham will amplify the law through performing *My charge, My commandments, My laws, and My teachings.*

At the Covenant Between the Pieces, God promises Abraham offspring and the land.[116] Abraham, in turn, will undergo the ritual of circumcision.[117] However, circumcision is a token of the covenant, a mark of the *everlasting pact.*[118] It does not include all the ramifications of the covenant for the exchange. These will remain unspoken until God employs the term *inasmuch*. At that moment Abraham's side of the bargain becomes clear: Abraham was to contribute to the shaping of a law which might be transmitted across the generations. *Inasmuch* as Abraham involves himself with *My charge; My commandments; My laws; and My teachings*—or, as will be discussed, engage with these four terms reflecting the whole gamut of law—there will be a divine blessing. Such an exchange entails more than simple obedience to the immediate command. Somehow—and this is the paradox of *inasmuch*—both submission to God's command and interpretation, the making of creative, adaptive, and emotionally compelling *halacha,* must coexist. The covenant then will be actualized through law.

Let us begin with unpacking the puzzling *inasmuch* by finding another place where it has been used to indicate an exchange of a divine promise for human legal action. Compare our passage from the promise to Isaac, *Inasmuch as Abraham listened to My voice* [*ekev asher shama Avraham be-koli*] *and kept My charge; My commandments; My laws; and My teaching,*[119] with a verse found just a few chapters earlier at the end of the narrative of the Binding of Isaac. There at the very end of the test, after the substitution of the sacrificial ram for Isaac, Abraham is promised his descendants will be blessed *inasmuch as you have listened to My voice* [*ekev shamata be-koli*].[120] Clearly, the first section of the two verses is virtually identical. Only the four-fold description of law, *My charge; My commandments; My laws; and My teachings*, which may be found as the concluding section of the verse we are focusing upon in the promise to Isaac, remains absent in the earlier verse concerning the Binding of Isaac. Not surprisingly, a number of commentators recognized this correspondence. They interpret *inasmuch as Abraham listened to My voice* in our verse as referring to Abraham's test during the Binding of Isaac.[121]

But this only poses a deeper question. The Binding of Isaac has only one phrase for Abraham's obedience—listening to God's voice while the other verse, pronounced many years later to Isaac, adds a four-fold list of the types of law Abraham obeyed. If the listening to the divine command is enough at the time of the Binding of Isaac to ensure a blessing, why—a generation later—should we also insist Abraham pursued law in all its other forms as a precondition to securing God's favor? In other words, what happens between the Binding of Isaac and God's promise to Isaac many years later which accounts for this difference? Why must the Patriarchs follow a capacious set of laws rather than simply listening to God's voice? And how do we distinguish listening to God's voice from keeping his commandments and teachings? The Binding of Isaac has often been seen as a meta-legal act, stepping beyond ordinary norms, and expressing the ineffable. For this reason, it has been cabined in all sorts of ways. It is a misconception, however, to say that just because a command cannot be emulated in ordinary circumstances that it does not impact upon the legal landscape. Our verse brings the Binding of Isaac back towards the realm of ordinary law. Abraham listens to God's voice as a supreme act of fealty, and then quite strikingly comes the cascading list of the four-fold forms of law.

Clearly, the grappling with a direct command in the narrative of the Binding of Isaac—the very definition of extraordinary law—reawakens memories of Adam's failure. The narrative of the Binding of Isaac begins with a command very different from Adam's first injunction. Adam might eat from *any* tree in creation with one exception. Abraham, on the other hand, had no substitutes for *your son, your only son, Isaac, whom you love,* although God would later decide a ram caught in the thicket might be consumed as a proxy sacrifice.[122] Moreover, Adam was charged with a negative commandment, *do not eat from it*—while Abraham must struggle with a positive command to execute the inconceivable, and to do so with such acts of devotion as waking early in the morning to set out on the journey or chopping the wood for the sacrifice himself.

Nevertheless, both Adam and Abraham were subjected to tests of obedience. God's voice is really God's command. It was too late when Adam heard the voice of God. After the transgression, Adam and Eve *heard the voice of the Lord God walking in the garden towards the cool of the day.*[123] Suddenly, caught in a web of fear and remorse, the gravity of the command became clear. In the story of the Binding of Isaac, however, Abraham hears God's voice three times: once to direct him to sacrifice Isaac as a burnt-offering; a second time to halt the sacrificial act—even as Abraham's hand was stretched forth with the knife; and, the third voice, to promise him *because you have done this thing and have not withheld your son that I will bless you and multiply your descendants as the stars in heaven and as the sand which is upon the seashore.* It is within this third voice, where Abraham hears the *ekev—and your descendants shall be blessed of all the nations of the earth inasmuch* [*ekev*] *you have listened to My voice.*

Why wait for the third voice for the *inasmuch*, and the bestowing of the blessing? The Binding of Isaac has been construed within many frameworks: the creation of a religious inner life; the historical sacrifice of the Jewish people; the subjugation of the rational.[124] However, for our purposes, it tells a great deal about the unfolding drama of realizing the making of norm-bearing human beings. Adam erred by interpreting the first decree for his own benefit. As discussed earlier, Malbim claimed Adam abused his interpretive power, seeking a reason to evade God's sole command through analyzing the language of the prohibition in such a way as to justify his consuming the fruit of the tree. For Malbim, the issue was whether Adam might marshal legal interpretation, not as the instrument of desire, but for the sake of transmitting and extending the law.

The word *mimenu* in Adam's command, *do not eat from it* [*mimenu*], which Malbim saw as such an interpretive stumbling block, has been redeemed by Abraham, who is praised by God because *now I know you fear God, and you have not kept back your son, your only one, from Me* [*mimeni*].[125] Only when it is clear that Abraham's interpretative capacity will not interfere with the enactment, and the action will follow as a consequence, can the divine voice now utter the *mimeni*, pronouncing its blessing without reservations. Throughout the narrative of the Binding of Isaac, Abraham demonstrated not simply that he was able to subjugate his own deepest attachments to a son who embodied the future, but also that he even had the fortitude to place at risk God's larger plan of imparting the law to the next generation. The beloved son, the fruit of Abraham's old age, was offered to God, standing as a proxy for Adam's fruit of the tree which was so wrongfully taken despite the divine proscription.

Abraham need not have suspended his legal interpretive capacities. Take, for example, the possible analysis of the verse *for I have known him to the end that he* [Abraham] *may command his children and his household after him that they may keep the way of the Lord to do righteousness and justice* which requires Abraham to transmit law. Was it not possible for Abraham to argue that these two injunctions, teaching and the sacrifice of a son, were seemingly incompatible?[126] After all, how could God command Abraham to teach his child on one hand and so unreservedly to demand his sacrifice on the other? In order to resolve this contradiction, Abraham might have interpreted the command *to offer him there for a burnt-offering* as simply meaning to ready Isaac as a figure dedicated to God.

Indeed, this was Rashi's suggestion: "[God] did not say to slaughter him; because the Holy One Blessed be He did not desire to slaughter him, but only to bring him up to the mountain in order to prepare him as a burnt offering."[127] Rashi suggests, therefore, that God's command was truly intended to set Isaac apart, like a holy sacrifice, not to have him consumed in flame. Isaac may have been designated for holiness—like the Biblical Nazirite or priest or even as the prophet Samuel would be in the future. Most certainly, there were other interpretive moves which could have been made. Nevertheless, Abraham suppressed his legal interpretive capacities in order to demonstrate absolute fealty to God.

In many ways, the Binding of Isaac permits the primordial problem of allegiance finally to be laid to rest. Adam's disobedience has been rectified by Abraham's unimaginable faithfulness. Abraham Isaac Kook makes a profound observation about the significance of the Binding of Isaac for establishing the future relationship between divine command and those who followed Abraham: "Were it not for Binding of Isaac, humankind would have stood in relation to the divine in either an untamed and wild emotional state, though with the strength of pulsating emotions, or in a somewhat diluted cool spirit devoid of profound life."[128] Untamed and unbounded religious intensity threatens God's plan. What might be wrongly sacrificed in the emotional whirlwind of pleading before God? Yet artless obedience also would result in failure. To simply follow law as a command, without interpretation and investment in the outcome, would turn humankind into a "cool spirit."

Constructing a covenant, therefore, requires more than a token of fealty—the removal of the outer sheath for the reproductive organ. It demands the offering of the very fruit of the organ as witnessed through Abraham's remarkable submission through the Binding of Isaac—and then, after all is said and done, the return from the immediacy of having *listened to My voice* to the realization of ordinary law. Abraham's descendants would need to learn the *via media* between the heat of desire and icy rationality; between impetuosity and an overabundance of interpretive caution. When God's face would become hidden, and everyday prophecy would cease, it would become impossible to rely upon hearing a commanding voice—and generations to come would need to depend upon their own internal voices as mediated through law. At that point, the other part of the verse—the four-fold description of law—would become still more important. If the Binding of Isaac has any significance for ordinary law, it tells us that through one remarkable act of submission and putting the issue of obedience to rest, deliberate judgment is now unleashed in the sphere of interpreting law.

This explains the difference between what is exchanged by God for his part of the transaction, the divine undertaking as a result of the *inasmuch*. In the case of the Binding of Isaac, *all the nations of the earth shall bless you and greatly increase your offspring like the stars of the heavens and like the sand on the shore, and your offspring shall inherit the gate of its enemy.*[129] Our passage, the promise to Isaac a generation later, reiterates the two promises of fertility and a blessing among the nations made to Abraham a generation earlier. But it appends a third element: *and I will give you all these lands*. Why add the promise of the land at this point? The explanation lies in the difference between what is being exchanged in the two verses. At the Binding of Isaac, absolute obedience with its willingness to place at risk of future generations through the act of sacrificing Abraham's heir, results in an assurance of future generations. Just as fertility was a blessing granted Adam in the course of creating a fragile natural world so was Abraham blessed as his obedience marked the beginnings of a religious-legal world.

The additional reciprocity of receiving the land in the later verse of the promise to Isaac, however, suggests the significance of the land for grappling with law in everyday life. We saw in our discussion of the readings for the fifth day how R. Ishmael identified law concerning the land, such as agricultural rules for leaving the land fallow during sabbatical years, as establishing a model for all subsequent *halacha*. Here, the verse to Isaac introduces an additional four-fold description of law. In addition to Abraham listening to God's voice, he followed four other kinds of norms: *my charge; my commandments; my laws; and my teachings*. For this his descendants were rewarded not just with the twin bounties of future generations and blessings, but also with the additional inheritance of the land. In other words, in exchange for the multiplicity of law—the four-fold description of law in its many forms—the descendants of Isaac will receive the Land of Israel with all its practical legal implications concerning everyday life.

How Did Abraham Know the Law?

Abraham's knowledge of the law was another conundrum for the exegetical mind. There were a number of ways to discern the law—through oral transmission; through written codes, commentaries, or treatises; or through logical analysis independent of any received tradition. Each of these valorizes one or another mode of legal thinking. Oral transmission reflects a *paideia* where practical wisdom is handed down from teacher to student through a combination of formal teaching and apprenticeship.[130] Allowing the transmission of intuitive reasoning and flexible custom rather than fixed norms, this notion would ultimately be embodied in the Talmudic ideal of *shimush,* the apprenticeship of disciples to master scholar.

Written codes are less mutable and subject to corruption. Commentaries and treatises focus on the logical structures shared among legal doctrines. They allow the law to expand through unpacking existing legal decisions. Analytic legal reasoning, like natural law, has the appeal of universality. All these models have advantages and disadvantages. How *did* Abraham know the law? Was he the heir to an ancient form of knowledge or a legal philosopher or a prophet receiving direct instruction from God? One midrash portrays Abraham seeing the Tower of Babel, and disdaining the builders as they gather stones.[131] The idea, of course, is that his rejection of an existing understanding of law—one which we earlier described as seeking to impose uniformity—might serve as the basis for a new *nomos*.

More telling, however, is a medieval debate about the age when Abraham embarked upon understanding the law. This debate illuminates the conflict between reason and prophecy as competing sources of Jewish legal tradition. As David Hartman has elegantly described, Maimonides portrays Abraham as a seeker of truth "without a teacher or anyone to instruct him" but who realized through reason that the world must have an architect. Having attained this knowledge, he spread his doctrine to others, "composed books on it and taught it to Isaac his son."[132] Maimonides states that Abraham was forty years old at the time of his election, and mature enough to think in philosophical fashion about the nature of the divine and the meaning of the law. For Maimonides, the God of Abraham was truly the God of the philosophers.

Abraham ben David of Posquieres, the medieval scholarly antagonist to Maimonides known as Rabad, disagrees, claiming Abraham was merely three years old. How did Rabad derive the beginning of Abraham's instruction at the age of three? The source for this again appears to be our verse: "*inasmuch as Abraham listened to My voice*. The numerical value of the word *inasmuch* [*ekev*] is one hundred and seventy-two." Since Abraham's life span was one hundred and seventy-five years, the Talmud subtracting the two numbers determines that he was instructed in the law at the age of three.[133] The difference in age is significant. It reflects the distinction between individuals with a capacity for reasoned analysis (Maimonides) and those whose knowledge of the law emerges from direct prophetic tutelage as encapsulated in the idea of listening (Rabad).

If we follow Rabad, how was Abraham tutored in the law? According to R. Simeon bar Yoḥai, God made his kidneys flow forth as two teachers.[134] "God provided Abraham with kidneys which were like two pitchers overflowing and filling him with wisdom and understanding all through the night, as it is said, *I will bless the Lord, who has given me counsel; even in the night my kidneys tutor me*."[135] Traditionally, the evening was the time for studying the oral law rather than the written law.[136] This instruction in law was more sustained over time than might be provided by the dream-like trance of the Covenant Between the Parts or the direct command of the Binding of Isaac; more full of detailed knowledge than the apprenticeship in judging experienced through the judgment of Sodom. It was said to include minute details of ritual observance. Abraham was taught the particulars of all the sacrifices except the tenth of the ephah; R. Simeon bar Yoḥai says even the tenth of the ephah.[137] Occurring every evening, this tutorial has an uncanny resemblance to the nightly Torah study of a dedicated scholar.

The appointment of the kidneys, however, suggests something beyond the practical rules of *halacha* is being transmitted. Kidneys are the seat of moral deliberation.[138] In Biblical imagery, God tests the kidneys and heart.[139] By making organs into teachers, the midrash suggests that law has both a divine source beyond the rational intellect—after all Abraham could not have determined these rules merely from the facts of nature—and the role of Abraham himself in the *paideia*. He has internalized the law, and now it flows through his being along with the bodily fluids. Nevertheless, it seems that only Abraham merited such an extraordinary mechanism of instruction which permitted the uncovering of legal principles without recourse to books.[140]

Even if Abraham has been able to assimilate the entire Torah in this fashion, he must figure out its transmission to others through more ordinary means. Not surprisingly, then, the idea of transmission was a *leitmotif* of the story of the law prior to Sinai.

Law was transmitted within the context of households. Various sources describe the tutoring of father to son among the pre-Sinai generations. Adam was said to know something of the Torah, and bequeathed it to his son Seth. "And he [Abraham] took the books of his father, and they were written in Hebrew, and he transcribed them, and he began from henceforth to study them, and I made known to him that which he could not [understand] and he studied them during the six rainy months."[141] One such bequeathed tradition concerned calendric calculations. "After the sun and moon were created, God "intercalated the years and afterwards He delivered the [calculations] to the first man in the Garden of Eden, as its is said, *This is the calculations for the generations of Adam*, the calculation of the world is therein for the generations of the children of Adam. Adam handed on the tradition to Enoch. . . . And Enoch delivered the principle of intercalation to Noah. . . . Noah handed on the tradition to Shem. . . . Shem delivered the tradition to Abraham; he was initiated in the principle of intercalation"[142] The focus on the calendar speaks to the anachronistic notion that the pre-Sinai generations observed festivals in their proper time. Such determinations may have required empirical observation of the sun and moon as well as calculations. To ascribe intercalations to the Patriarchs not only involved technical knowledge, it assumed the legal authority to render such binding decisions.

Abraham taught Isaac so that he was like him in all ways.[143] The "tongue of the creation," Hebrew, which was lost to general knowledge with the destruction of the Tower of Babel, was now reaffirmed as the language of law.[144] According to the midrash, the verse Abraham *armed his disciples* was interpreted as teaching them the portion of the Torah, Deuteronomy, Chapter 20, which discusses the laws of war.[145] Law seemed to follow life. The major focus was upon *shimush*, the apprenticeship of children and disciples with the domestic setting. Observing law in action was an important element in this training.

Nevertheless, the rabbinic legal imagination could not imagine a fully observant Jew without reference to the traditional means of investigating the corpus of learned law. Abraham is depicted as a sage who sat in the academy.[146] According to rabbinic sources, Abraham established a yeshiva, which continued through Isaac and Abraham's servant Eliezer to Jacob. Jacob, the dweller in tents, was said to be the prototype of the yeshiva student.[147] Traditional commentators claimed the existence of elders suggested a formal house of study. "From the days of our forefathers, academies did not depart from them. When they were in Egypt there was an academy with them, as it is stated, *go and gather the elders of Israel*; when they were in the Wilderness, there was an academy with them, for as it is stated, *gather to me seventy men from the elders of Israel.*[148] Not only was Abraham said to be the first to establish a clear chain of transmission, and perhaps to transfer this legacy through oral as well as written forms of Torah, but this communication between generations was an important touchstone for God's relationship with Abraham. *I know him* [Abraham] *for he commands his children and his household after him to keep the way of God.*[149] Knowing, as Rashi states, means more than simple awareness. It means divine intimacy.[150]

In a discussion of the rule of not allowing sacrifice to remain uneaten until the third day, Abraham was said to declare "I have found it written in the books of my forefathers (in the words of Enoch and in the words of Noah)."[151] There was a library, then, of legal books which impart the legal traditions of earlier generations. Presumably, these works focused on the Noahide law. Perhaps it was within the ambit of these texts that Abraham sought to expand the Noahide precepts into a more comprehensive code. "We have a tradition that Abraham's Talmud tractate of *Avoda Zara* contained four hundred chapters," commented R. Chisda in the Babylonian Talmud. "We have only learnt five and do not know what we are saying."[152]

This may reflect the notion that Abraham was surrounded by idolatrous nations and needed a more extensive legal text, such as *Avodah Zarah*, which deals with idolatry. However, such a statement also suggests that Abraham's extensive study created its own elaboration so that his oral law texts were even more well developed than those of the Talmud itself. Certainly, Abraham's role was evolving from the ideal type of Talmudic master who trained disciples through apprenticeship and engaged in oral debates to the authorial model of the medieval Jewish scholar. Maimonides claimed Abraham composed books of Torah.[153] Each generation fashioned Abraham in their own image.

None of these models—focusing upon an engagement with *lex scripta*—was suitable for those steeped in Greek legalism. Situating Abraham within a tradition of written law was itself a position fraught with controversy. The idea that a written text might be the highest authority, was "unthinkable for the Hellenistic mind."[154] Nevertheless, Philo, very much a citizen of broader Greek culture, was faced with the problem of justifying the authority of a written Mosaic law, which Philo calls "firm, unshaken, immovable, stamped, as it were with the seals of nature herself."[155] His response was to claim the virtues of the written Mosaic law are simply the fixed form of the unwritten law embodied in Abraham. For Abraham followed—and, in fact, established—the oral law which forms the foundation of its later written form.

Philo ends his *On Abraham* by describing Abraham's fealty to law as following unwritten nature: Abraham "did the divine law and the divine commands. He did them, not taught by written words, but unwritten nature gave him the zeal to follow where wholesome and untainted impulse led him. And when they have God's promises before them what should men do but trust in them most firmly? Such was the life of the first, the founder of the nation, one who obeyed the law, some will say, but rather as our discourse has shown [was] himself a law and an unwritten statute."[156] Oddly, Philo's claim that Abraham "was himself . . . an unwritten statute" shares a remarkable kinship with the Rebbe of Ger's suggestion, which we discussed earlier, that the oral law of the life of the Patriarchs preceded the *lex scripta* of Sinai.

Abraham resolved the triptych of obedience-transmission-interpretation which so bedeviled Adam. With the Binding of Isaac, the issue of obedience was laid to rest. Abraham demonstrated his subordination to the divine command through his willingness to sacrifice his son even when countervailing interpretations of the charge could have been made. Through his apprenticeship in the judgment of Sodom; delving into the *ta'amei ha-mizvot*, the rationales behind the commandments; and through his elaboration of the previously inert Noahide code within the scope of the performance of the law, Abraham learned the craft of legal interpretation. No doubt, Abraham sought to transmit the wisdom he had obtained. Nevertheless, his success, and indeed his redemption of the failure of Adam, may not endure. The problem was, of course, the limitations of human intellect in the absence of constant divine command. According to Maimonides in the *Book of Idolatry*, Abraham learned there was a God through gazing at the stars. He asked the question "is it possible that the celestial sphere should continuously be guided through its course without a guide?"[157] Maimonides follows an ancient tradition that sees Abraham as an astronomer or astrologer.[158] Abraham knew how to read the stars in order to achieve a true knowledge of the law.

But what if reason should deceive the star gazer? Much of the rest of the historical introduction to Maimonides *Book of Idolatry* is a cautionary tale. In the days of Enoch, idolatry began with the same fascination with celestial bodies. "Since God created the stars and celestial spheres to guide the world" these divine ministers should be set in a place of honor, praised, and glorified.[159] Looking at stars might result in the finding of a new religion—or in the corruption of old religious truths. Significantly, Maimonides seems to have seen the origins of idolatry much as Judah Halevi does in his well-known thesis about the Golden Calf—as the investing of proxies with divinity in the course of a search for a divine legislator.

Abraham, Maimonides insists, was able to attain perfection. However, his legal legacy was subject to corruption. Only the Tribe of Levi was able to retain some version of this oral law through its exile in Egypt. Abraham's model of obedience-interpretation-transmission was inadequate for the task. It required an extraordinary personality to be "himself an unwritten statute." Without constant recourse to either divine tutelage or the craft and discipline of a legal reasoning which rises above self-interest, and without an intact household willing to be subservient to the decision-making of the Patriarch, divine legislation would lose its force. Perhaps this problem of transmission explains why the Torah was given to the seed of Abraham—despite his extraordinary gifts—but not Abraham himself. As an individual, Judah Loew ben Beẓalel, known as the Maharal of Prague, explains, Abraham was susceptible to change. "But the Torah, which is God's eternal, unchanging plan, could only be given to someone who was himself unchanging. An individual is prone to change, unlike a people, whose destiny is fixed forever."[160] Clearly, the mortal vessel of law, a single individual such as Abraham, had to be replaced by a larger political unit whose law would reflect broader issues of governance over generations. The fluidity of oral legalism would be embodied in a fixed, yet more durable written code. If, as David Weiss Halivni has argued, Ezra's task was to repair a written Torah whose text had become corrupted over time, Moses may be said to have restored Abraham's oral legalism to its pure beginnings.[161]

It would be a mistake to see these twofold forms of legalism—household and national; oral and written; discretionary and prescribed; the law before the law and Sinai itself, as simply counterpoints. As Philo, Nachmanides, and the Rebbe of Ger would agree, the law of the Patriarchs became the grounding of the more elaborate legalism emerging after Revelation. After witnessing R. Eleazer ben Arakh expounding on Torah, Johanan ben Zakkai stood up and kissed his student on the head, saying "Fortunate are you, Patriarch Abraham, who have fathered Eleazer ben Arakh who knows how to understand and expound for the glory of his father in Heaven."[162] Descent from Abraham had become a metaphor. In a figurative sense, the exegetes in the Talmud belonged to Abraham's household.

Notes

1. Gen. 26:5.

2. *Midrash Mishle* (New York: Jewish Theological Seminary, 1990), 57; The *Midrash on Proverbs,* Trans. Burton L. Visotzky (New Haven: Yale University Press, 1992), 45.

3. PRK 12:1. *See*, also, Gen. R. 14:6, Abraham was worthy of being created prior to Adam. But he was created second in case Adam should fail and Abraham would be needed to repair the damage.

4. Abraham is the first man after Noah to speak directly with God, see: PRK 16:4. On the ten trials, *see Midrash Tehillim* 18, 25.

5. Joseph B. Soloveitchik, *Kol Dodi Dofek* in *Ish Ha-Emunah* (Jerusalem: Mosad Harav Kook, 1980/1), 86-87. Indeed, Soloveitchik posits a particularly modern understanding of the emotional underpinnings of pre-Sinai law. He describes the covenant of the Patriarchs, as opposed to the covenant of Sinai, as a setting apart. Even though Abraham followed the Torah, this observance was voluntarily and sporadic. Therefore, since the commandments did not reflect simple obedience to the divine will, their performance had an additional important purpose in distinguishing the Patriarchs from other peoples. This singularity was reflected in a loneliness which resided at the core of the covenant be-

tween God and Abraham. Joseph B. Soloveitchik, *Hamesh Ḍerashot* (Jerusalem: Makhon Orot, 1973/4), 85-97.

6. Gen. 15:2.

7. Nachmanides, Gen. 26:5. Similarly, see Rabbenu Baḥyya, Gen. 26:5.

8. Gen. 28:18. The prohibition reads: *and you shall not erect for yourselves a pillar, which the Lord, your God hates* (Deut. 16:22). *Sifre Devarim, piska* 146, recognizes this difference in observance between the generation of the Patriarchs and their descendants: the "pillar was loved by the Patriarchs and hated by their children."

9. *See*, for example, Gen. R. 84:13 which suggests Bilhah and Zilpah were sisters of Leah and Rachel. Forbidden in Lev. 18:18. From the fact that Jacob married two sisters, Ibn Ezra determined that this was an injunction "contingent on time or place or another matter" as opposed to incest with blood relatives. Abraham Ibn Ezra, *Yesod Morah ve-Sod Torah*, ed. Yosef Cohen and Uriel Simon (Ramat-Gan: Bar Ilan University Press, 2002), 119-22. Perhaps one of the most notable examples of a pre-Sinai figure violating Biblical law is recounted in the story of Reuben's sexual involvement with Bilhah (Gen. 35:22), *and it came to pass while Israel dwelled in that land, that Reuben went and lay with Bilhah, his father's concubine, and Israel heard.* According to Lev. 20:11, *a man who lies with his father's wife will have uncovered his shame; the two of them shall be put to death.* Anderson, "The Status of the Torah," 20-24.

10. Exod. 6:20.

11. Exod. 24:4. This was a particularly striking breach of the Deuteronomic injunction against erecting pillars since these twelve pillars were raised by Moses in the midst of the Sinai Covenant when the Jewish people accepted the Torah. This ceremony, and the use of twelve pillars as memorials, will be discussed in the last chapter.

12. Gen. 18:19.

13. Gen. 18:8.

14. Nachmanides, Gen. 28:18 and Gen. 26:5.

15. Nachmanides, Gen. 26:5. Forbidden in Lev. 18:18, *you shall not take a woman in addition to her sister, to make them rivals.*

16. Samuel Eliezer ben Judah Edels (Maharsha), *Ḥidushei Agudot,* Yoma 28b.

17. Gen. 18:8. *See*, *loc. cit.*, *Da'at Zekanim* (providing milk before the meat); *Ohr Sameaḥ* (providing a *ben pekuah*). The claim that the meat was from a fetus relies upon the language, *ben bakar*, child of a cow as referring to a calf. If we return to the dispute between Joseph and his brothers, which we discussed in the introductory chapter, then this proposition suggests that Abraham did follow the kosher laws according to the leniencies provided in the Talmud. Therefore, Joseph's brothers were simply following customary precedent inherited from Abraham. Joseph's criticism becomes all the more remarkable because it suggests that the situation was such in Abraham's time for Abraham

to avail himself of Talmudic leniencies; but his brothers' similar conduct was wrong in their own time. B. Ḥul. 33a establishes the legal norm.

18. *See* Nachmanides, Gen. 12:10 on Abraham committing a major sin by falsely identifying his wife as his sister; B. Ned. 32a on the transgression involving the arming of disciples. Baḥyya ben Asher blames the exile in Egypt of various of Abraham's transgressions, including identifying his wife as a sister, demonstrating a lack of faith by leaving Canaan for Egypt at the time of famine, and asking for proof (Gen. 15:8) that his descendants will inherit the land. Rabbenu Baḥyya, Gen. 12:13.

19. M. Kid. 4:14 on Abraham observing the Torah in its entirety. See, for example, the commentary of *Tiferet Yisrael, loc. cit.*, who links Abraham's reward with his fulfilling the commandments.

20. On Abraham granting a bill of divorce, PRE 216; Isaac tithing, *Yalkut Shimoni, Mishle* 938; Jacob and the Sabbath boundaries, *Pesikta Rabbati* 23.

21. Gen. R. 63:6; *Yalkut Shimoni, Toledot* 110.

22. B. B.B. 16b.

23. Gen. 1:29; Gen. 9:1.

24. Rabbenu Baḥyya, Gen. 28:6.

25. Gen. 15:5.

26. *See*, for example, Seforno's explanation that circumcision engraves the covenant on the reproductive organ because (1) "it symbolizes the eternity associated with the covenant;" and (2) since this organ is the reproductive one, the sign impressed upon it symbolizes the continuity of the covenant among later generations." Seforno, Gen. 17:14.

27. Franz Rosenzweig, *The Star of Redemption*, trans. William W. Hallo (Notre Dame: University of Notre Dame Press, 1985), 299-300. Leora Batnitzky, *Idolatry and Representation: The Philosophy of Franz Rosenzweig* (Princeton: Princeton University Press, 2000), 72-77.

28. Deut. 21:17. B.B.B., 126a. Indeed, the rabbis presumed that primogeniture was established in the time of the Patriarchs. When Isaac was born, Ishmael was supposed to have exclaimed that there was less reason for rejoicing because he was the one who would receive the double portion. Gen. R. 53:11.

29. Isaac Herzog, *The Main Institutions of Jewish Law* (London: Soncino Press, 1936), I: 50.

30. Num. 13:32.

31. *Seder Eliahu Rabbah*, ed. Meir Ish Shalom (Jerusalem: Warman Press, 1968/9), 29. Gen. 25:27, Rashi, Gen. 25:27.

32. Gen. R. 63:9.

33. Gen. 18:19.

34. Gen. 14:20. "Abraham set aside the first of great heave offering [one fiftieth of the crop], for he said to the Priest Melchizedek, *I have lifted up my hand unto the Lord* (Gen. 14:22), "lifting up" here connoting heave offering as

in the verse "you shall lift a heave offering of it for the Lord" (Num. 18:26). PRK 10, 6. On Abraham giving tithes, *see* also Jubilees 13:25.

35. Abraham's taking of a tenth as a tithe for Melchizedek would be compared to his demand for mercy if ten righteous men might be found in Sodom. PRE 27.

36. Rashi, Gen. 12:2.

37. Gen. 25:19 Why does the Bible say *And these are the offspring of Isaac son of Abraham—Abraham begot Isaac* (Gen. 25:19). Various commentators are puzzled by the redundant language. Why identify Isaac twice as the son of Abraham? As Rashi stated, "Since the text has just said, *Isaac, son of Abraham*, does it have to add, *Abraham begot Isaac*? But for the mockers of the generation who were saying, Sarah conceived from Abimelech—she lived with Abraham for many years without conceiving. What did God do? He formed Isaac's facial features like Abraham's, so that everyone testified, *Abraham begot Isaac*." B. B. M. 87a. While the similarity in features presents clear evidence of paternity, it poses a psychological problem. How can Isaac distinguish himself from his father while still retaining full fealty to the same ideals?

38. Exod. 14:13.

39. Gen. 26:5.

40. Gen. 9:6.

41. Gen. 18:25.

42. Ḥizkuni, Gen. 9:6. On God's name encompassing the idea of the central role of the magistrate, see Rabbenu Baḥyya, Gen. 1:1.

43. Gen R. 49:9.

44. Walter Benjamin, "The Storyteller: Observations on the Works of Nikolai Leskov" in *Walter Benjamin: Selected Writings*, 3: 143-66.

45. Gen. 18:18-19.

46. *See*, for example, Nachmanides, Gen. 18:19.

47. Gen. 18:21.

48. Job 9:24.

49. Tanḥuma, *Vayera*, 5. In traditional sources, God might be seen as consulting with others over such issues as the nature of creation, *see* Rabbenu Baḥyya, Gen. 1:26.

50. PRK 16:4, 268-69. See also, Gen. R. 39:6. Not every midrash views as wholly favorable Abraham's questioning God's justice in these cases. "You find that once Abraham pondered over the matter of divine justice. . . . Since you dare to reflect upon My actions, you must bring a burnt offering to Me. Therefore, He said: *Take now your son, your only son, whom you love, Isaac, and go to the Land of Moriah; and offer him there for a burnt offering upon one of the mountains I will tell you of*" (Gen. 22:2). *Tanḥuma*, Lech Lecha 10. This remarkable midrash suggests Isaac was an expiatory sacrifice. Alternatively, see Gen. R. 49:9, Abraham and Job made similar comments about the injustice of destroying the righteous along with wicked (Job 9:22). To explain why

Abraham was rewarded for what he said, and Job punished, commentators often state that Abraham spoke respectfully, Job disrespectfully.

51. Gen. 18:23 and 25.
52. On procedural justice, see Stuart Hampshire, *Justice is Conflict* (Princeton: Princeton University Press, 2000).
53. Gen. 18:17.
54. Rashi, Gen. 18:25.
55. Hampshire, *Justice is Conflict*, 19-48.
56. Rashi, Gen. 18:24-33.
57. Robert Cover, *Justice Accused: Antislavery and the Judicial Process* (New Haven: Yale University Press, 1975), 6-7.
58. Gen. 7:5.
59. Gen. 13:10.
60. Gen. 12:10. Mizraḥi, Gen. 12:10.
61. Gen. 19:1. Gen. R. 50:3. The word sat (*yoshev*)is written defectively (missing a *vav*), which alludes to the defective justice he performed. Also, Tanḥuma [Buber], *Vakyeira* 21 on Lot as one of 5 judges of Sodom.
62. Gen. R. 50:3.
63. B. San. 109b.
64. B. San. 109a, b.
65. Gen. 19:9. Gen. R. 50:3.
66. Rashi, Gen. 19:2-3.
67. Gen. 19:9.
68. Gen. 19:25.
69. Gen. 18:18-19.
70. Gen. R. 51:8 states that Lot's daughters thought the world would be destroyed as it was in the time of the flood. According to Nachmanides, Gen. 19:32, Lot's daughters determined that they might have sexual intercourse with their father as this was not enjoined under the Noahide code. Lot's daughters were seen as relying upon the exemption granted Cain for marrying his sister since this was necessary to sustain the world. B. San. 58b.
71. Gen. 19:31-35.
72. Rashi, Gen. 19:33 sees the elder sister as the more culpable since she initiated the sexual relations.
73. Gen. 19:37.
74. Seforno, Gen. 19:16.
75. Seforno, Gen. 18:33.
76. Gen. 21:9. Gen. R. 53:11.
77. Gen. 18:23. On the relationship between the use of *vayigash* by both Abraham and Judah, *see* Tanḥuma, *Vayera*, 4.
78. Gen. 27:21-22.
79. Gen. 27:8.
80. Gen. 44:18.

81. Lev. 26:46.
82. Deut. 12:1.
83. Gen. 18:19.
84. B. Yoma 28b. On Abraham knowing the entire: *Torah, see* Tanḥuma [Buber], *Lekh Lekha* 1, 11, 14, *Va-Yigash* 12, *BeHar* 3, *Pikudei* 5. *Yalkut Shemoni, Toldot* 111. *Also see* Syriac Baruch 57:1-2; Jubilees, 23:10. *Damascus Document* from the Dead Sea Scrolls, "Abraham was accounted a friend of God because he kept the commandments of God and did not choose his own will. And he handed them down to Isaac and Jacob, who kept them, and were recorded as friends of God and part to the Covenant forever." Geza Vermes, *The Complete Dead Sea Scrolls in English* (London: Penguin Press, 1997), 129. The dissection of the four-fold description of law may be seen in *Midrash ha-Gadol*, ed. Mordecai Margoliot, 10 vols. (Jerusalem: Mossad Harav Kook, 1997), *Toldot* 26:5, where *My charges* refers to extending beyond the letter of the law (*lefanim me-shurat ha-din*); *My commandments* refers to tithes (through comparison with Gen. 14:20); *My statutes* refers to incest (through comparison with Lev. 18:30); *My teachings* (or *Torahs*) refers to circumcision since it was said to be the equivalent of all the Torah.
85. *See* B. Yoma 28b, Ritva *loc. cit. See, also,* Seforno's comment (Gen. 17:3) that Abraham's circumcision of the reproductive organ, whereby the species is perpetuated, symbolizes the eternity associated with the covenant—and transmission to further generations.
86. Tanḥuma [Buber], *Lekh, Lekha*, 3.
87. Justin Martyr, *Dialogue with Trypho,* 16 *Writings of Saint Justin Martyr* (Washington: Catholic University of America Press, 1977), David Rokeah, *Justin Martyr and the Jews* (Leiden: Brill Publishers, 2002), 43-60. Justin Martyr inverts the circumcision from a *symbolica heroica*, an emblem of kinship to the divine law giver, into a mark of Cain—a signification of divine punishment rendering the Jews as social outcasts.
88. Rashi's view that *My charge* refers to second degree incest is based upon B. Yev. 21a, which finds parallel language used in both the Biblical passage discussing incest (Lev. 18:30), *'asu mishmeret le-mishmarti* (*you shall establish a guard for my charge*) and our passage, *va-yishmar mishmarti* (*My charge*). The Talmud identifies second degree incest as a rabbinic prohibition.
89. Seforno, Gen. 26:5. Rashbam, Gen. 26:5, also agrees with Seforno's non-anachronistic reading of Abraham's fulfillment of the commandments. In addition to the one direct commandment of circumcision, Abraham followed customary laws such as those concerning theft, sexual prohibitions, covetousness, civil law, and the rules regarding hospitality. In general, Rashbam is unsympathetic to anachronistic readings of the Biblical text.
90. B. Yoma, 28b.
91. Tanḥuma [Buber], *Lekh-Lekha*, 3.

92. Nachmanides, Gen. 26:5. Nachmanides' notion of discretion might also be seen in his reading of the narrative of Judah and Tamar. While under post-Sinai Jewish law the responsibility of levirate marriage obligates only the brother to offer matrimony to his sibling's widow, Nachmanides claimed pre-Sinai Patriarchs, "the ancient wise men who were prior to the Torah, knew of the great benefit in marrying a childless dead brother's wife," and believed that in those cases where the brother refused or was unable to meet this responsibility, the law applied to other near relatives. This explains how Judah, father-in-law to the widowed Tamar, came to marry her. Nachmanides, Gen. 38:7.

93. Rabbenu Baḥyya, Gen. 26:5.

94. Nachmanides, Gen. 26:5.

95. *See*, generally, Yitzhak Heinemann, *Ta'amei Ha-Miẓvot be-Sifrut Yisrael* (Jerusalem: Ḥorev Publishers, 1992/3).

96. Nachmanides, Gen. 26:5.

97. Nachmanides, Gen. 26:5. Gen R. 79:7. This passage interprets *and he encamped before the city* (Gen. 33:18) as setting the limits of the Sabbath boundaries.

98. For another example of Nachmanides' view of the importance of knowing the purpose behind the commandments, *see* his discussion of the marriage of Judah's son, Onan, to his brother's widow, Tamar. According to Nachmanides, Judah practiced the custom of "the ancient wise men who were prior to the Torah" which saw—it is hinted—transmigration of the souls as the basis for levirate marriage since the late brother's soul might become incarnate in the child issued from the union of a brother and deceased's widow. Knowing the mystical purpose of the law, prompted Judah's own marriage to Tamar after the death of Onan. The marriage of Judah and Tamar was, Nachmanides explains, also a form of levirate marriage which existed *before* the reception of written law. But the Torah later came to prohibit such father–daughter-in-law marriages. Nachmanides, Gen. 38:8.

99. Ḥayim of Volozhin, *Nefesh ha-Ḥayim*, 1: 21. Norman Lamm, *Torah Lishmah: Torah for Torah's Sake in the Works of Rabbi Hayyim of Volozhin and his Contemporaries* (New York: Yeshiva University Press, 1989), 107-10. On Ḥayim of Volozhin's idealization of Torah study, see Alan Nadler, *The Faith of the Mithnagdim: Rabbinic Responses to Hasidic Rapture* (Baltimore: Johns Hopkins University Press, 1997), 154-65.

100. B. Mak. 22b.

101. M. Kid. 4:14; B. Yoma 28b; B. Ned. 32a; Gen. R. 95, 3; *Maḥzor Vitry* 139. *See* Baal Ha-Turim, Gen. 26:5, where it states that *Abraham listens to my voice* in Hebrew is the numerical equivalent of *he fulfilled even eruv tavshilin.* According to *Midrash Tehillim*, 112, 1, this verse suggests that Abraham knew the entire Torah from the first letter to the last, and composed the acrostic from Prov. 31 for a woman of valor in honor of his wife, Sarah, who also knew the Torah. R. Moshe Isserles, the seventeenth-century legal authority known as

Rama, writes that Abraham knew all the commandments, even *eruv tavshilin*, but this referred only to Abraham. The individuals who lived within his household were only obligated to the extent of the Noahide code. Moshe Isserles, *Shealot u-Teshuvot Ha-Rema*, ed. Asher Siev (Jerusalem: Feldheim Publishing House, 1970), Responsum 10, 45.

102. On the role of unexpected and memorable speech in Jewish exegesis, *see* David Stern, *Midrash and Theory: Ancient Jewish Exegesis and Contemporary Literary Studies* (Evanston: Northwestern University Press, 1996), 55-71.

103. A dispute in the Talmud underscores the role of the rabbis in establishing the law of *eruv tavshilin*. Rabbah states that according to scripture, a person may cook on a holiday for the Sabbath since it is unclear whether there might be circumstances when the food might be used on the holiday itself. According to Rav Chisdah, there is a Biblical prohibition against preparing food for a weekday, not a Sabbath. Both agree that it was the rabbis who enjoined what was permitted preparation and then created a mechanism to circumvent the prohibition. B. Pes. 46b. On the reasoning behind the original prohibition, *see* B. Beẓ. 15b. R. Samuel Edels suggests that this shows the extent of the oral law Abraham followed since the *eurv tavshilin* has no basis in the essence of the written law. Maharsha, B. Yoma 28b.

104. Tanḥuma [Buber], *Lekh Lekha*, 14.

105. *Midrash Tehillim* [Buber], Ps. 1:13.

106. B. Beẓ. 15b explicitly derives the *eruv tavshilin* from the verse *remember the Sabbath day and sanctify it* (Exod. 20:8).

107. Tanḥuma [Buber], *Lekh Lekha*, 1.

108. Tanḥuma [Buber], *Noah*, 22-24.

109. Tanḥuma, *Noah*, 2.

110. Avraham Yitzhak Ha-Cohen Kook, *Igerot Ha-Rayah,* I: 134-35.

111. Gen. R, 11:7.

112. Gen. R, 64:4. Ḥatam Sofer states that Abraham was rewarded for observing the commandment of *erev teḥumim* by being granted boundaries of the land for descendants. You will be like the stars, I will grant you this land. See also, Gen. 14:15, where in the war with the Four Kings, Abraham divides the camp to remain within the *teḥum*.

113. Gen. 26:5.

114. *See,* for example, B. Kid. 22b.

115. M. Kid. 1:6.

116. Gen. 15:1-21.

117. Gen. 17:9-14.

118. Gen. 17:13.

119. Gen. 26:5.

120. Gen. 22:18.

121. See, for example, Judah Loew ben Beẓalel (Maharal), *Gur Aryeh*, Gen. 26:5. Malbim, *loc. cit.*, identifies the special merit of Abraham as the fact that

he did not derive his knowledge of God through inherited wisdom, but through various tests.

122. Gen. 22:2.

123. Gen. 3:8.

124. Aharon Agus, *The Binding of Isaac and Messiah: Law, Martyrdom, and Deliverance in Early Rabbinic Religiosity* (Albany: State University of New York Press, 1988), esp. 33-68. Shalom Spiegel, *The Last Trial: On the Legends and Lore of the Command to Offer Isaac as a Sacrifice: The Akedah*, trans. Judah Goldin (Philadelphia: JPS, 1967).

125. Gen. 22:12.

126. Gen. 18:19.

127. Rashi, Gen. 22:2.

128. R. Abraham Isaac Kook, *Igerot Ha-Rayah*, 2:43.

129. Gen. 22:17.

130. Cover, *Nomos and Narrative*, 105-10.

131. *Midrash Ha-Gadol*, Gen. 11:3.

132. Maimonides. MT I, iv, 1:2. David Hartman, *Israelis and the Jewish Tradition: An Ancient People Debating its Future* (New Haven: Yale University Press, 2000), 64-69. *See* B. Ned. 32a, "R. Ami bar Abba said: Abraham recognized his creator at the age of three, as it is said *inasmuch as Abraham listened to my voice*." The word *inasmuch* or *eikev* from our verse has a numerical value of one hundred and seventy-two, suggesting that he obeyed the commandments for this length of time. Since he died at age one hundred and seventy-five, Abraham therefore began to observe the law at the age of three. *Pesikta Rabbati*, Piska 21, suggests Abraham was either forty-eight years old or fifty when he became aware of God.

133. Ned. 32a. According to Tanḥuma [Buber], *Lekh Lekha* 3, "At three years of age, Abraham recognized his creator." *See* Tanḥuma [Buber], *Va-Yigash*, Buber/T284. Hasagat HaRabad, Mishnah Torah, *Avodah Zarah* 1:2. On Rabad, a major intellectual opponent of Maimonides, *see* Isadore Twersky, *Rabad of Posquieres: A Twelfth-Century Talmudist* (Cambridge: Harvard University Press, 1962).

134. Gen. R. 61:1; *Avot d'R. Nathan*, 33:1; *Yalkut Shemoni*, *Tehillim* 5214. Tanḥuma [Buber], *Va-Yigash* 12.

135. *Midrash Tehillim*, 16:7. According to Jubilees 4:19, Enoch, a vital figure in the chain of transmission, "saw in a vision of his sleep" what will happen to his descendants through the generations.

136. *Midrash Tehillim*, 19:7.

137. Lev. R., 3:3. This refers to the unit of volume for a meal offering. R. Shimon bar Yochai is suggesting that a meal offering accompanied the ordained sacrifices at the Covenant Between the Pieces.

138. Harry Austryn Wolfson, *Philo: Foundations of Religious Philosophy in Judaism, Christianity, and Islam* (Cambridge: Harvard University Press, 1947), 2:185.

139. Jeremiah, 11:20. *See* also on the role of kidneys: Psalms 73:21.

140. According to Menachem Nachum of Chernobyl, an important eighteenth-century Hasidic master, *Meor Enayim* (New Square: Meor Torah Institute, 1997), 81, being tutored through the kidneys allowed Abraham to see the Torah as it was conceived in the divine mind prior to its existence.

141. Jubilees 12:27.

142. PRE 8; Jubilees 4, 16-18. Intercalations involved the addition of an extra month to allow the Festivals to fall in their proper season. Sacha Stern, *Calendar and Community: A History of the Jewish Calendar 2nd Century BCE to the 10th Century CE* (Oxford: Oxford University Press, 2001), 47-62.

143. Exod. R. 1:1. Isaac was said to have studied more than Abraham, presumably this was partly because he benefitted from the presence of his father as a tutor. Exod. R. 2:6.

144. Jubilees 12:25-26.

145. Gen. R. 43:2.

146. B. Yoma, 28b.

147. Gen. 25:27. Indeed, Judah Loew ben Beẓalel (Maharal of Prague) suggests that Jacob learning the details of Torah in traditional yeshiva fashion would merit the Jews receiving the Torah while Abraham, the exemplar of law in action, would not. Judah Loew ben Beẓalel (Maharal), *Derekh Ḥayim*, ed. Ḥayim Pardes (Tel Aviv: Machon Mordecai, 1980), 112.

148. B. Yoma, 28b. Exod. 3:16; Num. 11:16. On Isaac learning directly from Abraham and Jacob's decision to supplement his training under Isaac with study at the yeshiva of Eber, see Exod. R. 1, 1.

149. Gen. 18:19.

150. Gen. 18:19, Rashi and Rabbenu Baḥyya.

151. Jubilees 21:10.

152. B. A. Z., 14b.

153. Maimonides. MT I, iv, 1:2.

154. Hindy Najman, "The Law of Nature and the Authority of Mosaic Law, *Studia Philonica Annual* 11 (1999) 55-73. Much of my discussion here owes its analysis to Najman's sophisticated exploration of Philo's dilemma concerning the place of oral law.

155. Philo, *De Vita Mosis*, II, 14.

156. Philo, *De Abrahamo*, 275-76.

157. Maimonides, M.T. I, iv, 1:2.

158. See, for example, Abraham searching the night sky for indications of future rain (Jubilees, 12,16); Abraham introducing Egyptians to science of astronomy (Josephus, *The Antiquities of the Jews*, 1, 8). Abraham looked at

constellations and through astrology, and saw that he was not fated to have children. B. Ned. 32a.

159. Maimonides, MT I, iv, 1:2.

160. Judah Loew ben Beẓalel (Maharal), *Tiferet Yisrael*, ed. Ḥayim Pardes (Tel Aviv: Yad Mordecai, 1984/5), 189.

161. David Weiss Halivni, *Revelation Restored: Divine Writ and Critical Responses* (Boulder: Westview Press, 1997).

162. T. Ḥag. 2:1.

Chapter Four

The Giving of the Commandments at Marah

And he [Moses] cried to God; and God showed him a wood, and he cast it into the waters, and the waters became sweet; there He made for them a statute and an ordinance, and there He tried them.[1]

After all the traumas of slavery, it is ironic that the Israelites encountered bitter water at Marah, a place whose very name means bitterness. Slavery, as evidenced in the bitter herbs eaten with the Paschal sacrifice, is itself associated with bitterness.[2] Should not the first encounter with freedom mean bitterness is left behind? Nevertheless, after only a few brief days of liberation the newly emancipated Jews at Marah experienced both bitter waters and the autonomy which comes with acquiring their own laws for the first time. Even before reaching Sinai, according to the rabbis, a variety of laws, including a civil law system, were given by Moses to the Jews in the wilderness at Marah.[3] For it says when describing the encampment at Marah, *there He made for them a statute and an ordinance*.[4] The Hebrew for *there He made* (*sham sam*) in our verse concerning Marah, the first encampment in the Wilderness, directly echoes the placing of man within the garden in the Eden narrative, *And He placed there the man* (*va-yasem sham*).[5] Marah was another opportunity to revisit the primordial giving of the first law to Adam.

There are parallels and significant differences between Eden and the oasis of Marah. In Eden, there was a single tree which was taboo amongst a large number of fruit-bearing plants. At Marah, there is no command issued against consuming a particular object. The water itself is permitted; but, as in the myth of Tantalus, it remains undrinkable. Dealing with the permissible in whatever new circumstances are encountered, evokes a more elaborate legal response than simple prohibition. What will be the reaction to this dangerous mix of temptation and adversity? Will it shatter the unity which the people shared as they embarked upon the Exodus? Marah demands a social law. The newly emancipated Jews cannot tear themselves apart as they respond to the strains of the journey out of Egypt. Unlike with Adam, no single command was issued to a single individual. Instead, laws will be furnished for governing a nation as a whole. Focusing upon the psychological posture within the framework of law, the Israelites at Marah must ascertain how to obey, interpret, transmit, *and* expand the substance of a legal code not simply within an individual or a domestic context, but as part of the complex fabric of civil society.

Quite remarkably, the law giving at Marah, like the Decalogue, consisted of ten sets of commandments.[6] As we will see, there are other parallels between Marah and Sinai, and the singularity of the revelation at Sinai collapses as we consider Marah as a prior encounter with receiving the law. This is significant because it places Jewish law within the framework we saw in the readings for the fifth day—as part of a series of stations where law is transmitted to Adam and Noah; to Abraham and the Patriarchs; and, through the millennia in the form of oral law and written law, customary law and codes, moments of intense immanence and moments where the reality of divine law-giving transcendence seems so overwhelming that even our own interpretive skills no longer are capable of furnishing comfort as we face the abyss of distance.

In his well-known response to Martin Buber's focus on the inner power of the Jews which is independent of law, Franz Rosenzweig suggested that Jewish legalism exists far beyond the reliance upon Sinai as the source of obedience, as a cabined moment when we become bound by external rules. Rosenzweig inventoried the Torah before Sinai. He found an ever-expanding corpus of well-developed, internal, and even contested legalism emerging both before and in the wake of Sinai, but outside the scope of immediate revelation. How, he asks, "can we really fancy that Israel kept this law, this Torah, only because . . . the six hundred thousand heard the voice of God on Sinai?"[7] The answer is the opposite of the rhetorical question posed to R. Judah which was discussed at the beginning of our investigation: the Torah was truly given multiple times.

Nevertheless, the law giving at Marah remains a half-forgotten episode. Indeed, this remarkable lacuna in the collective Jewish legal historical memory reminds us, more than any other incident, the way other sources of law might be eclipsed through a unitary and dramatic revelatory moment like Sinai. We will discuss below the particular laws which were given at Marah. Pivotal among these was said to be a corpus of civil law. This choice was particularly telling. Prior to the Exodus from Egypt, God's law was transmitted through a covenantal relationship between individuals and God.

As we have seen, Adam and his immediate descendants experienced the first encounter with law. Their successes and failures as they grappled with the triptych of obedience-transmission-interpretation, and with the problem of expanding the corpus of legal knowledge, often were difficult to convey to the next generation. Abraham, however, benefitted from the direct divine tutelage in law, learning the skills of judging and classifying, which he bequeathed to his children and members of the Patriarchal household. But such domestic transmission remained fragile. The covenant rested upon a succession of remarkable individuals. After God's intervention in Jewish history with the redemption from Egypt, the covenant became a national mission. Now the people as a whole would need to be fashioned into *nomian* beings.

This transformation was even more radical considering the recent experience of slavery. It might have been possible to replicate the condition of slavery, with its unceasing demand for obedience, in the *halacha* itself. But the Torah was to be a code where the law would be internalized, interpreted in manifold ways, and expanded through the legal analysis. In short, Marah demonstrated to the people, and God, that they were capable of becoming norm bearing in this particular fashion. No wonder, then, the narrative of legislation at Marah focuses on the experience of living the first Sabbath with little attention to the grandeur of revelation—so unlike the lightning and thunder of Sinai. For the endeavor of the people constructing a *nomos* must take place away from the overwhelming presence of an imminent God's law giving. This, we shall see, was the ultimate test mentioned at the end of our verse. Can the people live with their law, its interpretation and its use in everyday life, as the tempered command of a distant God, and—this may be the most difficult task—can they live under this legal regime with each other?

Exodus and Civil Society

Let us resume our story. The Patriarchal tradition of learning law has been interrupted by the experience of slavery in Egypt. Only a few remnants of early norms were said to have survived the rupture. According to traditional sources, these include the custom of preserving a Hebrew name, not to forsake their language, and—even with the terrible demands of taskmasters—to insist upon celebrating wedding feasts.[8] This survival is important for creating a bridge between past legalism and a perceived future commonwealth. The central feature of culture given first to Adam, the power to name; the particular language of Abraham; and the Patriarchal institution of marriage survive the dislocations of Egyptian slavery.

Moreover, the midrash claimed the Israelites established a covenant whereby they would only treat each other with kindness.[9] This suggests the Israelites were attempting to preserve at least some elements of civil society even in the midst of bondage. But the fragments of inherited legal knowledge from the Patriarchal period seems rudimentary indeed. Customary traditions are half-remembered. Moses is surprised when he encounters God at the Burning Bush for the immediate relationship with the divine law giver, the sort of apprenticeship Abraham experienced in judging or the tutorial in legal details delivered through his kidneys, has ceased. Clearly, the Jewish people inherited a dearth of legal foundations. If this were all the law the Jews were to receive, they might never have been able to devise the interpretive dexterity they would employ in law making as free individuals.

During their last days of slavery, however, the Israelites were given a series of commandments as part of their leave taking from Egypt.[10] They must calculate when the holiday of Passover begins; banish leaven bread from their homes; perform correctly the ritual sacrifice of the Passover offering; eat the offering as roasted meat without leaving over any of the offering for the next day nor breaking any of its bones; eat *matzah* and obey the prohibition against consuming leavened bread; and recount the narrative of the Exodus from Egypt. Two commandments were particularly important. For these, like the circumcision of Abraham or near sacrifice of Isaac, scripted a role of blood to seal the intimacy of the covenant. "They were bound closely to Me in Egypt by two precepts, by the blood of the Passover sacrifice and the blood of circumcision, as it says, *And when I passed by you, and saw you wallowing in your blood, I said to you: in your blood live*—this is the blood of the Passover sacrifice; *yes I said to you: in your blood live*—this is the blood of circumcision."[11]

Blood ties were critical in sealing covenants. Abraham's circumcision demanded a token of blood. Revelation at Sinai, as we shall see, would be marked by a sacrifice. Indeed the midrash links the dipping of the bundle of hyssop in bowls of blood and casting the blood upon the doorpost at the time of the Exodus with the blood gathered in bowls as Moses reads the *Book of the Covenant* at Sinai. When he concluded the reading of the *Book of the Covenant*—perhaps, as we discussed in the first chapter, enumerating all the law giving from Adam to the revelation of the Torah at Sinai—and the people called out *we will do and we will obey*—then Moses cast the blood upon them, saying *behold the blood of the covenant.*[12] Issued at the threshold of flight from Egypt, the paired precepts of both circumcision and the Passover both recall and anticipate other covenants, pointing backwards in time towards Abraham and forwards towards Moses. By performing these two commandments, the Israelites would merit redemption.[13]

According to the calculation of Maimonides, twenty commandments were given to the Israelites on the eve of their Exodus. These are largely concerned with the rules governing the first Passover in Egypt. The fact that so many commands were directed towards the departing Israelites, even as they stood on the threshold of their journey, suggests fealty to divine law would be a signal token of freedom. Yet the Passover commandments represent more than ritual precepts.[14] These laws might be understood as the initial step towards establishing rule of law for a civil society. The Passover *seder* was really a little commonwealth, a society in miniature, with Passover commandments regulating its governance. For Adam, law was a matter of individual decision making; for Abraham, it was concerned with the transmission of norms within the extended family. However, the *seder* demarcated a new stage towards constructing a social unit beyond the family. The essential requirement for consuming the Passover sacrifice was the creation of a fellowship called a *ḥaburah.*

In order to be a member of the *ḥaburah*, an individual had to register prior to the sacrifice of the Paschal offering. Registration for the *ḥaburah* created a fellowship that might shift, adding members or losing members, until the time of the sacrifice's designation. Defining the *ḥaburah* as a continuing entity composed of free citizens was especially important for marking the end of bondage. Registration for the *ḥaburah* may have functioned much like the Roman *manumissio censu* where enrollment in the list of free citizens provided for manumission of slaves.[15] Only those committed to Jewish law—the pre-Sinai *halacha* of Abraham—might register. In fact, even those non-Israelites who were strict adherents to the Noahide code were specifically barred from partaking in the meal—*a sojourner and a hired laborer shall not eat it.*[16] The *ḥaburah* was limited to Israelites, though inclusive of women and minors. Males were required to be circumcised. Circumcision, as we have discussed, signifies having the law inscribed on the flesh in much the same as it would later be carved into stone tablets.

Registration for the *ḥaburah* established a constructive kinship around which society might form. One of the laws of Passover forbids those registered from taking their portion elsewhere to be consumed—*in one house it shall be eaten.*[17] Even though registrants might be from different families, they are constructively considered as members of one household for the Passover evening. Compare the *seder* with its governing laws, and especially the registration requirement, to Abraham's *eruv tavshilin* or *eruv ḥaẓerot*. These legal devices involve establishing a symbolic meal which others might rely upon to prepare for the holidays or carry on the Sabbath within a quasi-public domain. However, such reliance does not demand registration or any sort of stake holding on the part of other individuals. In a sense, those relying upon Abraham's *eruv* would have been the equivalent of guests in *his* household—this being perhaps another *exempla* of Abraham's hospitality. Such individuals would not be common members of a mutual enterprise as was the case with the Passover sacrifice. Not surprisingly, then, the words *Torah* and *citizen* are used for the first time when describing the Passover commandments. *One law shall there be for the citizen and the proselyte who lives among you.*[18] The *ḥaburah* presaged the statutes which would be given at Marah for the creation of civil society.

As a society, the *haburah* would depend upon the equitable distribution of the sacrificial portion among its members. In this regard, it anticipates the division of the land over forty years later. Just as the paschal sacrifice must be divided in such a way that each member of the fellowship receives a similar portion so the land would be parceled out in the future to those families embarking upon its conquest. The connection between the *ḥaburah* as the model for civil society and the later establishment of a settled society also might be seen in narrative of how the second Passover, the *Pesaḥ sheni*, was instituted. Unable to participate in the Passover sacrifice at the ordinary time because they were ritually impure, a number of individuals approached Moses, saying *we are contaminated through a human corpse, why should we be diminished by not offering God's offering in its appointed time among the people of Israel*?[19]

Since the years of journeying from Egypt to the land of Israel would be so difficult, the commandment of bringing the Passover sacrifice would be suspended until entering the land except in the case of this first and only *seder* in the Wilderness. This is the only opportunity these individuals would have to consume the sacrifice within a *ḥaburah*. Instructed by God, Moses responds to the problem through creating a new legal rule. If a sacrifice cannot be offered during the first Passover, then a second Passover would be instituted one month later. Impure individuals might bring the Passover sacrifice at that time with other individuals who may have been rendered ineligible for various reasons.

The language of the grievance, and those who might miss the opportunity of a Passover *seder*, *why should we be diminished* (*lama nigra*) echoes another remarkable incident where the daughters of Zelophehad complain that they are unable to inherit their portion of land as women—*why should our father's name be diminished* (*lama yigara*)?[20] Moses again establishes a new legal principle, creating a system beyond agnatic inheritance. As has been pointed out elsewhere, the word *diminished* connects these two somewhat similar incidents of law making. The Hebrew word suggests becoming "cut off or separated."[21] Being barred from participation in the *haburaḥ* is analogous to disinheritance. Both call into question the membership of individuals in the polity. The small portion of the Passover sacrifice stands as a proxy for the portion of land, the *naḥalah*, granted each Israelite family. To lose one's portion is to lose a place in society as well.

The Exodus provided both the model for a commonwealth and the source of collective memory. Such a wondrous redemption has so marked the identity of the Jews that they are required to retell the story every year at the Passover *seder*, and remember it daily. It is recalled in prayers sanctifying the Sabbath. All this emphasis upon memory mirrors the remembering of God. He hears the groans of his people, and remembers his covenant with the Patriarchs. In turn, the people begin to cleave to a God which will never be forgotten. Only Pharaoh remains incredulous. Culminating in the terrible striking down of the Egyptian firstborn, Ten Plagues are required to liberate the Israelites. These miraculous plagues—conjuring frogs to hop out of beds and ovens; a sky darkened with locusts; the unexpected death of cattle—create the images for the story of remembering.

Remembering forms part of a meta-narrative which informs the entire course of Jewish history, a people endlessly exiled and who hopes to be redeemed. No matter how important this meta-narrative appears, however, we must be aware of its limitations. The meta-narrative of the Exodus could have led simply to fostering a sense of national identity without corresponding obligations; it simply could be used to prop up an imprecise sense of moral responsibility ("because we were strangers in Egypt"); or even become as ephemeral as any other historical happening which does not touch the everyday lives of the descendants of those who witnessed the event. Despite the fact that there was no greater overturning of the rules of nature, and no greater claim upon collective memory, than the splitting of the Red Sea, it may not have differentiated the Israelites from other people without the subsequent law giving moment at another body of water, Marah. As the midrash says about the verse in Song of Songs, *my love, my perfect dove,* God showed his divine love with the miracle at the Red Sea. However, "at Marah, where they received the commandments and became distinguished by all manner of precepts and virtues and good deeds like a dove which is distinguished from other birds."[22]

In the course of their redemption, the Israelites have often encountered water—so far with good fortune. The waters of Egypt had been turned to blood as the first plague. Aaron was ordered to *stretch out your hand over the waters of Egypt; over their rivers; their canals; over their reservoirs; and over all their gatherings of waters, and they shall become blood; and there shall be blood throughout the land of Egypt, even in the wooden and stone vessels.*[23] It was also water which effected what might be considered the penultimate punishment against Egypt: the destruction of Pharaoh and his army. Against outward logic, God directs the fleeing Israelites backwards towards the land of Egypt. This creates what might be called an unneeded miracle—for the miracle of the splitting of the Red Sea, unlike those of the plagues, was not necessary to effect the redemption from slavery. For without the return to the Egyptian border it need not have occurred.

Clearly, part of the divine plan was to bring about one more incident of God's imminence, a symbolic conquest of Pharaoh greater than all the others. Pharaoh gathers six hundred elite chariots and officers, and pursues the Jews. Witnessing the approach of the Egyptian army, the people cry out to both God and Moses. Moses stretches out his arm over the sea, it split, and the people entered into its midst in order to come out on dry land upon the other shore. The Egyptians follow. *Then the Lord said to Moses, stretch out your arm over the sea, that the waters may come back over the Egyptians and upon their chariots and upon their horsemen.*[24] Moses held his arm again over the sea, and the waters returned to their original place, drowning Pharaoh and his army. Deep waters covered them; they descended in the depths like stone.[25]

The spontaneous epiphany of the Song of the Sea marking the Israelite praise of their victorious God is one the most striking examples of anthropomorphism in the Bible. *God is a master of war. Your right hand smashes the enemy*. His nostrils blast forth in anger. Like Moses, if one may compare the two, miracles take place when God *stretches* [His] . . . *right hand and the earth swallows them.*[26] This anthropomorphism was not idolatry. However, even at the apotheosis of redemption, it also presented a warning of eidetic images and effusive language that might slip into pagan imagery. Instead of praising God, they may have praised the sea as a substitute or crafted false visual representations of God's power. The fact is that there exists a paradoxical relationship between divine immanence and idolatry. Those moments when God most clearly enters history—for purposes of redemption or revelation—unleash an exuberance of belief which might result in idolatry. There is a desire to hold on to the perceptible form of God as warrior at the Sea or as law giver at Sinai, and to seek a tangible object of attachment. The root of idolatry is the insistence upon a concrete representation of imminence.[27] Law, with its subtle shift from concrete to abstract and back to concrete again, serves as an antidote. Not surprisingly, then, the redemption at one body of water, the Red Sea, is followed by a law giving at another, Marah.

Prior to the splitting of the Red Sea, the Israelites are told *as you have seen Egypt, you shall not see them ever again.*[28] This is a puzzling phrase. For some, it is simply an assurance that the Israelites will not be returned to slavery. For others, such as Nachmanides, it is a commandment forbidding the Jews from permanently living in Egypt again.[29] Whether or not it constitutes an instance of pre-Sinai law giving, it seems odd that not long after hearing that they will not again see the Egyptians, the Israelites witness the corpses of the Egyptians washed ashore. The emphasis on the visual in the verse, cannot mean literally laying eyes upon the Egyptians. Rather, it may refer to the fact that the Jews will never again *see* the Egyptians in the same way. Without their slaves to mirror their own sense of grandiosity, the Egyptians can never be recognized as masters; rather, they are seen as those whom bondage trapped in a role where they are dependent upon the eyes of others.[30]

There needs to be a warning, if not a command, of not seeing the Egyptians as masters because after the experience of servility, it might be tempting for the Israelites to establish a simulacrum of Egypt within their new civil society. According to the midrash, the words *and Moses caused Israel to journey from the Red Sea* suggests that they only left under compulsion. The *Mekhilta* describes how some of the Israelites wished to return to Egypt in order to assume the places of their Egyptian masters whose corpses now lay before them on the shore of the sea. They even wished to make an idol to place at their head, much as they would do through making a Golden Calf at the base of Sinai. But Moses compelled them to travel onwards with his staff.[31] The very instrument of power against Pharaoh—the staff which ushered forth plagues or caused the Sea to split—was now being used against the Jews themselves. Perhaps it was difficult to leave the place where God had intervened most notably within the course of history. Moses eventually also would compel the people to leave Mount Sinai after receiving the Torah.[32]

There also may have been less admirable motives for remaining at the Red Sea. The now freed Jews, the midrash suggests, were intent upon scavenging the precious ornaments used to bedeck the Egyptian horses which were still being washed up on the shore. In any event, Moses already had to resort to duress in order to keep the Israelites moving. After departing from the Red Sea, the Jews marched for *three days in the Wilderness* until they arrived at Marah. The period of three days was a portent. It was the same span of time as the Jews had to prepare before the giving of the law at Sinai. Here, however, the preparation was not—as we shall see for Sinai—remaining in one place for the purification process. It may well have been that the purification at Marah took place through the parting of the waters, a kind of analogue to purification through immersion in a *mikveh*, and the journey simply provided for the required three-day hiatus prior to a law giving moment. Or, perhaps, a certain span of time was needed to psychologically distance oneself from bondage and the overpowering immediacy of the splitting of the Red Sea.

Bitter Waters Turned Sweet

They came to Marah, but could not drink the waters of Marah because it was bitter; therefore they named it Marah.[33] Imagine the people's surprise as they encountered water they could not drink. Should not all their needs have been provided through divine grace? God seems to have abrogated the role found in descriptions of the relationship of God to His people in the Exodus narrative: a nursing parent nurturing a suckling child.[34] Instead, the Israelites found themselves in a situation resonant of the Egyptian experience at the time of the first plague where the waters turned to blood.[35] The Israelites spilled out their resentment, and using the language they had preserved in exile called the first station of their journey a place of bitterness. The name of *Marah*, meaning bitterness, appears three times to mark the three day period during which no drinkable water might be found.[36]

But the word *Marah* has various etymologies. In addition to bitterness, it also signifies rebelliousness.[37] This suggests a simultaneous judging of God by the Israelites and of the Israelites by God. Why did it fall upon the fleeing Israelites to name the place? The midrash suggests that the water was not always bitter. God made it so in order to teach (the verse uses the word *instruct*) or, alternatively, in order to test (as the verse suggests in its final words, *and there He tried them*. Somehow this place of water, tantalizing within the midst of an arid desert, but undrinkable, would become an ideal location for the first revelation of law after leaving Egypt.

For the legal exegetical imagination, however, there is no doubt what this oasis evokes. Bitter waters were used in the ordeal for the suspected adulteress (*sotah*). According to archaic Jewish law, when a husband warns his wife not to be secluded with a particular man, and she does so nevertheless, the husband may issue an accusation of adultery. This begins the ordeal as a formal legal process. If the wife swears her innocence in an oath, a priest was chosen by lot to administer the bitter waters.[38] The woman's head was bared and she stood before the priest[39] Earth from the floor of the sanctuary was added to an earthenware vessel filled with water. Moreover, her oath was inscribed in parchment. These words were scraped into the water, which she proceeds to drink. If the woman is guilty, her stomach becomes bloated and her thigh collapses; if this does not happen, the accused wife is deemed innocent of the accusation.[40]

The sanction for secret adultery therefore was to be shamed with a public pseudo-pregnancy, a distending of the abdomen. At the same time, the adulterous woman would experience sterility. The innocent woman, however, will be blessed with becoming more fertile than she was before.[41] *Bitter waters which cause a curse* are transformed into a blessing. Nachmanides describes the Sotah ritual as the only commandment dependent upon a miracle.[42] Perhaps this contingency, and the uncertainty of legal process it implies, is the reason that the ordeal for the suspected adulteress was discontinued by R. Johanan ben Zakkai in the first century.[43] Even before then, it appears not to have been commonly administered. Nevertheless, the detailed exposition of its procedure, with an entire tractate of Talmud devoted to the *sotah* ordeal, suggests its hold on the legal imagination.

The bitter waters at Marah were like the bitter waters of the *sotah* ordeal. The same Hebrew root, *m-a-r*, described both bitter waters. Moreover, Israel has often been compared to a straying wife. *Like an unfaithful woman to her spouse so have you been unfaithful to Me.*[44] Idolatry was conceived as a hearkening after other relationships whereby the exclusive espousal of God to Israel was ruptured. The accused wife in the *sotah* ritual was found alone with a man suspected of being her consort. Similarly, the recent Israelite departure from Egypt, a country where they have been secluded with idolatry and impurity, has been seen by commentators as creating suspicion—especially since God seemed so distant during the course of the Egyptian bondage. They *may* have been unfaithful. God therefore places before them the bitter waters.[45]

In the end, the Jewish people are found innocent. Just as the bitter waters are only bitter to those wives who are guilty of adultery so will the waters at Marah be sweetened for them. Just as the wrongly accused wife will be blessed with a physical healing so did the Israelites receive the reward of being healed from the bodily inflictions they experienced as slaves.[46] Most importantly, just as the woman who has suffered under a false charge is blessed with fertility, the Jews, as has been suggested, will be made generative—granted the power of both biologic and cultural reproduction—with the giving of the law.[47]

The metaphor of the *sotah* was employed in another passage dealing with law giving at Sinai. When Moses came down from the mountain and witnesses the people worshiping the Golden Calf, he casts down in anger the Tablets of the Law and breaks them. Then, he took the calf which they had made, and burnt it in the fire, and ground it until it was powder, and strewed it upon the water, and gave it to the children of Israel to drink.[48] According to Rashi, Moses "intended to put them to the test as unfaithful wives."[49] Idolatry is adultery. If, as we have argued, the bitter waters at Marah reflected the idea of the *sotah* ordeal, how do we explain it taking place twice—once at Marah and once at Sinai after the destruction of the Golden Calf? To answer this question, we need to recall the two-stage process of marriage in Jewish law. The first stage, betrothal or *erusin*, constitutes a marital relationship where the husband and wife, while not yet engaging in intimate relations, remain exclusive to each other. Any extra-marital relationship is considered adultery. In *erusin*, the wife remains in her father's house. Complete marriage or *nisuin* marks the final stage whereby the wife enters the husband's house and the marriage is consummated. Sinai might be thought of as a complete marriage. In contemporary practice, the two stages have been united, though the earlier forms may still be seen in such rituals as the marriage canopy, which represents the bringing of the wife to the husband's domain.

The Israelites enter into complete marriage or *nisuin* at Sinai. There they had a marriage canopy, the clouds of glory, and are taken into God's domain—the domain of the *Torah*. The Tablets of the Law have been compared to a marriage contract. At Marah, however, the Israelites have not yet entered the home of their espoused. Nevertheless, they may still be accused of breaching the exclusivity of *erusin*—the *brit avot*, the Patriarchal covenental relationship forged before the covenant created through the revelation of the law at Sinai, the *brit Sinai*. Seeing Marah this way suggests the ways that the personal and household legalism of Abraham serves within this collective narrative. The Israelites are betrothed to God—but, more importantly, they are taught a legal warning—adultery/idolatry leads to bitter waters.

No doubt the threat of being cast off for failure to obey the law must have evoked memories of precedent. Adam experienced a divorce from the divine presence as a consequence of his transgression. The midrash interprets *and God drove out Adam* [from the Garden after his transgression] as referring to a bill of divorce granted a wife.[50] Before they make their way to Sinai, the Israelites are reminded of the importance of exclusivity though showing fealty to God through law. Perhaps it was this test, the *sotah* ordeal, which was referred to at the end of our verse: *and there He tried them.*[51]

What tree did Moses cast into the bitter waters to make them sweet? The language of the passage *the Lord showed him a tree* uses an unusual

Hebrew word for *showed—[va-yorehu]* which truly means *instructed*. In fact, *yorehu* is a cognate of Torah. Marah was a tutorial of sorts. Unlike the tutelage of Abraham through his kidneys, however, the instruction was visual. Each act of Moses—even the species of wood cast into the water—was laden with symbolic meaning. In the *Mekhilta*, a number of different possibilities are proffered. R. Joshua suggests a willow tree; R. Eleazar of Modi'in, an olive tree, though you can hardly find anything more bitter than the olive. R.Nathan proposes the wood thrown into the water came from a cedar tree. Some say a fig tree; others a pomegranate tree. The allegorists said, "He showed him words of the Torah which is likened to a tree, as it is said: *She is a tree of life to them that lay hold upon her*."[52]

If these proposed tree varieties reflected a lesson *instructed*, then we must decipher the symbolism of each one within the matrix of law and transgression. Each respective species represents a particular moment of trespass. For the exegetical mind, the fig tree was a candidate for the Tree of Knowledge of Good and Evil, where Adam and Eve committed the first wrong. Its leaves were used to sew the garments so they would not appear naked—and the early rabbinic commentators claimed the object which has done the wrong would cure the wrong.[53] The olive represents the leaves clutched by the dove after the Flood.[54] Now free of the ark, the dove returns with olive leaves, symbolizing the replenishing of the second creation after the diluge—though the residue of bitterness within the leaves recalls the sense of loss associated with the destruction. These two symbols, fig tree and olive tree, then recall the archaic law of those before Abraham. Perhaps the midrash is suggesting that the wrongs committed by the descendants of Adam and Noah might be sweetened, or corrected, through the efforts of a new generation which fully accepts the Noahide laws and obeys them. As we shall see, the seven Noahide laws were among the set of ten commandments given at Marah.

The cedar tree offers a different type of restoration. It was the wood used to burn the Red Heifer in order to create ashes used for ritual purification.[55] This hints that God's grace to the Jews during the test at Marah was more a matter of their undergoing purification, removing the impurities of Egypt, rather than creating a yardstick for legal compliance. Rashi sees the Red Heifer as one of the commandments given at Marah, and this fits well with the idea that cedar might have been the sweetening wood. In rabbinic literature, the pomegranate is said to contain as many seeds as the six hundred and thirteen commandments. The pomegranate, then, represents the totality of the law. Similarly, the willow was waved during the holiday of Sukkot, the festival where Jews cloaked themselves in the greatest number of commandments. Perhaps the idea was that only all the commandments in the Torah from Sinai—either in their command form like the pomegranate seeds or in practice like the willow—would be sufficient to undo the bitterness of slavery. Or, finally, it might be the healing effect of learning Torah, the tree of life, itself. While the fig tree and the olive tree point backwards to the earlier code of Noah, the cedar, pomegranate, and willow trees anticipate the law giving at Sinai.

It was no accident, Philo tells us, that "the lesson of the statutes of the law was given in a place whose name is bitterness, for injustice is pleasant and just-dealing is troublesome, and this is the most infallible law. For when they had gone out of the passions of Egypt" they encountered the test of the bitterness experienced through the limitations posed by law.[56] This passage seems to echo the antinomian themes we saw in Paul who saw law as a burden. But Philo takes an unexpected turn. Toil sweetens the bitter law—the water turns sweet—"for what is sweet in toil is the yearning, the desire, the fervor, in fact, the love of the good."[57] Law simply *seems* constricting. When it becomes the object of desire, it may be transformed into something beloved.

What was the lesson of Marah? Law might serve as a means of healing. Immediately after our verse, the people were told *if you hearken diligently to the voice of the Lord, your God, and do what is just in His eyes, give ear to His commandments, and observe all His decrees, then any of the physical infirmities I placed upon Egypt, I shall not bring upon you, for I am God, your healer.*[58] Water suddenly turned bitter was with a bitter stick of wood (especially the olive branch) turned suddenly sweet. Nachmanides calls this "a miracle within a miracle."[59] The bitterness of obedience experienced in bondage was to be undone by seeing the bitterness of obedience to divine commandments transformed into something pleasing. To be sure, this was a difficult instruction. But from it came the yearning for the law which would make revelation at Sinai possible. For Rashi, the giving of the commandments at Marah allowed the Jews to occupy themselves with the law. By studying the law in all its complexity, the Israelites would be less prone to internal strife. This is the basis of a normative rule in contemporary Jewish law. According to the *Mekhilta*, the Israelites had become "rebellious because they had been without Torah for three days."[60] Torah is likened to water—necessary for life on a nearly constant basis. From this experience *halacha* derives a normative principle in contemporary Jewish practice: the custom of reading the *Torah* on the Sabbath, the second, and the fifth days of the week—so three days would not elapse without Torah.[61]

Beyond whatever specific commandments they accepted at Marah, the Israelites were acquiring the ways to *learn* law—as an act of fealty towards a creator as might be seen in the lesson of the bitter waters; as a way to repair the world—as might be seen in the lesson of the wood which sweetened the bitterness; and the idea, expressed in the *Mekhilta*, that learning the law is an occupation—absorbing and engaging at the same time. Abraham redeemed the disobedience of Adam grasping the fruit of the Tree of Knowledge of Good and Evil through offering the fruit of his own loins. The wood, or tree, cast into the water at Marah redeemed the sin as well. For the Tree of Knowledge of Good and Evil had now been transfigured into the tree of tutelage in Torah. No wonder the rabbis described in their many descriptions of the messianic age that ultimately the water of the Great Sea, and even the Dead Sea itself, would be sweetened "just as God healed the waters of Marah through the hands of Moses our teacher."[62]

What Commandments were Received at Marah?

Marah stands halfway between the didactic legalism of the Patriarchal period, represented by the casting of the wood into the water, and the legislative impulse of Sinai. Just a few brief words describe the giving of the law at Marah: *There He made for them a statute and an ordinance.*[63] What law was revealed there? According to tradition, ten commandments were given at Marah. Perhaps the most frequently cited list of these may be found in the Talmud: "It was taught in a Baraita: Ten commandments were given at Marah; seven that the Noahides accepted upon themselves, and an additional three—establishing a legal system, the Sabbath, and the honor of the father and mother."[64] The Talmud explains that the latter two precepts were added because it states about both in the second rendering of the decalogue in Deuteronomy, *as the Lord your God has commanded you.*[65] This use of the past tense in describing the commandments at Sinai suggests that the Sabbath and duties towards parents were already established.

Moreover, it was argued that the revelation at Marah was necessary to make whole the numerical value of the six hundred and thirteen commandments in accordance with the verse, *Moses commanded us Torah.*[66] The numerical value of letters in the word *Torah* is six hundred and eleven. Add two commandments given before Sinai, circumcision (given to Abraham) and the Sabbath (given at Marah), and the total is six hundred and thirteen.[67]

Through appending these laws, however, the Talmud provides an even tighter connection between Marah and the Ten Commandments since their addition to the Noahide precepts creates almost an exact parallel to the Decalogue. The Decalogue's commandments recognizing God's sovereignty and not creating a graven image corresponds to the Noahide commandment against idolatry. The commandment against perjury or profane swearing is similar to the Noahide injunction against blasphemy. The commandment not to commit murder, has a direct parallel in the Noahide command against bloodshed. The commandment in the Decalogue against adultery might be seen as analogous to the Noahide prohibition against various sexual offences. *You shall not steal* and the commandment dealing with covetous desires echoes the Noahide directive against theft. The commandment against bearing false witness corresponds to the Noahide positive commandment to establish courts of law since these would presumably encompass proper laws of evidence. Only observing the Sabbath and honoring parents—so neatly added to the list of the commandments given at Marah—are missing to make the correspondence complete.

By accepting the Noahide code at Marah, the Israelites forged a link between Adam and Sinai. After all, according to tradition, Adam first received the Noahide commandments as primordial law which were given to him within hours of his creation. Having experienced the devastating Flood which destroyed a world bereft of law, Noah and his descendants were identified with a code meant for all humankind. The *Book of Jubilees* describes the way Noah sought to leave the Noahide code as a legacy. Abraham and the Patriarchs—following the understanding of one opinion in the Talmud and a number of commentators—observed the Noahide statutes even, as Nachmanides points out, they delved into the meaning behind the more elaborate Jewish law. In what appears to be a fragment of a petitionary prayer composed for protection in a time of flooding, the Talmud neatly shows how Marah was coupled with the Noahide code through the notion of water as a source of both retribution at the time of the Flood and as a life-giving source: "When more than a third wades in water deep/Remember the covenant [no flood again] and mercy keep/ We strayed from you as a wayward wife [who experienced the test of bitter waters]/Leave us not; as at Marah save our life."[68]

The Noahide code was therefore repeated at Marah, and again at Sinai. In light of its presence in the ante-Sinaitic legal landscape, the Talmud asks, "why was it necessary to repeat [the Noahide code] at Sinai?" The answer given as a general principle is paradoxical: "any commandment that was stated to the descendants of Noah, but not repeated at Sinai, was meant for Jews alone."[69] The Noahide code had to be repeated at Sinai in order for it to be legally binding for *non-Jews*. Why this odd transformation of Sinai into a place of law-making for gentiles? It was impossible that the Noahide code would include an aspect of the legal order that Jewish law, seen to perfect and supercede its predecessor, would lack. The Israelites were the recipients of a new covenant that would sweep aside the old. The previous covenant needed to be reaffirmed. Strikingly, the old ordering of precedent, from the Noahide commandments to the Torah, was reversed. The revelation of Sinai was now to be the foundation of the Noahide code itself.

However, the relationship between the Noahide code and what was given at Marah was also not an exact correspondence. The Talmud faces the problem of how to interpret the giving of an additional commandment of establishing a legal regime at Marah when the Noahide code already includes such a requirement. "Rav Nachman said in the name of Rabbah bar Avuha . . . [only three details concerning civil law were added at Marah] the number [of judges], [the requirements for] witnesses, and warning."[70] Jewish law differs from the Noahide code in all of these regards. Noahide law provided for a capital conviction for homicide in accordance with the ruling of one judge; based on the testimony of one witness; and without any prior formal warning.[71] In terms of the number of judges, under Jewish law twenty-three judges are required to try a capital case. Two witnesses, not merely one, are required for conviction. According to Jewish law, a formal forewarning is required before a capital crime in order to be executed. The potential offender must be told that the offense about to be committed subjects him or her to the death penalty. One opinion even adds that a person must be told the method of execution.[72]

In other words, the Talmud sees homicide as a paradigmatic juristic case. Even though the Israelites and the Noahides share a prohibition against bloodshed, the procedural aspects of the two systems are different. Jewish law requires many more procedural safeguards. To be sure, it might be possible to have a just system of criminal law without so many judges; a requirement for more than one witness; or a warning procedure. But this was considered a *de minimis* standard. The charge to preserve human life—what the law of homicide is all about—necessitates concern with the life of the defendant as well as in capital cases. The Talmud poses the question of where is the legal system that has been given at Marah. Are not these three conditions simply technical procedural safeguards applying only to homicide, and hardly a full bodied legal system? The combination of Noahide laws plus these paradigmatic technicalities provide the guidelines for interpreting and changing law. Bloodshed must be punished. The logical sanction might be one of equivalence, an offender who takes a life might lose his or her own. Nevertheless, there are other legal principles operating: exquisite attention to due process; anxieties of courts about taking the life of individuals created in the image of God; requirements of fair notice and culpable intent. R. Nahman does not see new substantive laws established at Marah; instead there are new procedural rules.

Rava differs with Rav Nahman about what was charged at Marah. The Baraita "was needed in order to establish a system of civil penalties."[73] While the Noahide code only required compensatory damages, Rava states punitive damages were added at Marah. Establishing penalties beyond compensatory damages, such as might be found in the traditional Mishnaic list of five forms of restitution—damages for injury, pain, medical costs, loss of time from labor, and emotional injuries—reflects a different sort of retributive justice that seeks to influence the conduct of those who might cause harm.[74] There is a focus on choice. Someone might be more careful or less, and the idea behind punitive damages is that a sanction may be imposed which is roughly proportional to the moral failing involved in the offence of placing others at risk—whether the results of such actions stems from negligence or recklessness. Perhaps compensatory damages alone were sufficient under the Noahide code because of the concern that courts might be unable to weigh these delicate issues of culpability, and that litigants might take advantage of the discretionary nature of punitive damages to either evade or impose additional penalties. However, as the Israelites construct a civil society they could not ignore the moral failure of indifference to the risk of others.

Whether it is criminal law procedural safeguards (R. Nahman) or a system of punitive civil law damages (Rava) both disputants would agree that the charge at Marah to establish a legal system extended far beyond the Noahide requirement of setting up courts of law for the purposes of adjudication between parties. Marah was not about undertaking a completed and unalterable inherited code. Rather, the commandments at Marah were a schooling in how a legal system *should* be assembled. Rashi makes this point rather clearly: Marah needed to combine two inheritances: the Noahide code and Abraham's charge to his children to do righteousness (*ẓedakah*) and law (*mishpat*).[75] After Marah, the courts—first mandated under the Noahide code—would be transformed. These would now adhere to fundamental standards of procedural and remedial justice.

For commentators, it was not just the seven Noahide commandments and the mandate to establish criminal or civil law rules which laid the foundations of a nascent legal system for the Israelites. As was pointed out above, the Baraita listed two additional commandments from the later Sinai revelation which were also said to be given at Marah, those concerning the Sabbath and the requirement to honor parents. These two commandments are linked since both point to the sources of authority for inherited legal rules. In return for raising children, parents are owed a corresponding debt of filial duty; God rested on the Sabbath which marked the completion of the creation cycle, and identified the divine as a progenitor for all of creation. God and the parents are described as "partners in procreation."

An intriguing midrash suggests that duty stemming from creation establishes the source of subsequent legal authority. The rulers of the nations of the world were not impressed by the first three commandments of the decalogue. However, when God uttered the commandment of filial piety, they remarked with approval, "in our codes of law it is set down that he who has himself inscribed by a sacred oath as belonging to the king must renounce his parents; but Israel's lawgiver solemnly declares and requires *honor your father and mother*. Thereupon, they rose up from their thrones and praised the Holy One, blessed be He."[76] This midrash suggests that this particular commandment reflects more than simply the authority of command, a demand to honor the divine lawgiver; but a requirement to honor based on equity—honor all those, parents and Creator, who have established you on earth. All norms flow from this fundamental sense of obligation.

Intriguingly, Rashi differs slightly from the customary list of commandments that were received at Marah: "He gave them a few sections of the Torah that they might engage in the study of them; the laws of Sabbath, the red heifer, and the civil law."[77] The red heifer substitutes for honoring parents in the Baraita's roster. This Rashi is clearly at odds with the Baraita which we have been unpacking, and there appears to be no other source. In fact, two commentators, Baruch Epstein and Moshe Sternbuch, suggest that the Rashi comment rests upon a scribal error. The abbreviation for the red heifer (*parah adumah* in Hebrew or p"a) would look remarkably similar to the abbreviation for honoring parents (*kibud av* or k"a).[78] However, even scribal errors need to make some contextual sense to survive. Perhaps the conundrum is better explained by returning to the original verse: *there He made for them a statute and an ordinance, and there He tried them.*[79] Ordinance (or *mishpat*) refers to civil law, and therefore might include the Noahide code and civil law procedure as the Baraita suggests. Statute or *ḥok*, as we have seen, refers to a law for which no rational purpose is known, and there is no more quintessential example than the burning of the red heifer, whose ashes miraculously transform the impure so as to make them pure.[80]

According to Rashi, the laws at Marah were given to those leaving Egypt so they might engage in study. Nowhere is this more true than with the case of the red heifer. One tradition sees the commandment of the red heifer—with its focus on preparatory purification—as the starting place for instruction in oral law.[81] More strikingly, the ashes of the red heifer will not be used for purification until the transgression of the Golden Calf.[82] In the words of the midrash, the mother, the red heifer, will atone for the child [calf].[83] Even at the law giving at Marah, it seems there is an expectation of the frailty of the Israelites in the face of a future revelation. The red heifer is law suitable for study since it is puzzling, connected with oral traditions, and waiting to be actualized. What about the Sabbath laws? Rashi may have seen the Sabbath—which was instituted as binding with the giving of the Manna, as the trial described in the last part of the verse, *and there He tried them*. Describing the Manna as a test, he says a core purpose was to see "whether they will keep the commandments related to it."[84] Rashi's understanding of the law revealed at Marah would therefore include not only civil law and procedure (ordinances); law in action through the Sabbath (trial); but also the divine decree which defies reason (statutes).

The systematic architecture of the legal code has shifted from Noah to Marah. No longer is the core a precise list of statutes. It is possible to construct a legal system around the abstraction of legal categories such as procedural and substantive law, criminal and civil law, oral and written. However, an intriguing *Mekhilta* suggests that what was granted at Marah was all the law, past and future, when God promised the Israelites that *if you listen carefully to the Lord, your God's voice, and do what is right in His eyes, lend ears to His commandments, and observe His statutes* then He will not bring down plagues upon Israel as he has with Egypt, and instead He will be manifest as *God your healer*.[85] The *Mekhilta* sees within this verse four types of law: *listen* . . . [to] *God's voice* refers to the Ten Commandments which were given in ten utterances; *do what is right* refers to the *aggada* or moral teachings which every person hears; *lend ears to His commandments* refers to decrees; *observe His statutes* refers to rabbinic legislation.[86]

What is wonderful about this mapping is that it focuses on the source of law rather than upon what is being regulated. There are direct commands from God; what everyone knows—either because it is customary or natural law; decrees ordained to resolve specific legal problems; and legislation which emerges from rabbinic interpretation. It is inclusive of all law. The law of Adam and Noah; of Abraham and his immediate lineal descendants; of the Israelites in Egypt and those statutes ordained by the waters of Marah; of Moses at Sinai; and of all future generations. Each might find its authority in this one brief verse from the law giving at Marah.

Whether it included a precise list of statutes or spoke to the idea of law, most commentators interpreted the law giving at Marah as a prelude to Sinai. The exception to this approach is Nachmanides. Perhaps seeing the task of establishing civil society as so daunting for a newly emancipated people, he suggests that the Marah commandments were deeply contextual, consisting of statutes needed to survive in the Wilderness. Nachmanides interprets the terms *statute* [*ḥok*] and *ordinance* [*mishpat*] at Marah as not referring to the "statutes and ordinances of the Torah, but rather the customs and ways of civilized society." "He established customs for them concerning how to regulate their lives and affairs until they come to a land inhabited." "It may mean," Nachmanides explains, "that Moses instructed them in the ways of the wilderness, namely to be ready to suffer hunger and thirst and to pray to God, and not to murmur. He taught them ordinances whereby they should live, to love one another, to follow the counsel of the elders, to be discreet in their tents with respect to women and children, to deal in a peaceful manner with the strangers that come into the camp to sell them various objects. He also imparted moral instructions, i.e. that they should not become like bands of marauders who do all abominable things and have no sense of shame, similar to that which the Torah commanded."[87]

Nachmanides sees a flexible, broadly discretionary core to the law giving at Marah. It consisted of whatever was necessary to survive the encounter with the Wilderness so civil society might remain intact. According to Nachmanides, the law of Marah was much like his understanding of the law of the Patriarchs, a law seeking to tutor its recipients through norms, rather than a collection of *per se* rules.[88] However, there was one major difference, the law of Marah was directed at a people rather than individuals. In a sense, then, the law of Marah was a common law, an *ius commune*, which transcended national boundaries and even preceded the establishment of a nation state. This place of bitter waters—wilderness magnified—was the site for the Israelites to be instructed and tested. It was not that this idea of a common law lacked a unifying coherence. Indeed, Nachmanides sees the absolute idea of the law giving at Marah as the principle that the Israelites would not become like other wilderness peoples. No doubt the Jews were surrounded by counter-examples. Amalek dealt with strangers through violence. The Midianites—even as Bilam praised the Israelites, *how goodly are your tents, Jacob* for their modesty—failed to show themselves "discreet in their tents with respect to women."[89]

By describing the law at Marah as those norms which defined the nature of Jewish law—its difference from others and its surmounting of foreign milieus—Nachmanides makes a powerful rhetorical gesture. *Halacha* is at its very core a *paideia*. Like Nachmanides' portrait of the Patriarchal encounter with legal study, the law giving was less a collection of rigid *per se* rules than a mix of procedural and substantive law; of everyday legal rules and the structures of civil governance; and of regulatory and moral issues. There is, however, a major difference in Nachmanides' understanding of the Patriarchal reception of law and the revelation at Marah. Prior to Marah, the most important actors in the drama of establishing an internalized *nomos* were individuals: Adam, Noah, Abraham, Isaac, and Jacob. Since such individual legal transmission was fragile, Marah signaled the intended role of the Jews was as a collective vessel for divine legislation. The Israelites must now create a jurisprudence for a settled civil society—not like the Patriarchal kinship networks they half-remembered; not like the slave society they left behind in Egypt; and not like the wilderness bands that surround them during their precarious journey to a homeland.

What does it mean to think of Marah as the first *national* Jewish law? On one hand, it is a recognition of the limitations of universal human reason to sustain legal norms. Baḥyya ibn Paquda suggests that law expands to meet human needs. Abraham did not need so many laws because he was pure of heart. The Israelites, on the other hand, required more regulation since they were exposed to luxury in Egypt.[90] Moreover, a civil society was a necessary prerequisite to both Sinai and settlement of the land. "R. Shimon bar Yohai said, what was the reason that civil law preceded all the commandments of the Torah? Because as long as there is litigation between one man and his fellow there is contention between them. Let the case be decided, and there peace is established between them. Therefore, Jethro said to Moses: *And all the people shall go to their place in peace.*"[91] To be sure, the entire Biblical narrative of Sinai seems to be framed by the problem of how to establish a permanent full-scale legal system. Before Sinai, there is the law giving at Marah and the institution of a system of adjudication through the appointment of judges at the suggestion of Jethro. After Sinai, there is a detailed enumeration of civil laws. Acknowledging the frailty of these emancipated slaves as bearers of law, both formal judging and written codes are seen as a means of addressing these limitations.[92]

Law as Test: The Experience of the First Sabbath

No doubt the Sabbath was an appropriate formative encounter with law because it served as the negation of the forced slavery in Egypt. It marks the liberation from labor, echoing the first Passover *seder* where the fellowship of celebrants addressed their own desires rather than those of Egyptian masters. Even the earliest Sabbath in the Wilderness, so soon after the Exodus, functioned as a time to *remember that you were a slave in Egypt and God has taken you out of there with a strong hand and an outstretched arm.*[93] In the Talmud, however, there is a disagreement about the precise scope of the Sabbath laws given at Marah. "For it is written [in the Ten Commandments] *Guard the Sabbath day and sanctify it as the Lord your God has commanded you.*[94] Rav Judah said in the name of Rav [that this verse was written in the past tense to mean] as He commanded you at Marah. One master [Rava] asserts that at Marah they were commanded to observe the primary laws of Sabbath, but they were not commanded concerning the law of the Sabbath boundaries. The other master [Aḥa bar Yaakov] argues that they were also commanded to observe the Sabbath boundaries."[95]

How do we understand this dispute? Rava claims the Jews at Marah were taught the thirty-nine primary laws of Sabbath. These were derived from the proximity of the section of the Bible commanding Sabbath observance to the building of the Tabernacle. Those necessary activities performed in the building of the Tabernacle are forbidden on the Sabbath, including, among others, agricultural pursuits involved in the making of the loaves of bread for the Tabernacle like plowing, sowing, reaping, grinding, and baking; those involved in making wool such as shearing, dyeing, and sewing; activities used to produce leather—trapping, slaughtering, and tanning; writing and erasing since the Tabernacle had to be built according to specifications concerning which post goes where; building and demolishing; and lighting fires and carrying within a public domain. From these primary rules are derived secondary rules (*toldot*), which further expand the list of prohibited acts. Aḥa bar Yaakov, on the other hand, claims Sabbath boundaries, the distance one can walk from a settled habitation on the Sabbath, was also taught.

Clearly, there are echoes here of our earlier debates about whether the Patriarchs knew the law. According to the Ten Commandments, the Jews had been commanded *in the past* to observe the Sabbath, *as God has commanded you.*[96] But what precisely was the nature of this command? Rava suggests the first command concerning the Sabbath pertained to the thirty-nine primary principles. Aḥa bar Yaakov revives a tradition we have discussed that the Patriarchs observed the Sabbath boundaries. These two areas of Sabbath law are quite different. The thirty-nine primary laws and all their attendant secondary rules require a highly analytic legal process. True, most of the Sabbath *halacha* might be derived through examining the similarity among activities; the purpose of the act; and the similarity of the objects acted upon. Such analysis through comparison of actions is an arduous process. R. Yochanan and Reish Lakish, two important figures in the Talmud, were said to have spent three and a half years studying the primary and secondary rules.[97] Indeed, their complexity was the source of an objection by later commentators, such as Naftali Ẓvi Yehudah Berlin (Neẓiv), who could not imagine untutored ex-slaves could have been taught these during their few days camped at Marah.[98]

The law of Sabbath boundaries, on the other hand, was rather simple. One approximates the distance from the last habitation, and according to the rabbinic standard goes no further than two thousand cubits in any direction. To claim, as Aḥa bar Yaakov does, that the law of Sabbath boundaries was included at Marah suggests that the people were reintroduced to the tradition that the Patriarchs observed the law of the Sabbath boundaries. Clearly, such an approach focused on the *past* rather than upon the analytic rules derived from the *future* building of the Tabernacle. This debate over the nature of the Sabbath law is not trivial. These two positions reflect competing understandings of legal doctrine: law as analysis versus law as precedent, deduction versus transmission; law in the books versus law in action.

The commandments at Marah are Janus-faced. On one hand, they look forward to Sinai, almost a harbinger of a much more significant law giving. Bits and pieces of the Sinaitic law—with the decalogue in its heartland—are transmitted at Marah. Nevertheless, on the other hand, Marah looks backwards to the law of the Patriarchs, and to the Noahide code that existed before them. Nachmanides emphasizes the backwards gaze. God gave the commandments at Marah "in the same way as He taught Abraham the Torah to familiarize them with the commandments and to know if they would accept them with joy and a glad heart."[99] Less important were the specific commandments endowed than how they were received. Nachmanides seems to be suggesting that the Israelites concentrated, like Abraham, upon the *meaning* of the commandments. The Jews had to ready themselves for revelation by transforming the law into something sweet like the waters. According to Nachmanides, this was the test. The reward for joyful acceptance of the law at Marah would be a much grander law giving at Sinai.

The Sabbath may well have been among the few commandments given at Marah because it lends itself so well to elaboration. It was, as we have seen, one of the major flaws of the generations after Noah that they failed to create a full-bodied legal system out of the seven commandments of the Noahide Code. However, there were other reasons for the presence of the Sabbath among these core statutes. In an intriguing passage in *The Guide of the Perplexed*, Maimonides stresses the universal significance of the revelation at Marah as the first set of commandments given to the Jews *after* the Exodus from Egypt—and, hence, in their capacity as a nation. He does so in order to shift the focus away from sacrifices such as the pascal offering and towards general legal norms.[100] The command to sacrifice a lamb was prescribed in Egypt when the Jews still had the status of slaves. But the first two injunctions to the people of Israel at Marah were the Sabbath (which establishes the underlying universal role of God as creator) and civil law. "It is clear from the Biblical text and tradition that the first matter that we were commanded had nothing to with the sacrificial cult, but rather . . . concerning the Sabbath and civil law . . . the latter to eradicate injustice."[101] What Maimonides is suggesting, of course, is the primacy of widely adhered to legal norms over distinctly Jewish ritual. Here, again, we see a debate over what is the first commandment—in this case, the earliest commandment given to the people as a whole. Maimonides' turn towards the universal contrasts directly with Rashi's well-known contention, *pace* midrash, that the recognition of when the month of the pascal sacrifice begins, leading to the sacrifice itself and ultimately to divine redemption, precedes all other divine legislation to the Jewish nation.

There is yet another significant reason behind the teaching of the Sabbath law at Marah. Unlike certain other laws, it would come into effect nearly immediately. Let us return to the last section of our verse: *And he [Moses] cried to God; and God showed him a wood, and he cast it into the waters, and the waters became sweet; there He made for them a statute and an ordinance, and there He tried them.*[102] How did God try them? What was the test associated with law? One way to understand this trial is to see it taking place directly at Marah. The incident at Marah itself, the absence of drinkable water, was the trial.[103] However, the idea of law as a trial—as a test of the ability to internalize norms—comes directly afterwards with the introduction of the manna. Seforno suggests that God wanted to see whether the Israelites would follow the statutes they were taught and prove themselves worthy of receiving further laws.[104] At Marah, the Israelites receive the injunction to observe the Sabbath. Their acceptance of the Sabbath—and the sanctifying of the Sabbath through performing the commandments associated with it—would serve as a prerequisite for the acceptance of the Torah at Sinai.[105]

Not long afterwards, in the course of their first Sabbath, and immediately after their first law giving, they are tried with the Sabbath injunctions concerning manna: *Behold I will cause to rain for you bread from heaven; the people shall go out and they shall gather a day's portion every day in order that I may test them as to whether they will follow My law or not.* On Sunday, we are told, the manna appeared, and for six days—corresponding to the six days of creation, the manna was gathered.[106] On the seventh day, this first Sabbath for the Jews would mirror the first Sabbath after creation, and be marked as a day of rest. Rashi sees the test in terms of the purpose as outlined in the *Exodus* verse, *as to whether they will follow my law or not*, "whether they will keep the commandments which are associated with it [such as] not leaving any [remaining manna for future use] and not going out on the Sabbath to gather it."[107]

Rashi's comment is telling. It is not the manna itself—but the idea that the gift of manna, like the Sabbath, is hedged by rules—that makes it a test. Will the rules be kept or will they not? Will the Israelites gather just one *omer*, as they are instructed, or—recalling the deprivations of Egyptian slavery, will they seek to horde the manna? Will they violate the Sabbath? To be sure, *some of the people went out to gather* [on the Sabbath], and they did not find it.[108] But most followed the law as taught at Marah. This example of law in action, even with its occasional lapse, created the first opportunity for the Israelites to hallow the Sabbath.[109]

Manna is again referred to as a test in a passage in Deuteronomy. Commentators debate the psychological impact of the introduction to the manna. God *feeds you manna in the Wilderness, which your forefathers knew not, in order to afflict you, and in order to test you, to do good for you in the end.*[110] According to one commentator, the difficulty is the dependency of man upon God for sustenance.[111] This comment reflects the beginning of the verse, God *feeds you manna in the Wilderness*. The problem here, of course, is that we are once again in a situation like that of the Garden of Eden where man as a ward of God must face the psychological dilemma of how to respond to the reimposition of dependency. For Nachmanides, manna tried the Israelites because it was a novel encounter: manna "was a trial to them, since they had no food in the Wilderness and were without recourse to any sustenance except the manna, which they knew not from beforehand and had never heard of from their fathers."[112] Nachmanides had interpreted the Sabbath command at Marah as evoking a common law of Sabbath observance inherited from the Patriarchs. But what might be done in a new post-Patriarchal legal landscape? Here was an unfamiliar foodstuff with unfamiliar rules. Clearly, Nachmanides is mooring his comment on the part of the verse *which your forefathers knew not*. Prior to Sinai, where the Israelites will be furnished novel statutes, they are being tried with a particular one.

Certain commentators, such as Seforno and Malbim, focus on the last part of the verse, *do good for you in the end*. When the Israelites receive the manna, will they use it for an ultimate good? The test is the "sustenance without effort."[113] Time freed from agriculture and the pursuit of fundamental human needs might be employed in idleness or in the pursuit of Torah. "Rabbi Shimon bar Yochai used to say, only those who have manna to eat are able to study the Torah. For behold, how can a man be sitting and studying when he does not know where his food and drink will come from, nor where he can get his clothes and coverings." He compared them to priests who exist upon tithes (*terumah*), and therefore have the leisure to properly serve God.[114]

The debate between Rashi, Nachmanides, and Seforno speaks to different sorts of trials. Rashi sees obedience to the law itself as a test; Nachmanides points to the application of the law in novel circumstances as the test—the strangeness of keeping the Sabbath within the framework of an unfamiliar material world; and Seforno sees the results of being sustained through manna as the test—the time created through this divine gift implies a command to use wisely freedom from necessity. Reading the narrative of the introduction of the manna, recalls the original commandment to Adam. The injunction against eating from the Tree of Knowledge of Good and Evil is paralleled through the instruction not to gather the manna on the Sabbath. In both cases, there lies the temptation to exert sovereignty over nature, and to consume all which might be consumed.[115] Even the command to *gather* the manna—a reminder that all sustenance after Adam's transgression must be earned through sweat of the brow—echoes the narrative of Eden.[116] Moreover, these two commandments from Eden and Marah demand obedience to a single law. "R. Joshua said, The Holy One Blessed be He, said to Moses: say to the Israelites, I have brought you out of Egypt, I split the Red Sea for you, I sent down the manna for you, I caused the well to come up for you, I have driven up the quail for you, I have fought with Amalek for you—how long will you refuse to keep my commandments and my laws? Perhaps you will say that I charged you with too many laws. But I charged you with this [one] Sabbath in Marah to keep it."[117]

Not all the Israelites obeyed God's command. It came to pass on the seventh day that some of the people went out to gather and they found none.[118] This partial compliance, however, did not lead to the kind of punishment that God visited on Adam and Eve. For the purpose of the trial of the manna was not simply to determine whether the Israelites *as a whole* were worthy. The collective aspect of the law giving at Marah, the presence of a larger part of the people who obeyed, seemed to distinguish the Israelites from Adam, who "was only granted one commandment, and he violated it."[119] The limitations involved in gathering manna served as a model for law in practice. Instead of an expectation of total subservience, it was full of success and failure, fears that the law would not result in sufficient sustenance, and even an expression of the divine legislator's disappointment, *how long will you refuse to keep my commandments and my laws*?[120] Like Marah itself, the first Sabbath was a moment for instruction, a proving and strengthening of a people to ready them for further encounters with law.

Indeed, the immediate response to the breach in compliance was to ordain another law. *Let no man leave his place on the seventh day.*[121] From this verse, the rabbis derive the law of the Sabbath boundaries. No individual is permitted to journey beyond two thousand cubits. Beyond the rules restricting the gathering of manna, there is now an additional injunction against travel itself. The derivation of the amount of the distance requires an incredible dexterity in using the exegetical device, the *gezeira shava*, which relates one verse to another when there is a shared word.[122] In fact, the derivation is so fanciful that various medieval commentators, including Maimonides and Nachmanides, argue about whether the law is of Biblical or rabbinic origin.[123] However, there remains a connection between the laws of manna instituted for a moment and the law of the Sabbath journey—which for all time serves as a remembrance of our reception of the law at Marah. All this talk of metes and bounds, whether for gathering or journeying, recalls the limitations in space evoked by God's very creation of a limited, finite world. This is the point made in *Sefer ha-Ḥinukh* where it states the purpose of the *Sabbath boundary or tehum* was to recall through these limits God's creation of the world *ex nihilo.*[124]

A *piyut*, a liturgical poem, recited on the Sabbath during the holiday of Sukkot summarizes the role of the Sabbath in defining the law before the law:

> *As you saved Adam, your handiwork, to be his shield;*
> *On the holy Sabbath you brought forth for him forgiveness and grace;*

This refers to the first Sabbath after Adam's transgression when he repented.

As You saved the distinctive nature which sought freedom;
With wisdom they anticipated the choice of the seventh for rest;

This verse refers to the Patriarchs who knew the idea of Sabbath, as we have seen, in the form of the requirement to rest and—according to some sources—as even the observance of rabbinic ordinances such as the *eruv tavshilin*. It suggests that Abraham and his descendants embodied a distinctive wisdom that led them to the notion of a day of rest. Through embracing the Sabbath law, the Patriarchs presaged the later law giving of both the written law and the oral law.

As You saved the people whom You guided like flock to contentment;
and You issued a statute at Marah beside tranquil waters;

Here is a description of the law giving at Marah which included the Sabbath law. However, the contention at Marah has been replaced by the image of a shepherd watering his flock. The waters turn tranquil. God and the people rest from a second creation—the Exodus from Egypt—and mark that rest with the transmission of the law of the Sabbath.

As You saved Your portion in the encampment at the Wilderness of Sin;
They acted wisely and gathered double bread on the sixth [day];

No mention is made of the imperfect compliance of the people. Instead, the Israelites' setting aside manna on the sixth day in preparation for the Sabbath imitates God's setting aside them as a special portion. In time, as the *Mekhilta* recounts, they will be rewarded for their observing the command to collect a double portion on the sixth day by God providing additional bounty on the sixth year of the Sabbatical cycle.[125]

As You saved those who derived the rules of preparation through their wisdom
Their shepherd blessed their talent and deferred to them;

As it is stated in *Exodus*, the Israelites were required *on the sixth day when they prepare what they bring and it will be double what they gather every day* so as not to require any gathering during the Sabbath.[126] This is an especially intriguing verse because it eludes to the idea that preparations must be completed only on an ordinary day and not on a holiday that precedes a Sabbath. This legal idea was derived from the experience of the giving of the manna, and would lead to the creation of the *eruv tavshilin*, a legal mechanism which permits preparations on a holiday for the Sabbath.[127] As the poem suggests, we have gone full circle. The generation of the Wilderness, used the commands concerning manna to invent the legal fiction of the *eruv tavshilin*, remarkably echoing its place in the legal thinking of the Patriarchs.[128]

As You sustained on the day of delight
With the guarded manna,
Whose appearance did not chance
And whose aroma did not sour;

As You saved those who study the laws;
Regarding the burdens of the Sabbath;
They are content and they rest,
Guarding domains and boundaries;

The Israelites—as they will do at Sinai itself—established firm boundaries which circumscribes their movement. *Guarding domains and boundaries* refers to the passage in Biblical discussion of the manna, where the people are commanded *Let every person remain in his place; let no person leave his place on the seventh day.*[129] The *Mekhilta* interpreted this as eluding to the limits of the Sabbath boundaries, a limitation which would later be inscribed in rabbinic law.[130]

As You saved those permitted to hear
The fourth pronouncement at Sinai;
The [dual] notions of remember and observe
To sanctify the Sabbath;

To be sure, the giving of the manna, the first true Sabbath for the Jewish people, might be seen as the apotheosis of the law giving at Marah. It is a foretaste of the later commandment concerning the Sabbath which would be given at Sinai in two forms, remember and observe.[131] The Sabbath memorializes so much: creation and exodus; God's role in history and God's model of a figure who rests outside of the world of action. As the touchstone of legalism from Adam to Abraham and from Abraham through Marah, it also serves as a memorial for the giving of the law in all its guises. The Torah itself, not surprisingly, was given on the Sabbath.[132]

Nevertheless, the establishing of the law giving at Marah, and its enactment through the gathering of the manna with its Sabbath regulations, represented more than simply a station on the road to Sinai. Marah needed to be memorialized in a particular and tangible way. *Take one vessel and put a full omer of manna in it as a safekeeping for your generations. As God had commanded Moses, Aaron placed it before the ark of testimony for safekeeping.*[133] Perhaps it was no accident that the amount of manna preserved, one *omer*, was the same quantity that the people were commanded to gather. For it commemorated the way the law was observed in practice. Most strikingly, the vessel of manna was placed near the Tablets of the Law. These Tablets, both whole and broken, served as memorials for the giving of the Torah at Sinai. Might we not think, then, of the vessel of manna as corresponding to the Tablets of the Law? As the monument marking the earlier law giving at Marah?

Notes

1. Exod. 15:25.
2. Exod. 12:8.
3. B. San. 56b.
4. Exod. 15:25.
5. Gen. 2:8. *See* Radak, loc. cit. that *placed him* means placed him in charge. In other words, the placing was the moment of establishing dominion which, as we have seen, was also the moment of command.
6. B. San. 56b; B. Hor. 8b. The reckoning of these commandments vary, as we shall see below. But B. Sanhedrin 56b lists them as the seven Noahide commandments, the precept of honoring one's father and mother, Sabbath regulations, and civil laws. *Yalkut Shimoni*, however, *Beshalach* 237, enumerates eleven commandments, including the seven Noahaide laws, circumcision (commanded to Abraham), the prohibition against eating the sciatic nerve (commanded to Jacob), and honoring parents, and Sabbath regulations.
7. Franz Rosenzweig, "The Builders," in *On Jewish Learning*, ed. Nahum Glazer (New York: Schocken Books, 1955), 78-80.
8. TdE 123.
9. TdE 123.
10. According to the Palestinian Talmud, *RH* 17, the first commandment given to the Israelites in Egypt was for them to emancipate their own slaves as a precondition for the liberation of the entire people. This example of the law before the law was said to be crystallized in the later commandment to free

every Hebrew bondsman after seven years of service (*see* Jeremiah 34:14). This first commandment is described in *Menachem Kasher*, *Torah Shelemah*, vol. 9 (Appendix), 116-17.

11. Song of Songs R. 5:2. Also, PRK 7, 4. Ezekial 16, 6. The image of blood is an ever-present one, binding both God and Israel. As the vivid imagery in Ezekial suggests, blood is associated with birth. Perhaps this helps to explain its role in founding legal moments.

12. Exod. 24:4-8.

13. Exod. R. 1, 36. Exod. 12:21-23 and 23:4-8.

14. Aaron Halevi, *Sefer Ha-Ḥinukh*, Commandments 4-21. Two additional commandments, 22 and 23, are concerned with the redemption of a firstborn donkey. The author of *Sefer Ha-Ḥinukh* links these commandments to the Exodus by suggesting that they served to remind the Jews of their redemption through the plague of the destruction of the Egyptian firstborn males.

15. H.F. Jolowicz, *Historical Introduction to the Study of Roman Law* (Cambridge: Cambridge University Press, 1932), 136. Of course, Roman *Manumissio Censu* required the consent of the master.

16. Exod. 12:45.

17. Exod. 12:46. Exod. 12:4 serves as the basis for the registration requirement. B. Pes. 89b.

18. Exod. 12:49. *Citizen* is also used earlier, Exod. 12:19, describing the individual who will be punished through excision for eating leaven during Passover.

19. Num. 9:6-14. According to the Talmud, these individuals were made impure through engagement in a public duty as either bearers of Joseph's coffin or burying an unattended corpse. B. Sukkah 25a.

20. Num. 27:1-11.

21. Michael Fishbane, *Biblical Interpretation in Ancient Israel* (Oxford: Oxford University Press, 1985), 98-99.

22. Song of Songs R. 5:2.

23. Exod. 7:19.

24. Exod. 14:26.

25. Exod. 15:5.

26. Exod. 15:1-19.

27. Kenneth Seeskin, *Searching for a Distant God: The Legacy of Maimonides* (Oxford: Oxford University Press, 2000), 3-22.

28. Exod. 14:13.

29. Nachmanides, Exod. 14:13. Maimonides sees this requirement as founded upon three Biblical passages, Deut. 17:16 and 28, 68 as well as Exod. 14:13, and therefore it may not reflect a command given at the moment of the Exodus. He limits the restriction to permanent settlement. *Hilkhot Melakhim*, 5:7-8. The emphasis on *how* Jews will perceive their relationship with Egypt is

strengthened by the notion in Deuteronomy that a monarch might be willing to accede to sending Jews into service abroad in pursuit of his own aggrandizement.

30. David Brion Davis, *The Problem of Slavery in the Age of Revolution 1770-1823* (Ithaca: Cornell University Press, 1975), 560-64.

31. Mek., *Vayassa* 1.

32. Deut. 2:2.

33. Exod. 15:22.

34. Ilana Pardes, *The Biography of Ancient Israel: National Narratives in the Bible* (Berkeley: University of California Press, 2000), 40-50.

35. Mek. 2:89.

36. U. Cassuto, *A Commentary on the Book of Exodus*, trans. Israel Abrahams (Jerusalem: Magnes Press, 1997), 183.

37. Ba'al Ha-Turim (Exod. 15:23) sees the origin of Marah as rebelliousness, citing Jeremiah 4, 17, *For she has rebelled (marata) against Me.*

38. T. Sot. 1:2.

39. Num. 5:16-18.

40. Num. 5:11-21.

41. T. Sot. 2:3.

42. Nachmanides, Num. 5:20.

43. M. Sot. 9:9 ascribes suspension to an increase in male adulterers; T. Sot. 14:2 cites the increasingly public nature of adultery. The marginality of the *sotah* ordeal from a practical legal point of view may be indicated by the decision in the Talmud (B. Sotah 3a) that a husband is forbidden to warn his wife against secluding herself with another man and, as a consequence, to initiate the circumstances necessary for the ordeal to take place. B. Ber.19a states the rabbis identified the ritual with both those who convert and those who are originally Jewish. On the interpretive cabining of the practical uses of the *sotah* ordeal, *see* Moshe Halbertal, *Mehafkhot Parshaniut be-Hithaveten*, 2nd revised ed. (Jerusalem: Magnes Press, 1999), 110-13.

44. Jeremiah 3:20. *See*, also, Jeremiah 2:20. On the common use of the metaphor relating idolatry and adultery, see Moshe Halbertal and Avishai Margalit, *Idolatry* (Harvard University Press, 1992), 25-30.

45. Moshe Sternbuch, *Sefer Ta'am ve-Da'at*, Exod. 15:25. Daniel Boyarin has maintained that the inner ambiguity of the Biblical passages prompted divergent readings in the *Mekhilta* which suggests either that the people were rebellious without cause or, through their three days of thirst, recognized their dependence upon God. Boyarin calls this the "double-voicedness" of the narrative. Indeed, the legal association with the *Sotah* tribunal suggests a similar set of ambiguities. For the wife may be truly unfaithful or falsely accused, and the investigatory aspect of the ordeal will seek to harmonize this ambiguity. Daniel Boyarin, "Inner Biblical Ambiguity, Intertextuality, and the Dialectic of Midrash: The Waters of Marah,"*Prooftexts* 10 (1990): 29-48.

46. Exod.15:26.

47. Perhaps this partly explains why the commandment to be fruitful and multiply, *return to your tents*, comes with the revelation at Sinai. *See* the extended discussion of this commandment in Chapter V.

48. Exod. 32:20.

49. Rashi, Exod. 32:20.

50. Gen. 3:24; TdE 3. The Hebrew root for the verb casting out, *g-r-sh* is used for divorce as well as Adam's exile. *See*, for example, Lev. 21, which bars priests from marrying *one divorced [gerushah] from her husband.*

51. Exod. 15:25.

52. Proverbs 2:18; II, 92. In opposition to the Jewish identification of the tree as the Torah, Christian commentators saw the bitter waters as symbolizing the law, and the tree as the Cross, which would sweeten these demands for obedience. Bernard P. Robinson, "Symbolism in Exodus 15:22-27 (Marah and Elim)," *Revue biblique* 94 (1987): 376-88.

53. Rashi, Gen. 3:7.

54. Gen. 8:11. *The dove in the evening came back with an olive leaf it had torn [taraf] in its mouth.* For the rabbis, the word *torn* or *taraf* evokes images of primordial violence. *Gen. Rabba* 38:6.

55. Num. 19:6.

56. Philo, *The Preliminary Studies*, 542-45.

57. Ibid.

58. Exod. 15:26.

59. Nachmanides, Exod. 15:26; Mek. 2:90. Rabbenu Baḥyya, Exod. 15:22 sees the importance of something bitter making bitter water sweet as underscoring the non-rational nature of the miracle, and testing the people's faith in God.

60. Nachmanides, Exod. 15:25.

61. Mek. 2:90. Abraham Sperling, *Sefer Ta'amei Ha-Minhagim* (Jerusalem: Eshkol, 1981/2), 63-4.

62. B. Ber. 55b.

63. Exod. 15:25.

64. B. San. 56b.

65. Deut. 5:12 and 5, 16.

66. Deut. 33:4.

67. *Midrash Tehillim*, I: 227. On the Sabbath, *see* also: "And after this law [Passover], I made known to you the laws of the Sabbath days in the desert of Sinai, which is between Elim and Sinai" Jubilees 50:1. This appears to be a reference to Marah.

68. B. M.K., 25b.

69. B.San. 59a.

70. B.San. 59a.

71. Gen. R. 34:14. Contrary to Jewish criminal law, conviction may also occur for homicide carried out through an agent and for the death of a fetus.

72. T. San. 11:1.

73. B. San. 56b. R. Moshe Isserles (Rama) sees the civil law given at Marah as being identical to that given at Sinai, *see* Asher Siev, *Shealot u-Teshuvot Ha-Rema* 10 (Jerusalem 1970), 46.

74. M. B.K. 8:1.

75. Rashi, B. San. 56b.

76. PR, Piska 23/24. Judah Loew ben Beẓalel (Mahara), *Tiferet Yisrael*, 360, states that more than other commandments, the honoring of parent—a duty which presumably attaches at birth—is a legal obligation founded upon reason.

77. Rashi, Exod. 15:26. Rashi does not seem to be alone in trying to distinguish between the statute and ordinance. Look, for example, at a dispute in the *Mekhilta* concerning our verse, *there he made for them a statute* [*ḥok*] and *an ordinance* [*mishpat*]. R. Joshua interprets *ḥok*, or a statute, as the Sabbath. R. Eleazar sees *ḥok*: or statute as incest (*arayot*); and ordinance or *mishpat* as robbery, fines, and torts. Mek. 3:1.

78. Exod. 15:26. See Moshe Sternbuch, *Ta'am ve-Daat* and Torah Temimah, Exod. 15:26.

79. *Mekhilt. Vayassa*, 1 also makes a distinction between a statute and an ordinance. "R. Eleazar of Modi'im says, *a statute*, means the laws concerning incest, as it is said, *that you do not any of these abominable customs* (Lev. 18, 30). *And an ordinance*, means laws about robbery, laws concerning civil fines, and laws concerning torts." Clearly, the *Mekhilta* sees incest as a matter of decree rather than founded purely upon reason.

80. Moses was said to have known the reason for the commandment concerning the Red Heifer. PR, Piska 14; PRK 4, 6. *Keli Yakar*, Exod. 15:25, states that the idea of a commandment whose authority rests upon a paradoxical feature—such as the Red Heifer's ashes transforming the impure into the pure—might be seen first in the remarkable demonstration at Marah of bitter waters being made sweet.

81. PRK 4:6. *See* Braude and Kapstein's analysis of this problematic passage, PRK 80-1, where they suggest that R. Eliezer, a descendant of Moses, began his instruction of the Mishnah with a discussion of the Red Heifer in much the same way as Moses used the powder of the golden calf, in lieu of the Red Heifer, to purify the Israelites after their transgression.

82. Keli Yakar, Num. 19:2; PRK 4:6.

83. *Pesikta Rabbati*, 14:14.

84. Rashi, Exod. 8:4.

85. Exod. 15:26.

86. Mek. [Horowitz], 157.

87. Nachmanides, Exod. 15:25.

88. Nachmanides, Exod. 15:25. Naphtali Ẓvi Yehudah Berlin (Neẓiv) elaborates upon Nachmanides' approach: the Law of the Wilderness given at Marah,

included "what would regulate the nation in general, between them and their Father in heaven, between one individual and his fellow, that they should have fit and proper customs," Exod. 15:25. Baḥyya ben Asher suggests Moses instructed the people on how to conduct themselves within the relationships between husbands and wives and between parents and children. Rabbenu Baḥyya, Exod. 15:25. For Joseph Baer Soloveitchick, following the Lithuanian tradition of valorizing Torah learning, the object of the giving of the pre-Sinai commandments at Marah was primarily for Torah study. Joseph Baer Soloveitchick, *Shiurim le-Zecher Aba Mari z'l*, 2 vols. (Jerusalem: 1983-5), 2:207. On Nachmanides' reading of the events at Marah, *see* Elchanan Adler, "Be-Inyan ha-Miẓvot she-Nitnu be-Marah," *Or Mizrach* (2003), 4:18-41.

89. Num. 24:5. Rashi uses this verse to describe how the doors of the tents were positioned so as not to be directly across from each other as a sign of modesty. Nachmanides, Exod. 15:25.

90. Baḥya ibn Paquda, *The Book of the Direction to the Duties of the Heart* (London: Littman Library, 1973), 422. "What is the difference between our asceticism and that of our predecessors? Our predecessors, like Enoch, Noah, Abraham, Isaac, Jacob, Job, and their companions, were men of pure minds, and thus a few laws were enough to keep them in perfect obedience to God. . . . When their offspring went down to Egypt and lived there through the age of Joseph, about seventy years, in peace and luxury, their desires grew stronger, and their instincts overcame their minds. . . . [T]o counteract their desires and to fight their strong instinct . . . the Creator added for them a few commandments by revelation."

91. Mek. 3:2.

92. J.H.H. Weiler, "On Being a Judge—Jethro's Lesson," 2 *Green Bag* 291-96 (1999).

93. Deut. 5:15.

94. Deut. 5:12.

95. B. Shab. 87b. Jubilees, which might be said to be a work dedicated to the law before the law, places particular importance on the Sabbath. The Sabbath rest of God at the time of creation frames the beginning of the book. It ends with a description of the importance of the Sabbath law, which was given in the Wilderness prior to Sinai, Jubilees, Chapter 50.

96. Deut. 5:12.

97. Y. Shab. 9b.

98. Nevertheless, B. Pes. 117b suggests that the thirty-nine categories of labor reflect the tasks imposed upon the Israelites by the Egyptians.

99. Nachmanides, Exod. 15:25.

100. This position is followed by Radak, who says the first commandment concerned Shabbat—collecting manah; and that this is because this is the essence of the mitzvot, not matters of sacrifices [*divrei olah ve-zevakh*]. Radak, Jeremiah, 7:22.

101. Maimonides, *Guide*, III, 32:531.
102. Exod. 15:25.
103. Rashi, Exod. 15:25.
104. Seforno, Exod. 15:25. Nachmanides links the incident of Marah and the lack of water with the absence of food and the receiving of manna a number of verses later. Exod. 15:25 Nachmanides. For a similar approach linking Marah and the manna as two tests, *see* Ralbag, Exod. 15:25.
105. This theme is elaborated at length in Zalman Sorotzkin, *Oznaim la-Torah*, Exod. 15:25 and 16:28.
106. Rabbenu Baḥyya, Exod. 16:5.
107. Rashi, Exod. 16:4.
108. Exod. 16:27.
109. According to the School of R. Ishmael, God "blessed it [the Sabbath] with the manna and hallowed it by the manna. He blessed it with the manna, since on the other days of the week there was only one *omer* per a head, but for the Sabbath there were two *omers*. And hallowed it by the manna: *And it did not rot, neither was there any worm therein* (Exod. 16:24). PR, Piska 23.
110. Deut. 8:16. See, also, Deut. 8:2: *you shall remember the entire way which God led you for forty years in order to afflict you, to test you, to know what is in your heart, whether you would observe His commandments or not.*
111. Mendelssohn, Biur, *loc. cit.*
112. Exod. 16:4.
113. Deut. 8:16 Seforno. See also, loc. cit. Malbim.
114. Mek. 2:104. See, also, TdE, 102, which states that after the manna ceased, the study of Torah ceased. *Keli Yakar*, Exod. 16:4, contrasts the ethereal nature of manna which is conducive to Torah study with heavier, more earthly foods.
115. Yeshayahu Leibowitz, *Sheva Shanim shel Sichot al Parshat ha-Shavua* (Jerusalem: Keter Publishing Company, 2000), 273.
116. Mek. 2:116.
117. Mek. 2:121.
118. Exod. 16:27.
119. *Midrash Seder Olam* [Ratner], 5.
120. Exod. 16:28.
121. Exod. 16:29.
122. B. Eruv. 51a.
123. Maimonides, *Sefer Ha-Mizvot,* negative commandment 321; *See* Nachmanides's statement that the law of Sabbath boundaries or *teḥum* is of purely rabbinic origin. Nachmanides, *Sefer Ha-Mizvot le-Rambam ve-hasagot Ha-Ramban*, ed. Ḥayyim Dov. Chavel (Jersualem: Mosad Ha-Rav Kuk, 1981), 479. *See* also Rashi, Exod. 16:29.
124. *Sefer Ha-Ḥinukh*, commandment 24.

125. Mek. 2:122; Lev. 25:21, *I will ordain My blessing for you in the sixth year and it will yield a crop sufficient for the three year period.*

126. Exod. 16:5.

127. B. Eruv. 38b.

128. A similar connection is made by the Baal Ha-Turim (Exod. 16:28) who points to the use of the term *my teachings* (*torati*) only two places in the Bible—the narrative of the manna and the proof text for Abraham's knowledge of Torah—where it is presumed that Abraham observed the *eruv tavshilin*.

129. Exod. 16:29.

130. Mek. 2:198.

131. Radak, Ezekiel, 20:13.

132. B. Shabbat 86b.

133. Exod. 16:33-34.

Chapter Five

Law as Collective Memory

> *Only be careful for yourself and be very careful for your soul, lest you forget the things yours eyes have beheld, and lest you remove them from your heart all days of your life; and make them known to your children and your children's children the day that you stood before the Lord your God at Horeb when God said to me, 'Gather to Me the people and listen to My words, so that they shall learn to fear Me all the days which they live on earth, and they shall teach their children.'*[1]

Sinai did not eclipse the earlier experiences of law giving. That revelation was preceded by earlier legal norms—since the Jewish people traced its biological genealogy backwards to Adam and its cultural genealogy to Abraham—should come as no surprise. As we have seen, Jewish commentators saw *halacha* as full of *before* and *after*. Abraham's primordial encounter with law—leading to the triptych of obedience-transmission-interpretation would define in the abstract the relationship between mankind and law. Noah's legal code marked a point in time balanced between Adam and Abraham. Unlike Adam's law, it was meant as the foundation for a system of social governance; unlike Abraham's law, it remained limited, almost stunted. Commentators looked backwards and forwards, then, across time with all the figures which populated the Biblical narrative. Abraham—who lived before Sinai was vested with legal knowledge as if he experienced the event. Nevertheless, there was an acute recognition of Abraham's difficulties in the transmission of his covenant to future generations. This issue was addressed through envisioning the creating of a civil society in the aftermath of the Exodus. The giving of the law at Marah anticipated the revelation at Sinai.

Here is a narrative of multiple law giving. *Midrash Rabbah* describes Jewish law as a distinguished lady with a retinue both preceding and following her.[2] While there is no doubt that the chief aristocrat, the matron in this allegorical image, is the law giving at Sinai, it remains equally true that she stands among attendants who represent other moments of legislation before and after Sinai. Bits and pieces of prelegalism were allowed to survive as a result of the conservatism of Jewish legal thinking. In part through appropriation by later codified law, in part through the kind of anachronistic exegesis described throughout this book, and in part because oral traditions will retain such a powerful lure across the generations even as a written code comes to the fore, references to pre-Sinai law became embedded in Jewish legal culture. But such a preservationist impulse cannot alone account for the preoccupation with the law before the law. Earlier normative sources were retained within the archeology of *halacha* because they have explanatory power. The pre-Sinai encounter with law, I have proposed, anchors the psychological readiness of the people for Sinai. To tell the story of the law before the law, is to witness the achievement of internalizing norms.

In order to receive so many new commandments at Sinai, the Israelites had to become practiced in grappling with law as an idea. This was a long and arduous process. Baḥyya ben Asher suggests the image of a people emerging from a darkened room who must gradually become acclimated to the growing light. The commandments were therefore transmitted little by little. Both the law giving at Marah and the revelation at Sinai introduced the Israelites to a limited number of laws. The remainder of the six hundred and thirteen commandments would be taught by Moses over an extended period of time.[3] Nonetheless, the law before the law did more than ready the individual—it constituted the Israelites into a people. By adopting laws governing civil society at Marah, the Israelites were able to come to Sinai with a sense of social organization rather than as a rabble. They stood around the holy precinct of the mountain in a fixed formation. The encampment at the foot of Mount Sinai, like the Passover fellowship in Egypt or like the gathering of manna in the Wilderness, asserted the fact that this was a social unit governed by norms. Those commandments delivered at Sinai were layered upon the commandments inherited from before Sinai.

To be sure, the shadow cast by Sinai—and the idea that God demands obedience in a thunderous voice from a mountain—has often cribbed our own envisioning of law outside of this singular moment. In this regard, the law before the law is not just a precursor. It is a counter-tradition, playing itself off of the dominant tradition of Sinai. Even in the narrative of revelation itself, however, a concern with law other than the higher law of the Sinai code, was preserved through recording the ordinances mandating preparation for the revelation itself and those ordinary laws which directly followed. All these ordinary laws compass the higher law of the decalogue and locate it within a broader normative framework. The distinguished lady, the decalogue as envisioned by the midrash, does not stand alone even at the moment of her glory. While the Sinai pericope marks the apotheosis of the people's encounter with law; it still represents the distinguished matron crowded by attendants.

According to the Biblical account, God ordered the Jews to set boundaries around the mountain which would not be breached and to abstain from marital relations. The moment of divine legislation was hedged by another, albeit less notable, law giving even if the preliminary injunctions would not become permanent commandments. These charges were not insignificant. Boundaries serve as a guiding metaphor for law. In the case of revelation, these boundaries were established to sustain the right position of the people as they faced an imminent law giver. They could not come too close to the mountain out of desire nor retreat too far out of fear. Like the setting of boundaries, the injunction of sexual abstention reflected the importance of the human element at Sinai. Again, there is a command involving the setting of proper distance within an intimate relationship. Its purpose, moreover, was to ensure that the Israelites would be purified so as to be appropriate vessels for the law. Like the priesthood, receiving the Torah was a holy office. The purification prior to the announcement of the Ten Commandments—as with the thunder and lightening—created a necessary sense of awe to sustain the immediacy of revelation across the generations.

Preparatory commandments bind the people through borders, purify them like priests, and thus allow the Israelites to stand at Sinai. But what will the Israelites achieve through revelation? If much of the law of the Torah was known prior to Sinai, and law might be transmitted through means other than a dramatic revelatory moment, then what was the purpose of giving the Torah in this fashion? The contribution of standing at Sinai was the very reception of law experienced through an emotional epiphany.[4] Revelation brought forth a swirl of feelings. Some of these were contradictory—such as desire and fear—and some were so powerful as to almost push aside the substantive law itself. Sinai was an euphoric sensory experience full of visual images, and even those laws which were given earlier, such as the Noahide commandment against bloodshed or the Sabbath laws, will receive new authority from being transmitted in the proximity of a trembling mountain and within the midst of thunder and lightening.

Here lies one of the contradictions of law giving. The human element in law is of critical importance through determining whether a norm will be obeyed or the nature of interpretation. But this role also animates a sense of uncertainty. It is one matter to establish norms, even in the most dramatic fashion, and another to have them followed. Would the commandments be observed despite the vicissitudes of national existence—and even of exile? Might a future generation be able to extend fundamental legal principles? To borrow a phrase from Aristotle, would the Jews, contrary to the historical failure of Adam, be able to establish a "law [of] . . . reason unaffected by desire"?[5] The purpose of the visual was to engrave the emotions surrounding law giving permanently upon the people. Not surprisingly, the notion of a test was invoked again in reference to law—just as it was with the gift of manna—this time concerning the revelation at Sinai. *Moses said to the people, do not fear, for in order to test you, God has come; so that awe of Him shall be upon your faces, that you might not transgress.*[6] The Israelites were tried by God to see if they could become norm bearing not just for a moment or even for a generation—but forever.

What ensues after the intense moment of revelation—but truly as part of the Sinai experience—is a concern with bridging the chasm between a unique moment of law giving and the construction of ordinary law. Immediately following the revelation, the Israelites would receive two laws. Their first command, *return to your tents*, is ambiguous with little indication that it is indeed a statute at all. It creates closure for divine revelation as the Israelites are meant to resume normal marital relations. However, legal interpreters saw *return to your tents* as implying not simply the completion of the period of sexual abstinence; but something more—an affirmative command for procreation.

The second law, *you shall not make of Me* [images] *of gods of silver and gods of gold, you shall not make for yourselves*, is unquestionably stated in the form of a command as an injunction against idolatry. However, the language of this statute, both elusive and repetitive, poses difficulties. On one hand, it might be treated as ordinary law stemming from the decalogue's Second Commandment since the two bear a strong resemblance. But this approach itself leads to a conundrum: how, then, does it differ from the injunction against idolatry in the decalogue? On the other hand, treating this statute standing alone requires even more interpretive prowess in unpacking its confusing language. Both the implied charge to procreate, where the statute itself does not even mention the language of command, and the ambiguous language of the injunction against idolatry place a burden upon the Israelites to immediately interpret these statutes. This critical role of interpretation is important, it will be argued, for it frames the shift from an imminent legislation to ordinary law, and because legal interpretation allows the Jews after Sinai to endure even as they experience a distant God.

Finally, as we will see in the last section of this chapter, there remains the difficult question of what happens to the law before the law in the wake of Sinai. The question of Sinai's significance across the generations continues to be dominated by the issue of how to fashion a norm bearing individual. A medieval debate over whether there is indeed a commandment to remember Sinai provides a way of addressing this problem. Amending the list of six hundred and thirteen commandments constructed by Maimonides, Nachmanides adds the commandment of remembering the revelation at Sinai. He cites as proof text the verse: *be very careful for your soul, lest you forget the things yours eyes have beheld, and lest you remove them from your heart all days of your life.* What does this commandment mean? How does it alter the relationship between the law before the law and the moment of divine legislation at Sinai? Nachmanides, and other sources as well, focus upon the eliciting of the emotional *experience* of Sinai—the awe, the sense of fear, the desire—as the people respond to what they had seen. Within this particular understanding of Sinai, it will be argued, lies a deeper evocation of the law as experienced as opposed to an unadorned roster of rules, and this includes all which has occurred in the past as well as those future laws which will be enacted outside of the shadow of Sinai.

Preparing for Legislation

The preparations made as the Israelites encamped before Sinai reflect the general statement God made to them at that time: *you shall be to Me a kingdom of priests and a holy nation.*[7] Since perhaps the most notable device used to distinguish the priesthood was separation it is not surprising, then, that this was also the hallmark of the prefatory injunctions to the Israelites at Sinai. God has taken this people from others, setting it apart for a special purpose. Now it is Israel's turn to segregate themselves. This comes as a command when Moses was instructed *Go to the people and sanctify them today.*[8] Like the priests, then, these instructions entail specific references to clothing as an insignia of office. By donning their vestments—described in detail in the Torah—the priests are said to have inaugurated their service. In similar fashion, the Israelites are ordered to wash their garments, and, while their dress was not distinct in itself, the newly cleaned attire marks the beginning of their preparation for the giving of the law at Sinai. Although not explicitly stated in the Biblical text, the rabbis presumed an immersion of the body which corresponds to the washing of the garments.[9] Just as priests immerse in a ritual pool before their service so did the Israelites immerse prior to revelation. Both priests and Israelites at Sinai separate from their wives at the time of service. Nachmanides elaborates still further on the correspondence between priests and the Israelites at Sinai. The metes and bounds of Sinai mirror the different precincts of the Temple.[10]

At the beginning of the Hebrew month of Sivan, the Israelites arrived at Sinai. On their first day at the mountain, Moses did not relate to them the laws of preparation at that time "because of the exhaustion of the journey."[11] The next day, Moses summoned the people. He recounted God's words: *You have seen what I did to Egypt, and how I have borne you on eagles' wings and brought you to Me.*[12] God had determined that *you shall be to Me a kingdom of priests and a holy nation.*[13] Two acts of separation, therefore, were realized. The Israelites who had been redeemed from Egypt and traveled through the Wilderness were now sequestered from other peoples in an unpopulated region. In turn, God would set them apart and distinguish them through granting a unique law, and separate from the nations of the world. The people responded together: "everything which God has spoken to us we will do."[14]

On the third day, in a Talmudic rendering of the chronology of revelation, R. Yose relates that Moses ascended the mountain and God let it be known He would appear in "the thickness of the cloud." God instructed Moses to tell the people that they *shall set boundaries for the people roundabout*. Then Moses returned to the people, whereupon the Israelites accepted the command of boundaries. On the fourth day, Moses again ascended the mountain. He informed God that the people had accepted the covenant. God instructed Moses to command the people to abstain from sexual relations for two days. *Sanctify them today and tomorrow.* Moses did so, establishing a first day of abstinence. The fifth and sixth days marked the completion of three days of abstinence. On the seventh day, the Sabbath, the Torah was given.[15]

Even here, in the shadow of Sinai, law giving takes place through incremental stages. The setting of boundaries might be conceived as an acceptance of the law in microcosm. *You shall set boundaries for the people roundabout, saying beware of ascending the mountain or touching its edge; whoever touches the mountain shall surely die. A hand shall not touch it for he shall surely be stoned or thrown down; whether by animal or person he shall not live.* By demarcating how close they will come to the mountain, the Israelites set limits on their activities. Moreover, refraining from sexual relations—like the borders around the law giving presence of an imminent God—reflect restrictions on intimacy. Boundaries are a formative metaphor for so much about law—its line drawing and its limitations; its sense of broadly recognized norms with signposts and the threat of sanctions for those who trespass them. It is impossible to imagine a law without boundaries. Who shall be eligible as a spouse for marriage? What is the extent of property rights? And how can we distinguish between pure and impure, between the holy and the profane, between what is permitted and what is forbidden absent boundaries? To be norm bearing is to be bounded.

Of course, our earlier images of the law before the law are packed with boundaries. Adam is bounded with the fruit he cannot consume and, wrongly believes, he cannot touch; Abraham sets the boundaries of the *erev tavshilin and erev ḥaẓerot*; the Passover sacrifice in Egypt cannot be eaten outside the constituted bounds of the household as defined by the *ḥaburah*. Legislation at Marah vividly invoked such borders in its Sabbath law. The Sabbath was marked by boundaries in time distinguishing between day and night. A boundary in space was set through limitations on the distance one may walk on the day of rest, and there were clear restrictions on the collection of manna related to the Sabbath. Perhaps an allusion to the ever present role of boundaries in Jewish law—and its earlier place in the law before Sinai—might be found in a description of how Moses ascends the mountain on two of the three days prior to revelation. Why did he not do so on the last day? The Talmud answers that Moses was occupied in the "task [of preparing] for the Sabbath."[16] Since this was a Friday, like others he was involved in the ordinary duties of the Sabbath law as given at Marah, and was busy gathering a double portion of manna for the next day—all this within ordinary Sabbath law's set bounds.

According to R. Yose, whose chronology of the giving of the Torah differs slightly from another in the Talmud, the third day was marked by Moses reporting to God the people's promise of obedience. God then said to Moses, *Behold, I shall come to you in a thick cloud so that the people will hear as I speak with you, and they will also trust in you forever.*[17] In addition, God instructed Moses on how the people should prepare themselves for the revelation through sanctifying themselves and setting boundaries around the mountain. There is a rabbinic debate about the authority for establishing three days of preparations. R. Yose suggests God ordained only two days of preparation. "Moses added an additional day [of abstinence from sexual relations] on the basis of his own understanding."[18]

This shows a remarkable assertion of legal interpretive authority on the part of Moses. Of course, the addition of a preparatory day is not the only time when Moses takes it upon himself to determine legal rules. Both the innovation of the second Passover, providing for the bringing of the sacrifice a month later when individuals are ritually impure and unable to consume the Pascal lamb at its proper time, and the introduction of the rule providing for inheritance of property through women in the narrative of the daughters of Zelophehad, suggest that law might be determined through legal reasoning as well as divine fiat.[19] In both cases, the rabbis justify legal innovation by suggesting that while the law would have been included as part of the Torah in its entirety, it was a special divine honor to allow the individuals bringing the cases to serve as the mechanisms for ushering in new legal rules. Law had to reconcile compliance with an ascribed duty when the individual, for no fault of his or her own, cannot fulfill the duty.

For the second Passover, the individual might be impure for such laudatory reasons as performing a burial or unable to bring the sacrifice because of a long journey for the purpose of collecting charitable funds; for the laws of inheritance, the woman—like the Biblical Tamar—seeks to preserve the name of a dead spouse even if the couple was unable to have a male child. The Talmud, however, suggests that Moses added an additional day of abstinence at the moment God ushers in His uttermost imminence. What is particularly striking is that, a clear direct command was amended. Moses must have believed the need for readiness in receiving the law so important that he was even willing to alter the date of the revelation. It is the capacity of the people—rather than an alignment of the constellations or even a divine plan to reveal the law on a given date—which animates the timing of God's legislation.

Perhaps this surprising choice might be understood by looking at Seforno's explanation as to why Moses remained celibate rather than return to cohabitation with his wife after the law giving at Sinai—despite the command to return to your tents, which is interpreted as a charge to resume ordinary sexual relations.[20] According to Seforno, Moses believed he would serve as the vessel of prophecy, speaking to God face to face, and his own preparation for prophecy set aside the divine injunction. Indeed, the Talmud compares Moses' appending an addition day to the preparatory period to two other situations in his life. First, when Moses ignored God's command to renew ordinary sexual relations after the revelation at Sinai, despite the implied command of *return to your tents*, and determined to undertake permanent celibacy. Secondly, when Moses descending from the mountain encountered the Israelites worshiping the Golden Calf, and he hurled the Tablets to the ground, breaking them into pieces.[21]

If Moses' decision to add another day to the period before revelation is puzzling, so is God's final command: *descend, warn the people, lest they break through to gaze at God, and many of them shall fall.*[22] Why an additional warning? God has already instructed the Israelites to set boundaries and not to touch the border. The statement of Moses seems to register surprise at this repetition, when he says to God: *the people cannot ascend Mount Sinai for You have made this known, saying set a boundary around the mountain and sanctify it.*[23] However, God repeats His warning yet again: *Go descend. Then ascend, you and Aaron with you, but the people shall not break through to ascend to God.*[24] A hint of the purpose comes in the singular use of the Hebrew word *shall fall* (*nafal*) in the midst of the warning.[25] The people had arrived and—as a famous comment by Rashi suggests—camped as one, "as one person with one heart," since here again the singular was used, *and Israel encamped (ve-yiḥan) there* [at Sinai].[26] As Rashi explains, this unity emerged from repentance over the failure to act properly in the period of the Wilderness prior to Sinai. It is critical that the revelation be granted with a singular field of emotion, and that the people do not splinter in their perceptions, their *gaze*, of the moment of divine legislation.

The people need to desire the gaze as one, but this creates its own risks. Are they strong enough to accommodate the divine presence? Will the reaction to revelation turn into an unthinking crowd response? Perhaps both Moses's decision to decree an additional day of preparation and the reiteration of the warning against breaking through boundaries were meant to address the disorienting emotions which would be unleashed by the desire to gaze upon God. Ironically, however, while the people sought the visual experience of revelation, they found themselves unable even to undergo the aural part of the giving of the law. *On the third day when it was morning, there was thunder and lightening and a heavy cloud on the mountain, and the sound of the shofar was very powerful and the people trembled.*[27]

The people remain in the camp. Is it fear, agitation, or simple awe which prevents them from approaching the mountain? Are they suffering from a form of emotional paralysis? It seems as if all the concerns about marking boundaries is unnecessary for the people need to be led by Moses from the camp to the mountain, *Moses brought the people from the camp toward God, and they stood at the bottom of the mountain.*[28] Even after the revelation, the Israelites do not know if they can bear the revelation: *The entire people saw the thunder and the flames, the sound of the shofar and the smoking mountain; the people saw and trembled from afar. They said to Moses, speak with us and we shall listen; let God not speak to us lest we die.*[29]

No single emotion is associated with the revelation. Even the earth gyrated between trembling and moments of calm.[30] The people experience desire and fear at the same time. According to Baḥyya ben Asher, shame emerges in the course of revelation as individuals recognize the consequences of transgression.[31] The Israelites might break through the boundaries at the moment of desire—for as the Talmud says love involves the rupture of borders; but equally powerful is the press for distance, they turn aside from the overwhelming experience of law giving.[32] In an intriguing midrash, fear prompts the people to retreat at hearing each of the commandments of the decalogue. With the assistance of angels, the people are propelled forward, regrouping and returning to their original position until the next commandment is uttered. With each commandment, then, the people travel twenty-four miles—and they do so ten times in total.[33] This bewildering back-and-forth motion speaks to the whirlwind of emotions encountered at Sinai.

The people have the opportunity to receive the law through Moses as an intermediary. But as the revelatory moment unfolds they reject this approach. *God said to Moses, behold, I will come to you in a thick cloud that the people may hear when I speak to you, and also believe in you forever.* The original blueprint, then, was for God to appear before Moses and for the people to simply overhear the revelation veiled in a thick cloud. *And Moses told the words of the people to God. And God said to Moses, go to the people and sanctify them today and tomorrow, and let them wash their clothes. And be ready against the third day. For on the third day, God will descend before the eyes of the people.*[34] The people were told; but they did not agree. From the fact that God changed from so *the people may hear* to *before the eyes of the people* means that there was a shift from the aural to the visual. We are not told what the Israelites said when they objected to God's original proposal. Rashi explains this lacuna in the narrative. Moses said to God, "I have heard from a reply to this statement. It is their desire to hear [the commandments] from You and not from me. One who hears from the mouth of a messenger is not the equivalent of one who hears [directly] from the mouth of the king."[35]

Here, again, is another contingent element in the emotional relationship forged at Sinai. Moses adds another day of preparation; the people ask for a direct visual revelation. However, the sensory experience is visual in a surprising way. The people's decision to *see* has transformed even sounds into sights.[36] *The entire people saw the thunder and the flames, the sound of the shofar and the smoking mountain; and the people saw and trembled from afar.*[37] The thunder becomes like the flames; the blasts of the shofar like the smoking mountain. Even this does not mark the end of the transformation. Now prepared as priests, the people internalize the visual. Baḥyya ben Asher understood the revelation at Sinai as bracketed by two aspects of the eidetic. In the beginning, God tells the people *You have seen what I did to Egypt, and how I have borne you on eagles' wings and brought you to Me.*[38] At the conclusion, *the Lord said to Moses: Thus shall you say to the Israelites: you yourselves saw that I spoke to you from the heavens.*[39] The core feature of both verses is *seeing*. But the desiring gaze is no longer solely the source of transgression as it was in the past—for it has been domesticated through preparation and boundaries. At the time of creation, Adam learned about the link between law and the visual sense. The Tree of Knowledge of Good and Evil was a *delight to the eyes*, and Adam proved unable to resist following his eyes within even just a few short hours of being enjoined against its consumption.

Nothing better symbolizes this transmutation of the gaze than the metamorphosis of one visual image seen at Sinai. *They saw the God of Israel, and under his feet was the likeness of sapphire brickwork, and it was like the essence of heaven in its purity.*[40] Instead of the other striking images from the theophony, such as the lightening, this one focuses upon color—the intense blue beneath God's feet. This blue will be replicated upon the ritual fringes, which will serve as a mnemonic device for the commandments of the Torah.[41] These fringes were intended to remember all the commandments of God and to perform them; and not to seek after your heart and your eyes after which you stray.[42] Instead of the eyes fixing upon an object of desire, they will now focus on a representation from the moment of revelation. What has been *seen* at Sinai—hedged through the fear that the desiring gaze might lead to crossing boundaries—provides the visual images which serve as the basis for remembering Sinai for future generations.

Sinai and Covenant

Fear and law giving are thickly interwoven. At the time of the revelation, the people experienced terror. Nevertheless, the closure of the revelatory experience leaves them bereft. This paradox makes psychological sense. When the terror of Sinai recedes, the sense of missing God's immediacy comes to the fore. In terms of the genesis of norms, the cessation of the moment of law is also a liminal moment full of both danger and promise. Closure therefore creates as many dilemmas as preparation. When does the revelation come to an end? Having once received law directly from God, how might the people be able to flourish without this imminent presence? What is the relationship between the law giver and the law receiver after Sinai?

Such questions about closure, and our earlier discussion of preparation, frame an intriguing exegetical debate over the timing of the Sinai covenant. Away from the immediacy of revelation, a covenant is forged between the Israelites and God:

> *And Moses came and told the people all the words of the Lord, and all the ordinances; and the people responded with one voice, and they said, all the words which the Lord has spoken we will do. And Moses wrote all the words of the Lord, and rose up early in the morning, and*

> *built an altar at the foot of the mountain, and twelve pillars corresponding to the twelve tribes of Israel. And he sent the young men of the children of Israel, who offered burnt offerings and sacrificed peace-offerings of oxen to the Lord. And Moses took half the blood, and put it in basins; and half of the blood he dashed against the altar. And he took the Book of the Covenant, and read it within the hearing of the people; and they said: 'all that the Lord has spoken we will do and obey.' And Moses took the blood, and sprinkled it on the people, and said: 'Here is the blood of the covenant, which the Lord made with you in agreement with all these words.'*[43]

We have encountered this Biblical passage before. This description of the Sinai covenant is the same Biblical passage upon which rests the *Mekhilta*'s description of the readings for the fifth day. The *Mekhilta*, of course, has served as a road map for our understanding of the various forms of law prior to Sinai. A special reading was ordained for the occasion of the revelation. As with the earlier covenant with Abraham, the Covenant Between the Pieces, there are burnt offerings sacrificed and the division of the sacrificial object—in this case the blood. Half the blood returns to God when it is dashed against the altar; half is sprinkled upon the people. The Israelites affirm their full assent to the giving of the law.

Philo envisions the sacrifice as an allegorical text describing the awakening of the senses which allow the rational acceptance of law to divert irrational desires. His reading is so remarkable that it warrants quoting at length:

> Marvelous too is the equal distribution of the sacrificial blood which the high priest Moses, following nature's guidance, made. He took, we read, half of the blood and poured it into mixing-bowls and half he poured upon the alter to show us that sacred wisdom is of a twofold kind, divine and human. The divine kind is without mixture or infusion, and therefore is poured as an offering to God, who knows no mixture or infusion and is in His isolation a unity. But the human is mixed with infusion and thus is scattered abroad upon us, who are a mixed compounded product of infusion, to create in us oneness of mind and fellowship, and in fact a "mixing" of our various parts and ways of conduct. But the part of soul which is free from mixture and infusion is the mind in its perfect purity. . . . The mixed kind is the senses, and for this nature has created the proper mixing-bowls. The eyes are the "bowls" of sight, the ears of hearing, the nostrils of the

> sense of smell, and each of the others has its fitting vessel. On these bowls the Holy Word [*logos*] pours of the blood, desiring that our irrational part should be quickened and become in some sense rational, following the divine courses of the mind, and purified from the objects of senses, which lure it with all their deceitful and seductive force.[44]

In place of the *sedra* or written readings of the law for the fifth day, Philo rivets attention on the ceremonial aspects of law giving. The Israelites at Sinai undergo a ceremony of purification which establishes a unity of pure thought reflecting the divine will. This reflects our discussion of Abraham's source of legal knowledge, the Greek cultural valorization of unwritten law. By sprinkling the blood on the people until they have been purified, they are transfigured into receptacles for the commandments.[45] The idea of the *logos* is difficult to understand; but there appears to be a collapsing of the actor and the object—of the people and the law—until there becomes a unitary identity for the two.[46] Philo's powerful vision of the Sinai Covenant reflects the importance of the psychological reception of the Torah.

When does this covenant take place? The Biblical passage depicting the Sinai covenant is embedded a number of chapters after the narrative of revelation and after the listing of the commandments found in the decalogue. This is an odd location, suspended in the midst of unrelated surrounding material. It is not clear how it fits within any sort of chronological scheme. Indeed, the immediately preceding sections are not even narrative; but list in detail the injunctions of a civil code. This creates a conundrum. Even though the commentators agree that historical narratives are often out of chronological order in the Bible, there are few internal hints to determine whether the Sinai covenant occurs prior to the revelation at Sinai or afterwards. Is it part of the preparation for revelation or does it constitute closure through a sealing covenant? A clear split has emerged among exegetes. French commentators see this covenant taking place prior to Sinai while Spanish commentators place it later in the day of revelation after the decalogue.[47]

A French exegete, Rashi identifies the Sinai covenant as transpiring immediately following the preparatory commands at Sinai; but prior to the enunciation of the decalogue. The people are told—according to Rashi—about the pre-Sinai law much as R. Judah suggests in the *Mekhilta* when he lists the readings for the fifth day, *All the words of the Lord.* These are the commandments of separation [mandating a hiatus for] marital relations and the setting of the boundaries [at Sinai]; *and all the ordi-*

nances, the seven commandments which were commanded to the descendants of Noah, and [the laws regarding] the Sabbath, and the honoring of the father and mother, and the red heifer, and the laws which were given to them at Marah."[48]

Rashi sees the covenant as marking preparation. Recounting a version of the law before the law as the readings for the fifth day, he provides a roster of various moments of law giving prior to Sinai, including the quite recent occurrence as the people stand before the mountain—the giving of the two commandments of sexual abstinence and boundary setting. Rashi's understanding of preparation parallels the procedure established for studying conversion.[49] The people have fulfilled the requirements of conversion through both easy and difficult commandments—the former, perhaps, being the Noahide commandments they already follow, the latter being honoring parents and observing the Sabbath; undergoing circumcision—which was instituted as a precursor to the first Passover in Egypt and seems to be reinvoked with the sprinkling of blood; immersion—which was implied as one of the preparatory commandments at Sinai; and the sprinkling of blood.

Spanish commentators, and here Abraham Ibn Ezra and Nachmanides serve as our examples, claim that the covenant at Sinai transpires *after* the revelation. "The act of the covenant took place on the day after the giving of the Torah, and on that day was the ascent, when Moses went up to the mountain and he stayed there for forty days."[50] Nachmanides states that the readings are not those of R. Judah; but instead the law delivered following the decalogue, most notably the law against idolatry, discussed below, and the civil code. The model is not Rashi's paradigm of conversion, but the idea that a covenant is a seal marking an agreement to the preceding revelation. Both positions recognize a need for a covenental moment away from the instance of absolute imminent law giving.

However, there is an important philosophical difference in the postures of the French and Spanish exegetes. The French are concerned with the dilemma of preparation; the Spanish commentators with the dilemma of closure. For those arguing for a pre-Sinai reading of the *Book of the Covenant*, there is a perfect moment where the people are able to proceed with a covenant—having undergone the conversion ceremony and having not yet experienced the rupture of the transgression of the Golden Calf.[51] According to the Spanish commentators, law can never be fully accepted without knowing the terms of a significant body of norms. Instead of coming to law as converts, Nachmanides Israelites are approaching it as students. But for both, quite remarkably, the covenant represents the shift from fear to knowledge as the basis for assent to the full burden of the law.

Quite remarkably, the Biblical description of the Sinai Covenant includes Moses erecting *twelve pillars corresponding to the twelve tribes of Israel.* To erect a pillar is an offense listed in Deuteronomy, presumably because of its relationship to idolatry, *do not erect a pillar which God hates.*[52] How do we understand this presumed transgression even in the midst of the very acceptance of the Torah? It may be, as has been suggested, that the Sinai Covenant takes place prior to the handing down of the law, and therefore such an action is still a matter of personal discretion. Or it might be, as Nachmanides proposes, that the ban against raising pillars only emerged later in response to the encounter with idolatry that took place when the Jews entered the Land of Israel.[53]

In any event, these memorials then have a double-voiced aspect. Erected out of stone, they represent the immutability of the Covenant; while at the same time, the pillars would illustrate the changing face of law since their erection would soon become a transgression. Such a reminder of the mutability of law over time has important consequences for the evolution of ordinary law. How can a person of flesh and blood be a law maker after the very idea of establishing norms has been seen to be a divine gift? In the absence of a divine commanding voice, how do we recreate legal certainty? The authority of *halacha* will now depend upon interpretation and human decision making. Such a shift from the posture of command—with its fixed reciprocal duty of obedience—to the creation of norms through interpretation, transmission, and expansion must also be seen as part of the revelatory experience. If Sinai is depicted as the apotheosis of imminent law giving, it is also the place where the Jews first felt the pull towards a distant God—and, as a result, the reliance upon their own craft in making law.

Between Closure and Interpretation

Two statutes mark the closure of the intense law giving surrounding the decalogue. Interestingly, both of these statutes are variations on commandments we have seen prior to Sinai—the command to be fruitful and multiply, and the command against idolatry. Both statutes are ambiguous. Sinai frames these laws in a new fashion, adding further details.[54]

As discussed earlier, the people were told to *return to your tents*—or, in other words, to resume marital intimacy.[55] This marks closure. No longer must the Israelites maintain a pure state for direct communication by God. However, the renewal of sexual relations also means the fulfilling of the directive of procreation. This commandment—so elusive in its articulation as simply a return to the shared tent—does not specifically instruct the people about the goal. Nowhere in the Biblical narrative is there any discussion of reproduction—just simply *return to your tents*. But the commentators are puzzled by the fact that this charge is needed at all since the Israelites were told to abstain from marital relations for three days, and the resumption of intimacy would have been automatic. The Talmud learns from this that even when a court establishes a prohibition with a clearly defined terminus there still needs to be an affirmative decision to permit the resumption of the previously enjoined behavior.[56]

However, marking closure at the end of revelation with a command for procreation reflects something further. As with the new world that God creates for Adam, the unfamiliar territory of the Torah, its legal rules and interpretations, must be settled. *Return to your tents* means reproduction will be consumed within the task of preserving the Torah granted at Sinai for future descendants; but the novel idea of finding a binding rule embedded in this elusive phrase hints that this is not a matter of communicating unthinking obedience—rather the true preservation of law demands *interpretatio iuris*. Indeed, as will be argued, the transmission *with* interpretation of law across the generations will become a signal feature of remembering the revelation itself.

If renewing intimacy signifies a proper cultural reproduction of the Sinai moment, idolatry represents a false replication. An idol is "that which is not."[57] The first clearly enunciated statute after the giving of the Ten Commandments reflects an initial entering into ordinary law. *God said to Moses, say this to the Children of Israel, you have seen that I have spoken to you from heaven. You shall not make of Me* [images] *of gods of silver and gods of gold, you shall not make for yourselves*.[58] Clearly, this first statute is related to the Second Commandment where the people are told *You shall have no other gods before Me*. The Second Commandment continues with a prohibition against any *graven image or manner of likeness of any thing that is in heaven above or that is in the earth below* and enjoins prostration or service to idols.[59] Like Adam, who only hours after his creation had to wrestle with legal interpretation, the Israelites experienced their first brush almost immediately after the disorienting experience of revelating and had to explain a statute in terms of the decalogue. It could not be a simple repetition for such a repetition would violate the principle of economy in the use of legal language. Moreover, the phrase *gods of silver and gods of gold* cannot imply a limitation so that gods created of any non-precious metal fall outside the ambit of the injunction and are therefore permissible.[60] This statute demands interpretation.

Indeed, the language of the statute itself is perplexing. *You shall not make of Me*—the singular, unitary God—plural images of *gods*. There is no smooth transition from legal command to legal interpretation. The statute is full of gaps and ambiguities. Much as linguistic difficulties gives rise to Biblical interpretation in the form of midrash; legal uncertainty forces more daring readings of law. To resolve this lack of clarity, the Talmud, Nachmanides, and a number of other commentaries see this as a commandment against creating intermediaries.[61] In the tractate *Avodah Zarah*, for example, the Talmud envisions this verse as teaching that "you shall not make images of My servants who serve before me on high such as the *ofanim*, *seraphim*, *ḥayot ha-kodesh*, and the ministering angels."[62] God's servants—either angels or planetary bodies such as the moon—may not be represented as intermediaries. Such an interpretation is read against the literal meaning of the statute which refers to *gods* rather than intermediaries.

Why should this be the first clearly articulated commandment after the Ten Commandments? Here, the problem is not the idolatrous practices of other peoples. Instead, it is the possibility that images might be used to bridge the chasm between God and man. Individuals would seek to create mnemonic devices to recall the moment of intimacy at revelation. It would be reasonable to create images to achieve this purpose "for there are a number of commandments in the Torah [designed to elicit] memory" such as the consuming of the Paschal sacrifice or the building of tabernacles like those used in the Wilderness.[63] The goal is legitimate—the longing for God's presence—but the means are improper. The commandment against this sort of idolatry, making intermediaries, reflects a recognition of the deep craving for the divine law giver which emerged after Sinai. Here the danger lies in another odd turn of phrase in the statute, the dangling last clause *for yourselves*. We would create intermediaries as instruments of our own, seeing them as *gods*. Perhaps as a recognition of our own implicit frailties we might wrongly countenance images from within our own tradition, and with the awareness that these are only God's servants, we might be tempted to cross the boundaries established at Sinai.

A third element of the wording strengthens this reading of the statute—the preface with its clearly stated reason. *You have seen that I have spoken to you from heaven*. Here we are faced with the difficult to fathom idea of the Israelites having *seen* God's voice. The very seeing of the invisible—the language of spoken law—suggests the problem with representing God through any sort of medium. All alloys, even precious metals, cannot even remotely express the divine. Differing from Nachmanides and those that suggest the statute bars the making of images of intermediaries, Maimonides, for example, bases a commandment of not making human figures in relief upon this particular verse.[64] The human form, of course, was created in God's image and therefore includes an element of the divine. This medieval difference of opinion between Nachmanides, who sees the statute as a ban on the representation of intermediaries, and Maimonides, who sees it as enjoining the representation of the human form, shows how elusive even later commentators found the statute's interpretation.

Both commandments—for procreation and against idolatry—are ambiguous. Why does ordinary law begin with such uncertain legislation which requires resorting to statutory analysis? Why begin the process of teaching ordinary law with measures which evoke disagreement among interpreters? It seems as if the task of legal interpretation was part of the closure of revelation. The law concerning reproduction does not even mention this requirement, and seems to be simply a call for the Israelites to return to their tents. But this simple phrase, seen as redundant, is given normative meaning. The injunction against idolatry is certainly structured like any other law. However, its language and its relationship to the commandment in the decalogue are unclear. The relationship between the Second Commandment, a higher law principle, and the particulars of our statute had to be examined. Did the statute, a sort of subordinate rule, limit or expand the more general rule against idolatry? How did the ascribed purpose of the law comport with its practical implementation?

Moreover, the difficulties with the language of the injunction against idolatry, for example, suggests the need for sophisticated readings, and indeed a multiplicity of interpretations. Idolatry is a form of false pluralism. The singular God is seen in so many manifestations that these must be described through a plethora of representations. Some of these forms may be juxtaposed against each other. God represents mercy and justice; a figure of deliverance and vengeance. This is what has called the "error of multiplicity."[65] If God's image cannot be parsed into different forms, however, His will may be understood through law as competing interpretations reveal a statute's plural guise.

Law stands in opposition to idolatry in an even more powerful fashion. Maimonides often focuses upon idolatry as a failure of abstraction. Yet within the context of revelation, idolatry seems to be more than ever a misrepresentation and a mis-seeing. It is a mis-remembering. For that reason our statute begins, *God said to Moses, say this to the Children of Israel, you have seen that I have spoken to you from heaven*. If future generations would properly recall the epiphany at Sinai in its full form, they would recognize the inability to express the standing at Sinai through any material form. For such figures cannot serve as even a mnemonic device since the essence of the revelatory experience was the acceptance of law—not the image of the divine figure who delivered it to the people nor the setting. In other words, legal interpretation was a fitting consummation of the revelation at Sinai. The people, and their legal scholars, were empowered with construing norms because that is what the limitations of divine legislation requires. Just as God apprenticed Abraham in the craft of judging during the judgment of Sodom so were the Israelites introduced to the difficulties of pursuing the literal meanings of statutes in the midst of a code-making enterprise. Like judging, statutory construction is an act of *imitatio dei*, which recaptures the meaning of this one singular moment through trying to unpack the meaning of the written law.

No doubt the immediacy of divine legislation would end with the conclusion of the revelation at Sinai. In fact, two events signal the finality of this closure. The Israelites would be compelled to leave the mountain, and Moses himself—who had seen God face to face—would now wear a veil for the rest of his life.[66] Leaving Sinai was abrupt, a simple command. God said, *enough encircling this mountain, turn yourselves northward.*[67] The verb *encircling* hints at the remaining desire for immanent law giving. The people did not simply stand at Sinai; they fixed their camp around it. Without the direct, almost impatient, divine command telling them to resume their travels, they were reluctant to leave. The people journey northwards—which is the place where the Land will be settled and the Temple built. Both might be conceived of as replacement for Sinai. The Land, as we have seen, will be the place where law is actualized; the Temple will be the source of awe. But something does change. *North* is also the word in Hebrew for hidden. Even though there will be other focal points there will never be another similar experience of receiving the law with such emotional intensity.

This abrupt closure was paralleled by Moses taking the veil. *And when Moses finished speaking with them* [the people of Israel after his descent from the mountain] *he placed a veil upon his face. When Moses would come before the Lord to speak with Him, he would remove the veil until his departure; then he would leave and tell the Children of Israel whatever he had been commanded.*[68] Like other Biblical figures who have received law, Moses's physical form is altered. Abraham lost part of his generative organ through circumcision in the course of making the covenant; Isaac—who midrash says had his sight impaired during the binding—turns blind; Jacob, when he receives the commandment not to eat of the sinew, suffers an injury upon his thigh that leaves him limping for the rest of his life.[69] The Israelites were right. Law giving is a dangerous business. The veil is explained as protection, a means of shielding the people from Moses's radiant face, which shone forth with intensity after Sinai. But the veil speaks to more than this sense of risk. Its lasting significance is that it marks the end of the Sinai moment, evoking a permanent sense of loss.[70] The veil is also a separation. Moses's face, like the divine law giving face, has become forever hidden. Now Sinai must be relegated to memory. Through interpreting law, through both expertise in the analysis of statutes and the practical wisdom of applying law to everyday life, we will see that the Jews will be able to keep the memory of Sinai alive. Law is not simply the antithesis of idolatry. It is the solace which allows us to live with a distant God.

Remember Standing at Sinai

According to rabbinic tradition, the Biblical commandments number six hundred and thirteen. "Six hundred and thirteen commandments were revealed to Moses at Sinai, these being three hundred and sixty five prohibitions, corresponding in number to the solar days, and two hundred and forty eight positive commandments corresponding to the limbs [and organs] of the human body."[71] During the middle ages, a genre of literature emerged which enumerated these commandments with the most influential of these being Maimonides' *Book of Commandments*. Serving as a preface to his monumental code of Jewish law, the *Mishneh Torah*, Maimonides' list of commandments was derived through a variety of hermeneutic methods. However, various challenges were made to Maimonides' choices concerning the inclusion or exclusion of particular commandments. In particular, Nachmanides in a number of instances amended the list of precepts on theological or philosophical grounds. One of his notable additions to the *Book of Commandments*, which we will examine at length shortly, was his addition of the commandment not to forget the law giving at Sinai.

It seems peculiar *not* to have a precept to recall the revelation at Sinai. For Sinai is above all an historic beginning, and therefore like other mythic origins should elicit a commemorative ceremony. Moreover, there are numerous other commandments to remember or not to forget. The Jews are enjoined to remember the Sabbath; to remember and not forget the aggression of Amalek; and to remember in numerous ways the Exodus from Egypt. Memory seems to multiply within the Biblical text. The Sabbath, for example, leads to a double remembering. The command to remember the Sabbath prompts in turn the recalling of both Creation and Exodus. Sometimes there is a reciprocal remembering where the Covenant demands Israel must remember God; and God remembers Israel. Even the history of the people begins with memory. The genealogy of Abraham is inaugurated with God remembering Sarah just as the Exodus unfolds with God recalling his Covenant.

Moreover, since memory requires focusing consciousness, there are a variety of commandments intended to constitute mnemonic devices. Abraham's covenant is marked by circumcision. Some of the most common Jewish ritual objects—such as ritual fringes, phylacteries, and signs upon the doorpost—surround individuals as vivid and constant reminders.[72] Phylacteries are called a *memorial* or *zikaron*.[73] Other moments of recall are more sporadic, recalled at specific dates on the calendar. Amalek is remembered through reading the section of the Torah dealing with his attack against the Israelites in a special assigned reading and through the recitation of the scroll of Esther on the holiday of Purim. If memory abounds, and as has been claimed, is the principal medium for Jewish ritual to engage with the past, then Maimonides' omission becomes all the more puzzling.

How do we explain this? Although not identified as a command to remember, Maimonides seems to have seen the ceremony of *hakhel* as fulfilling the duty to remember Sinai. Described in the Biblical text as a gathering, this ceremony takes place infrequently during the year following the Sabbatical year. *At the end of seven years, at the time of the Sabbatical year, during the festival of Sukkot when all Israel comes to appear before the Lord your God, then in the place that He will choose, you shall read this Torah before all Israel, in their ears. Gather together the people—the men, the women, and the small children, and the stranger who is within your gate, in order that they will hear and that they shall learn to fear the Lord your God all the days that you live on the land to which you are crossing the Jordan, to possess it.*[74] *Hakhel* reverses the *we shall understand, we shall listen* of Sinai. Instead, the ritual begins with listening to the Torah reading and ends with *they shall learn to fear the Lord.* But it seeks to memorialize through recapturing the sense of awe which marked the original revelation. The fact that this commandment is one of the last two in Torah—the other being the writing of the Torah scroll itself—alone suggests its role in ensuring collective memory.

Maurice Halbwachs's classic study of collective memory underscores the importance of ceremonial as a mechanism for remembering. While individual memories, no matter how strong, might fade, group commemorations of past events serve to redefine the historical moment in ways that individuals might assimilate as their own. Writing largely in the aftermath of the First World War, Halbwachs, a French sociologist in the Émile Durkheim tradition, saw collective commemorations as essential for establishing a common usable past.[75] Individuals would remember a shared experience through the medium of collective ceremonial. The performance aspect of *hakhel* with its ritual re-enactment fits neatly in this model. It creates what Pierre Nora called a *lieu de mémoire*, a realm of memory, which might be defined as a symbolic receptacle for the heritage of a community.[76] Trumpets are sounded, perhaps echoing the thunder at Sinai, and the people assemble around a large wooden platform whereupon sits the king. A Torah scroll is passed from one official to another, each one of higher rank, until it reaches the High Priest. The High Priest delivers the scroll to the king, who then opens it to the appropriate place, recites a blessing, and reads the passages of the Torah with concluding blessings.[77] It was an aural and visual experience much like the revelatory moment at Sinai. There is the sound of the laws of the Torah and the sight of the king in all his majesty. It is possible to imagine the jostling of the crowd as they seek to catch a glimpse of the monarch or to imagine the snatches of comments about his comportment.

It was not a precept which might be performed alone—for how would it then be possible to recapture the awe surrounding the reading of the Torah? Nor was it like Passover performed within the circumscribed limits of the household fellowship of the *seder*. *Hakhel* established a collective and ritual image of remembrance for *all* who had been at Sinai and were now standing at the Temple Mount.

Such a commemorative remembering requires the presence of others from a variety of different social categories, including commoners, priests, and the monarch. This is not surprising. Memory is about the demands of relationships—with both contemporaries, and past and future generations.[78] Indeed, like the traditional understanding of the revelation at Sinai, it also demands the attendance of women and children.[79] The boundaries of the platform and the area below resembles the metes and bounds around the mountain. In place of Moses, the king delivers the law. Even the readings for the ceremony suggest its role in establishing collective memory. Selected passages are read from the Book of Deuteronomy. The beginning of Deuteronomy to the middle of the sixth chapter traces the events of the Jews in the Wilderness; tells of the epiphany at Sinai and repeats the decalogue; and concludes with the *Shema*. Other less contiguous passages include the ceremonial proclamation of blessings and curses on Mount Gerizim and Mount Ebal (Deut. 27:15-26) which echoes the revelation at Sinai; the laws concerning tithes (Deut. 14:22-27 and 26:12-15); and the Chapter of the King (Deut. 17:14-20).

Clearly, these readings reflect a collective history surrounding Sinai and the duties of commoner and monarch upon the land. It is therefore quite striking, though not surprising, that these selections return us to our point of departure at the beginning of this book—the suggested readings for the fifth day from the *Mekhilta*. Without doubt, there are strong parallels between the readings at *hakhel* and two of the three readings we have seen were suggested in the *Mekhilta* as the *Book of the Covenant* read at Sinai. R. Jose's idea of an overarching narrative is reflected in the readings of the march towards Sinai, the giving of the Torah, and its subsequent reaffirmation on Mount Gerizim and Mount Ebal. Again, we have a turn towards narrative. Just as R. Jose wished to describe the period from Genesis to Sinai, the readings in the *hakhel* ceremony relate the historical tale of the Wilderness and its relationship to Sinai. The ceremony's very position in the calendar at the end of the holiday of Sukkot reminds us that it is meant to recall the Wilderness where the Torah was given.

R. Ishmael's proposed readings for the fifth day, as we recall, provided a sample of the law and concerned those ordinances regarding the land—such as the sabbatical year, the jubilee, and the law of bonded labor. Paralleling R. Ishmael's readings in the *Mekhilta* are sections read by the king as part of the *hakhel* ceremony dealing with tithes and the role of the monarch. The *hakhel* readings focus upon the establishing of a settled, even stratified society upon the land. Tithes, like the laws of the sabbatical year, reflect duties associated with the possession of agricultural land. The tithes include the annual tithe set aside to be consumed at the sanctuary as well as the tithes granted to the poor and the Levites. Moreover, the law of bonded labor might be seen as neatly corresponding to the legal restrictions set upon the monarch. Limiting the king in the number of horses and wives, in part, is meant to prevent the placing of his subjects in slavery—and, perhaps, even the *return* [of] *the people to Egypt in order to increase horses.*[80] The *hakhel* passage also enjoins the monarch to study Torah so as to rule justly on the land. Intriguingly, both R. Ishmael's readings and the *hakhel* readings include an admonition.

According to the *Mekhilta* selection for the fifth day, God warns *if you consider my decrees loathsome, and if your being rejects My ordinances, so as not to perform all My commandments, so that you annul My covenant, then I will do the same to you.*[81] A number of curses are threatened—panic, swelling lesions, burning fever, the heavens hardened into copper, the death of livestock and children, and the land shall become desolate.[82] Within the *hakhel* ceremony, the readings recall the dramatic moment when the twelve anathemas were proclaimed from the two mountains, Mount Gerizim and Mount Ebal, warning the people to follow the law as they enter the land of Israel. Each anathema begins with the word *accursed* and, like the admonitions of R. Ishmael, threaten *one who will not uphold the words of this Torah, to perform them.*[83] The people between the two mountains—standing within as formal an array as the *hakhel* ceremony would later require—answer each curse with *amen*.

R. Judah's proposal for the readings of the fifth day—the selection describing pre-Sinai law which provided the roadmap for this book—is strikingly absent. There is no parallel to any of the readings assigned for the day of *hakhel*. The law before the law is missing. No doubt this is because the *hakhel* ceremony stresses the remembering of Sinai to the exclusion of earlier law giving. In so many ways, *hakhel* tells a diametrically opposing story to the law before the law. *Hakhel* focuses on written law, as evidenced by the Torah scroll, rather than oral law. As a commemorative ceremonial, it seeks to recapture the awe of the singular revelatory moment rather than the multiplicity of law giving; enunciates prescripts regarding ascribed social hierarchies and duties, such as tithes or the laws of the monarch, which sustain norms within the context of settled society; stresses clear rules rather than interpretation; and relates the narrative of the Wilderness generation making its progress to Sinai instead of the stories of the Patriarchs.

The collective-performative ceremony of *hakhel* requires ritualized behavior from its actors, and remains outward directed. However, this is not to suggest that *hakhel* ignores the psychological dimension of law giving. *Hakhel* is meant to evoke a sense of inner awe. Maimonides describes that those witnessing the ceremony "must make ready their heart and give ear with their ears to hearken in awe and reverence and trembling joy, as on the day when the law was given on Sinai."[84] Yet *hakhel* is a remarkably formal performance which is enacted only once every seven years. It would be impossible to sustain a similar level of wonderment at the re-enactment of the giving of the Torah if it would take place more often.

Nachmanides' claim that there is a specific commandment not to forget the giving of the Torah at Sinai refers to personal memory, not the commemorative memory of the *hakhel*. It concerns the internalization of law rather than outward performance. Nevertheless, this distinction would not be sustained, and the addition of another commandment made to the list of precepts, if there was not a Biblical verse which serves as its basis: *Only be careful for yourself and be very careful for your soul, lest you forget the things your eyes have beheld, and lest you remove them from your heart all days of your life; and make them known to your children and your children's children the day that you stood before the Lord your God at Horeb when God said to me, 'Gather to Me the people and listen to My words, so that they shall learn to fear me all the days which they live on earth, and they shall teach their children.*[85] As Nachmanides describes, this prohibition enjoins Jews "not to forget the law giving at Sinai nor to permit it to depart from your consciousness."[86] While its purpose is legal transmission from one generation to the next, it is predicated, as Nachmanides points out, upon the idea that "the study of the fundamental basis for belief in Torah constitutes the study of Torah."[87]

Other exegetes have interpreted this verse as ordinary law or, indeed, not as law at all. Rashi reads the verse as merely hortatory: "Only then if you will not forget [the commandments] and you will observe them properly will you be considered wise and full of understanding; but if you do them corruptly, because of forgetfulness, you will be considered fools."[88] There is no specific commandment to remember standing at Sinai—only a general evoking of a need to be careful when performing any part of the law. Not all reminders are commandments. For example, *remember, do not forget, that you provoked the Lord, your God, in the Wilderness* with its demand of double recalling—remembering and not forgetting—gives the impression of a commandment.[89] It is treated, nevertheless, as the hortatory beginning of Moses's parting words to the Israelites. Even if our verse does have legal significance, it may be subordinate to another law. Maimonides reads the verse as part of the general obligation to transmit the law to one's children, providing an additional detail that "just as it is a person's duty to teach his so is he obligated to teach his grandson."[90]

In his commentary to the Book of Deuteronomy, however, Nachmanides again makes clear that he—unlike Rashi or Maimonides—sees the verse *Only be careful for yourself and be very careful for your soul, lest you forget the things yours eyes have beheld* as a command:

> This verse, in my opinion, is a negative commandment in which he [Moses] admonishes [us] severely [as follows]: For, as he stated, that we should be careful concerning all the commandments and be heedful to perform the statutes and the ordinances, he again stated: "Only I warn you exceedingly to take heed and guard yourselves very, very much to remember whence the commandments came to you, that you should not forget the revelation on Mount Sinai, nor all the things which your eyes saw there—*the thunderings, and the lightning, His glory and His greatness* and His words that you have heard there *out of the midst of the fire*. And you should convey all the things which your eyes saw at that glorious revelation *unto your children and your children's children* forever." He explained the reason [for this prohibition]: God made the revelation so that you might learn to fear Him all the days and teach your children during all generations. Therefore, do so [remember the revelation and teach your children] and do not forget it. Thus before mentioning the commandments which were proclaimed there [on Mount Sinai] He admonished with a negative commandment that we are not to forget a thing from the revelation, and we are never to remove it from our hearts. He further charged in the form of a positive commandment that we should inform all our children

> from generation to generation of everything that happened there—what we saw and what we heard.[91]

Nachmanides' focus is upon the visual. What should not be forgotten is the sensory experience of Sinai—*the thunderings, and the lightning, His glory and His greatness*. There is no substitute for this moment. Nothing can aid our memory beyond the need to remember itself. This remembering is personal and immediate. In this sense, it differs from the commemorative memory as required by Biblical command. We recall Amalek through evoking its name. Amalek, who attacked those who could not keep up with the main body of the Israelite company as they left Egypt, is remembered through oral evocation with the special reading of the Sabbath before Purim and is not forgotten—the other commandment according to Maimonides—through recollecting Amalek in our minds.[92] However, there is no legal requirement which demands that we feel the same fear as the Israelites in the Wilderness as Amalek swoops down from the distant reaches of the desert, and slays the weak or elderly. Indeed, the ritual of collective remembering seems to channel the mood of vengeance into a set of circumscribed acts.

We are asked by Nachmanides to recall not the commandments, not the law giver, not the multitudes assembled, not even the Tablets of the Law. The precept is to remember the thunder and lightening, and how it feels to hear words come forth from the fire. Such atmospherics are not simply the window dressing for revelation. Baḥyya ben Asher, who so often echoes Nachmanides, sums up the requirement nicely. Our obligation is to recall the *experience* of standing at Mount Sinai.[93] On its face, then, observing this commandment seems so overwhelming. How can the revelatory moment again be felt? What means are at our disposal to evoke an eidetic moment we have never even seen? How should we recall the awe, truly the fear, of law giving? Even at Sinai, as we have seen, it was difficult for the people to sustain the presence of an imminent God. There is no ritual to mediate this commandment. It must be faced by every individual on its own, and the difficulty lies in our own limitations. For, as Yosef Hayim Yerushalmi has so elegantly reminded us, "memory is problematic, usually deceptive, sometimes treacherous."[94]

However, Nachmanides hints at a way around this dilemma. It must be an experience we can convey to our children—"all the things which your eyes saw at that glorious revelation *unto your children and your children's children* forever." In other words, legal transmitter domesticates the verse of awe.The Talmud's rendering of this verse unpacks the ways this precept of *not to forget* Sinai might be fulfilled:

> R. Yehoshua ben Levi said: Anyone who teaches his grandchild Torah, Scripture considers it as if he had [himself] received the Torah from Mount Sinai. As it is written, *you shall make them known to your children and your children's children*, and adjacent to this *the day that you stood before the Lord your God at Horeb*. [It once happened] that R. Chiya bar Abba encountered R. Yehoshua ben Levi who had [hastily] thrown a cloth upon his head, and was escorting his grandchild to the synagogue [to study]. [R. Chiya bar Abba] said to him: What is all this about? [R. Yehoshua ben Levi] replied to him: is it a small matter [to fulfill] that which is written *and you shall make them known to your children* [*and your children's children*], and adjacent to this *the day that you stood before the Lord your God at Horeb*? From this, R. Chiya bar Abba [established the custom] of not tasting a delicacy at breakfast until he had read with his grandchild [what had been learned before] and taught him additional [scripture as well]. R. Rabbah bar Rav Huna [had the custom] of not tasting [the same] delicacy at breakfast until he had brought his grandchild to the study hall.[95]

This is a remarkable passage. The awe of experiencing Sinai, the thunder and the lightening, is remembered through the most ordinary of acts, the taking of a grandchild to school or even the delaying of a breakfast delicacy until a passage of scripture is taught to a grandchild. Nowhere were the rabbis in this tale told how to perform the commandment of *not to forget* Sinai. The sages themselves determined how to follow the precept. Obedience, interpretation, and transmission of law occurs through their own discretionary sense of the meaning of the command to remember, and these renderings, so seemingly trivial, take upon themselves the full weight of command.

There is a striking contrast between the infrequent *hakhel* ceremony marking commemorative memory and the sort of pervasive individual re-enactments described here. To create a sense of awe, *hakhel* relies upon the presence of kings. The *hakhel* ceremony is formal and stylized, a ritual commemoration. It takes place according to the dictates of the calendar, not as a result of an inner emotional need to express memory. For all its drama, *hakhel* seems a pale reflection of the intimacy of the giving of the law. Recalling the experience of Sinai, however, invokes an imminent God, who is ruler of the universe. The Torah scroll read in an assemblage cannot resemble the emotional whirlwind of encountering God's presence. This stands in contrast to the intimacy of Nachmanides' command to remember. The reliance upon hierarchy within the *hakhel* ceremony legitimates the existing social order while the Nachmanidean commandment recreates the centrality of domestic transmission *to your children and your children's children.*

Indeed, we are suddenly thrust back to the time of the law before the law. The understanding of law is immediate and highly personal. R. Chiya encounters R. Yehoshua ben Levi escorting his grandchild. As a result, he learns a *halacha*. The commitment of the grandfather—the image of the sage engaged in the everyday business of interpreting and transmitting the law—has a formative effect upon the grandchild. In contrast to other ways of remembering, such as the Passover *seder* or the ritual of bringing the *bikurim*, the performance of the commandment does not recall the event through the tools of narrative. There is no story of what occurred at Sinai long ago.

Unlike the commemorative ceremony of *hakhel*, the command to remember makes no attempt to re-enact the overpowering awe of the revelation at Sinai. Instead, it summons up even more ancient historical memories concerning law. The legalism evoked here is what we have been describing as the law before the law. It is concerned with an oral *paideia* rather than written codes; is discretionary rather than formalist; relies upon the legerdemain of interpretation rather than command; speaks to a form of transmission related to kinship or personal relations; and provides for a pluralism of legal actions while retaining a shared marrow of normative language.

The psychological attitudes of the legal actors are important. If as has been argued—turning Cover's syllogism on its head—*nomos* precedes narrative, the invocation of an historical moment through the making of norms shows the absolute power of the *nomos* of the law before the law to reassert itself. The word *remember* is not mentioned in this commandment. Instead, the individual is required to *only guard yourself.* This echoes God's statement concerning Adam who was placed in the garden to work it and *to guard it*. Indeed, the refraining from eating a delight suggests that legal interpretation might now circumscribe desire rather than—as was the case of Malbim's narrative of Adam and the fruit of the Tree of Knowledge of Good and Evil—serving as its instrument. Adam rushed to sample the forbidden fruit; R. Chiya bar Abbu refrains from taking a taste even of what is permitted. The cloaked R. Yehoshua ben Levi seems to be an implicit rebuke to Noah. While the rabbinic figure will not even walk through the streets without proper garments reflecting the dignity of a sage, Noah debased himself through exposure of his private parts. For R. Yehoshua ben Levi does not simply inherit a code—and, after all, the code of six hundred and thirteen commandments from Sinai is so much greater than Noah's seven commandments—but adds to these statutes as well. Unlike the Noahide code, the law of Sinai expands in incremental fashion.

It is common in earlier societies for grandparents to play a significant role in the education of young persons. While parents are occupied with other tasks, and without formal educational institutions, grandparents would take charge of transmitting tradition within the household. Nevertheless, the tale of R. Yehoshua ben Levi tells us that even where there are houses of study, it is still necessary for elders to impart the sense of having been at Sinai. Strikingly, the legal transmission described here most closely echoes that of Abraham. Just as Abraham taught the law through his example so do the two grandfathers. In a domestic setting, a highly interpretive and discretionary move is made—and one that expands the law—where a new practice might be established. Abraham's covenant to his children and his children's children seems to have become the basis for tutoring future generations. In fact, in this particular passage from the Talmud it is the written texts of the law from Sinai, studied in the synagogue or in the home before breakfast, which are cabined by a fertile *lex non scripta* expressed through personal comportment. This story, then, reflects a turn towards orality—an oral approach to the written commandment with its roots deeply grounded in pre-Sinai legalism.

Written law and oral law, legislation and common law exist side by side in an uneasy equilibrium. Through retaining its archeology of past legal forms, it has sustained the jostling of different notions of the *idea* of law—and sustained creative pluralism as a result. The question of determining the law before the law, I argued earlier, arose because it posed a conundrum for the legal mind to understand how law, so central to Jewish culture, was interpreted by generations prior to revelation—by Adam or the Patriarchs or the Israelites leaving Egypt. In addition to the puzzle itself, there may have been deeper reasons for expending so much effort—even in scattered sources—upon the project of thinking about archaic law. Pre-Sinai law speaks to the psychological question of how we internalize norms and become norm bearing. It cannot be asserted that there is a simple, one-dimensional normative claim that results from eliciting the paradigm of this earlier law. However, it *is* the case that we might think about Jewish law somewhat differently if we can remember—as part of our received tradition of its history—that an earlier customary law at its core embodied the notion that law must not simply be commanded, but internalized as well.

Sinai has not obscured the sort of law making experienced as archaic law. It has not, or at least need not, become the basis of a call for simple obedience, the curbing of the interpretive impulse, or establishing a purely written and learned legal culture to trump various oral or customary traditions. The notion of multiple moments of law giving, which was the idea behind R. Judah's readings on the fifth day, habituates the people to legal rules, and prepares them for the burden of Sinai. But the need for this habituation does not end with Sinai. The simple *exempla* depicted in the Talmud's description of the everyday behavior of grandparents has much the same purpose. It domesticates Sinai and places the extraordinary moment of law giving within the ambit of ordinary behavior.

One should not be deceived by the simplicity of the Talmudic tale—or the awkwardness of the anachronistic narrative of pre-Sinai legalism. Quite remarkably, the commandment to remember the revelation at Sinai serves to recall the modes of legalism from a pre-Sinai past. Sinai suggests the model of the apotheosis of divine command. Nevertheless, and here lies the most telling irony of all, its remembrance serves as the legal justification for making new law in the manner of the law before the law.

Notes

1. Deut. 4:9-10.
2. Exod. R. 30:3.
3. Rabbenu Baḥyya, Exod. 3:1 and 18.
4. Yehezkel Kaufmann, *Toldot ha-Emuna ha-Yisraelit* (Tel Aviv: Dvir Publishers, 1969), 69.
5. Aristotle, Politics, 175.
6. Exod. 20:17.
7. Exod. 19:6.
8. Exod. 19:10.
9. Nachmanides, Exod. 19:10.

10. Nachmanides, Exod. 25:1.
11. B. Shab. 87a.
12. Exod. 19:4.
13. Exod. 19:6.
14. Exod. 19:8.
15. B. Shab. 88a.
16. B. Shab. 88a.
17. Exod. 19:9.
18. B. Shab. 87a.
19. On the second Passover, *see* Num. 9:6-14; On the daughters of Zelophehad, *see* Num. 27:1-11 and Num. 36:1-2.
20. Seforno, Exod. 19:11.
21. B. Shab. 87a. It is astonishing that Rashi concludes his classic commentary on the Pentateuch with a description of the impressive acts of Moses committed *before the eyes of all Israel* by focusing on the destruction of the first set of Tablets. "His [Moses's] heart inspired him to break the Tablets in their sight, as it is said, *and I broke them in your sight* (Deut. 9, 17), and the Holy One Blessed Be He agreed with his opinion, as it is said, *which you did break, may your strength be firm for having broken them* (Exod. 34, 1)." The destruction of the Tablets, which took place upon Moses's own initiative, is seen as an act of creative destruction, and as evidence of Moses's greatness—presumably, a greatness found in making legal decisions beyond direct divine command.
22. Exod. 19:21.
23. Exod. 19:23.
24. Exod. 19:24.
25. Rashi, Exod. 19:21.
26. Rashi, Exod. 19:2.
27. Exod. 19:16. Scholars of religious visual culture have suggested that a special gaze signals the projection of religious conventions which determine the status of the viewer. David Morgan, *The Sacred Gaze: Religious Visual Culture in Theory and Practice* (Berkeley: University of California Press, 2005), 2-6.
28. Exod. 19:17.
29. Exod. 20:15.
30. B. Shab. 88a.
31. Rabbenu Baḥyya, Exod. 20:17.
32. B. San. 105.
33. Rashi, Exod. 20:15.
34. Exod. 19:9-10.
35. Rashi, Exod. 19:9. Ironically, the Israelites circumscribe the importance of an intermediary; but it is the absence of Moses, the intermediary, which arouses the fears which some commentators have seen as the reason behind the transgression of creating the Golden Calf.

36. See Rashi's comment, "although sound is not visible, this was visible," B. Berachot 6b.

37. Exod. 20:15. The importance of the visual in establishing the grounding of the law cannot be overestimated. Pierre Legendre, whose work brings to bear the relationship between psychoanalysis and the law, describes the primary importance of the image in establishing law through reflecting the self within another image—much as the water reflects Narcissus. By reflecting opinions in the form of the other, the law, norms are therefore vested with authority. Nevertheless, as we will discuss below, iconic renderings of law or law giving itself also raise the problem of idolatry. Pierre Legendre, *L'Inestimable objet de la transmission*: *Etude sur le principe généalogique en Occident* (Paris: Librarie Fayard, 1983), 51-68.

38. Exod.19:4.

39. Exod. 20:19.

40. Exod. 24:10-11 describes what Moses, Aaron, Nadav and Avihu, and the seventy elders saw upon their partial ascent.

41. Song of Songs R. 17:5.

42. Num. 15:38-39.

43. Exod. 24:3-8.

44. Philo, *Quis Rerum Divinarum Heres* [*Who is the Heir of Divine Things*], IV:373-75.

45. *Targum Onkelos*, Exod. 24:8, adds that the function of the sprinkling of the blood is atonement, "and he sprinkled the blood on the alter as an atonement for the people [*le-ḥapra al ama*]." Moshe Alsheikh explains that this atonement is to rectify Adam's transgression. Alsheikh, *Torat Moshe*, Exod. 24:3. In anthropological terms, the enactment of death through blood sacrifice serves as a denial of the transient self so as to provide for the re-emergence of individuals as components of a transcendent entity. Maurice Bloch, *Prey into Hunter: The Politics of Religious Experience* (Cambridge: Cambridge University Press, 1992), 4-7.

46. Harry Austryn Wolfson, *Philo* (Cambridge: Harvard University Press, 1982), 2 vols., I: 258-59.

47. Abarbanel, Exod. 24:1. Abarbanel's characterization of French and Spanish schools cannot be taken as rigid categories; but they may serve as useful devices to describe different sides in this debate. Maimonides's son, for example, proposes like the French exegetes that the Sinai covenant took place before the giving of the decalogue, while Samuel ben Meir (Rashbam), a grandson of Rashi, follows the Spanish commentators that it occurred afterwards. Abraham ben Moshe ben Maimon, *Perush al Ha-Torah*, Exod. 24:1. Rashbam, Exod. 24:1.

48. Rashi, Exod. 24:3, based upon B. San. 56.

49. Moshe Sternbuch, *Sefer Taam ve-Daat*, Exod. 24:1. B. Yevamot 47b; B. Keritot 9a.

50. Nachmanides, Exod. 24:1. For a similar timing, see Ibn Ezra and Seforno, Exod. 24:1.

51. Zalman Sorotzkin, *Oznaim la-Torah*, Exod. 24:1.

52. Deut. 24:4.

53. Nachmanides, Gen. 26:5.

54. Idolatry is cited in the Talmud as a law given as part of the Noahide code and repeated at Sinai. B. Sanhedrin 59a, b.

55. Deut. 5:27. B. Beizah 5b; B. San. 59b.

56. B. Sanhedrin 59b.

57. Carlo Ginzburg, *Wooden Eyes: Nine Reflections on Distance*, trans. Martin Ryle and Kate Soper (New York: Columbia University Press, 2001), 95-108.

58. Exod. 20:19-20.

59. Exod. 20:3-5.

60. B San. 7b.

61. See, for example, Seforno and Neẓiv on Exod. 20:19-20. Moshe Halbertal and Avishai Margalit, *Idolatry* (Cambridge: Harvard University Press, 1992), 190-97.

62. B. A.Z. 43b.

63. Rabbenu Baḥyya, Exod. 20:4.

64. Maimonides, *Sefer Ha-Miẓvot*, negative commandments #3. Also, *Sefer ha-Ḥinukh*. This verse has grammatical difficulties as well. The first part of the verse *You shall not make of Me* [images] is one clause; *you shall not make for yourselves* is a second clause. But it is unclear where the middle section, *of gods of silver and gods of gold*, should be appended—whether it should be part of the first clause or the second. The verse demands interpretation simply to understand the proper punctuation. *See* John Van Seters, *A Law Book for the Diaspora: Revision in the Study of the Covenant Code* (Oxford: Oxford University Press, 2003), 58-60.

65. Halbertal, *Idolatry*, 110.

66. Exod. 34:33.

67. Deut. 2:2.

68. Exod. 34:33-34.

69. Gen. 17:11; Gen. 32:25-26.

70. Ibn Ezra, Exod. 33:21.

71. B. Mak. 23b.

72. On ritual fringes, Num. 15:37-41; phylacteries, Exod. 13:9-16, Deut. 6:4-9 and 11:13-21; *mezuzot*, Deut. 6:9 and 11, 20.

73. Exod. 13:9.

74. Deut. 31:10-13.

75. Maurice Halbwachs, *On Collective Memory*, trans. Lewis A. Coser (Chicago: University of Chicago Press, 1992), 43-51. Also, Paul Connerton, *How Societies Remember* (Cambridge: Cambridge University Press, 1989), 6-

71. It is risky to read, academic scholarship with the lens of ethnic identity. Nevertheless, French fin-de-siècle Jews were broadly concerned with collective memory and the connection between religion and modernism. Ivan Strenski, *Durkheim and the Jews of France* (Chicago: University of Chicago Press, 1997), 149-59.

76. Pierre Nora, ed., *Realms of Memory: Rethinking the French Past* (New York: Columbia University Press, 1992), trans. Arthur Golhammer, xvii.

77. Maimonides, MT IX, ii, 3:4. M. Sot. 7:7-8.

78. Avishai Margalit, *The Ethics of Memory* (Cambridge: Harvard University Press, 2002), 40-63, discusses the importance of cultivating shared memory in defining the contours of social relations.

79. Rashi, Exod. 19:3 describing the presence of women.

80. Deut. 17:16.

81. Lev. 26:15-16.

82. Lev. 26:14-53.

83. Deut. 17:26.

84. Maimonides, IX, ii, 3:5.

85. Deut. 4:9-10.

86. *Sefer Ha-Miẓvot le-ha-Rambam ve-Hasagot Ha-Ramban,* ed. Chayim Dov Chavel (Jerusalem: Mosad Ha-Rav Kook, 1981), 396. Yonah ben Avrahram of Gerona, a relative of Nachmanides, states that forgetting a matter studied results in the violation of the commandment *lest you forget, see* Yonah ben Avraham of Gerona, *Shaarei Teshuva*. (Jerusalem: Eshkol Publishing House, 1977/8), 3: 28, 57.

87. *Hasagot HaRamban*, 386.

88. Rashi, Deut. 4:10.

89. Deut. 9:7.

90. Maimonides, MT, I, ii, 1:2.

91. Nachmanides, Deut. 4:9.

92. Maimonides, *Book of Commandments,* Negative Commandment #59; Positive Commandment #189.

93. Rabbenu Baḥyya, Deut. 4:9.

94. Yosef Hayim, Yerushalmi, *Zakhor: Jewish History and Jewish Memory* (Seattle: University of Washington Press, 1982), 5.

95. B. Kid. 30a. Baḥyya ben Asher suggests that the Hebrew word for mountains (*horim*), like Sinai the sources of instruction in law, and another source of law, parents (*harim*), are related. Parents refers to both the patriarchs and the actual parents of children. Rabbenu Baḥyya, Exod. 3:1.

Conclusion

The Once and Future Law

> *In this normative world, law and narrative are inseparably related. Every prescription is insistent in its demand to be located in discourse—to be supplied with history and destiny, beginning and end, explanation and purpose. And every narrative is insistent in its demand for its prescriptive point, its moral.*[1]

This book has sought to uncover a tradition of legal interpretation which focuses upon pre-Sinai law. At root, the questions asked by commentators were all normative. How did the first human beings encounter the idea of rules? What does it mean to be—like Abraham—a founder who missed the Sinai founding? And what are the normative moves necessary for constructing a legal system for a new-found society, especially when this society consists of those freed from slavery and whose previous experience with social regulating structure was based upon the model of the household? These norms might seem scattered, fragmentary, or barely even legal forms. However, as I have tried to show, almost every Biblical passage hinting at a law before the law has given rise to sophisticated claims of a preexisting law. The giving of the law did not efface the law before the law.

The law before the law was seen as much more fluid, oral, customary, discretionary, rooted in the particularities of an earlier social reality, deeply enmeshed in a web of legend, predicated upon the compass of individual psychology, and indeterminate than the received tradition of Sinai legalism. Its reinscription served, as I have suggested, as a laboratory for experimenting with alternative understandings of law. A wide array of jurisprudential issues were probed, representing nearly the entire gamut of concerns about law which Jewish law later faced. Visions of early Jewish law touched on issues such as statutory interpretation, legal transmission, the role of custom, citizenship, the relationship between civil and criminal law, and how norms came to be widely accepted.

To borrow a psychoanalytic term what I have described at many points is a kind of palimpsest legalism. Peel off one layer of law and another might be discovered underneath. The anachronistic use of precedent simultaneously both legitimizes and subverts the Sinai narrative.[2] It legitimizes the Torah by finding still deeper historical roots among Jewish progenitors. Imaginary depictions of early Jewish law, on the other hand, suggests that law is more than the command of a superior to an inferior. It reflects a complex appeal to the psychological dimension of individuals and societies which might change over time. In modern times, especially, traditional Jewish legalism has been predicated upon the idea of immutable commandments handed down at a moment of revelatory law giving. To the contrary, the idea of the law before the law suggests that even the most remarkable narrative of legal origins might be tempered by focusing upon the reception of law by individuals.

Introducing new interpretive methods within formal doctrine, legal realism, and the natural law's siren-like appeal to universal legal norms are only some of the mechanisms for bringing flexibility to traditional law. In addition, there is real normative ballast in revitalizing a robust customary law through uncovering earlier legalism. With numerous examples of textual *lieux de mémoire*, Jewish commentators excavated a buried legal past. However, as I suggested briefly in the preface, other legal traditions might also recover earlier legalism to counter contemporary norms. Common law might be used to challenge statutory law, seventeenth-century English ancient constitutionalism posited alternative tribal legal histories against common law itself. By reenacting the interpretive drama and customary law, I have tried to posit a paradigm for both Jewish legalism and common law thinking in the modern world.

But I am not the first to take the pre-law historical turn. Such nods towards imagination, such acts of recovery reflect a past of their own. In the Jewish context, Elias J. Bickerman, one of the most prominent twentieth-century historians of ancient Judaism, posited its origins in the Hellenistic period.[3] According to Bickerman in *Der Gott der Makkabäer* (*The God of the Maccabees*), those trained in Greek culture, and especially Jewish reformers themselves under Antiochus IV, around 200

B.C.E. attacked the exclusiveness of the commandments. To the Greeks, Jewish legal particularism was a misfortune. Jewish law's particular customs—such as dietary laws, circumcision, the Sabbath, and family law—separated Jews from other peoples. Drawing upon a Greek historical trope, legal rules promoting social exclusion reflected a declension from following universal laws of nature to adopting rules which were particular and transient. A band of Jewish Hellenists internalized these Greek norms.

In response, Jews aware of Greek culture but with a sense of fealty to their own traditions, crafted a counter-legal history, arguing that primal Jewish law was ancient and inherently particular. They elaborated upon a narrative of the Patriarchs following detailed, gradually accumulating rules which ultimately culminated in the giving of the law at Sinai.[4] The antiquity of the Torah was emphasized. "While the Greeks resented the religious separatism of the Jews, which they regarded as misanthropic, the Jews resented the political privileges of the Greeks, to which they regarded themselves as having equal right in light of their ancient culture."[5] This novel evolutionary history of the law before the law was the basis for the *Book of Jubilees* and the *Testaments* of *the Twelve Patriarchs*. Since the Torah itself presented evidence against the Patriarchs following Mosaic Law, exegetical acrobatics were necessary to rewrite the legal historical narrative of the Jewish people so as to provide a *before life* for the law giving at Sinai.

It is not my purpose here to discuss whether Bickerman was correct in his interpretation. As might be expected of such a powerful thesis, it has elicited vigorous debate. What is important for our purposes is that Bickerman's assertion that the God of the Maccabees was not the God of the natural law philosophers was itself an artifact of an historical period. Published on the eve of World War II in 1937, Bickerman's book celebrated a certain version of the German-Jewish synthesis. Jews who operated in two cultural traditions—much like committed German Jews in Bickerman's time—embarked upon a formative period of extraordinary creativity in legal thinking, acts of courageous exegesis, which would serve as a harbinger of the audacious re-readings found in the rabbinic tradition. If we had any doubts about the contemporary implication of *God of the Maccabees*, the comparison of Jewish adherents to Greek culture with nineteenth-century German Jewish reformers, such as Abraham Geiger or David Einhorn, is explicitly made. Of course, Bickerman's own work might itself be seen as a species of historical rethinking, not so very different from historiographic legerdemain which he attributes to those in the time of the Seleucids.

Only two years later in 1939, Freud published *Moses and Monotheism*. This was Freud's last sustained work. According to Freud, Moses was an Egyptian adherent of Akhenaten's Ra cult who was ultimately murdered in the desert by the Jews. The Egyptian cult represented a pure form of monotheism. But the Jews were unable to accept this demanding religion, and after their homicidal act turned to a crude, blood-thirsty, and primitive Semitic god. Freud sought to strip Moses of Semitic particularism and recover a form of pure monotheism. Moses was a cultural ombudsman who brought the universal Egyptian values. While Bickerman saw particular Jewish myth-making in the time of the Maccabees as the primal interpretive act, Freud, oddly enough, saw the muddy world of Hebrew mythopoesis as leading to a cultural retreat from common moral values and to the murder of the Jewish people's founding father.

A moment of law giving is a moment of danger, an overriding sense of rupture.[6] The rupture of Sinai marked a sudden upending of values and resulted in trauma. This trauma ultimately elicits another trauma through the slaying of Moses and the corruption of a universalistic legalism by a tribal law. The homicide gave rise to subconscious guilt embedded in the Jewish collective consciousness. Deep within Rabbinic legend, as with an individual's dreams, lie the marks of the trauma of law giving. Both the death of the universal and the death of Moses are acts of terrible violence. "The distortion of a text," Freud writes, "is not unlike murder. The difficulty lies not in the execution of the deed but in the doing away with the traces."[7]

Writing in the lengthening shadow of an impending crisis which ultimately would result in the destruction of European Jewry, Freud and Bickerman were two modern voices in a very old debate about the law before the law. Freud sought to uncover the pure beginnings of Judaism. He suggested that there was an unsullied earlier law, now corrupted, which might be reclaimed by sifting like an archeologist through the layers of law and legend. Despite claims to the *reality* of an *ur*-law, his narrative is truly an act of faith. Freud *believed* in the primacy of universalism over particular law. Even more than the death of Moses, the reader of *Moses and Monotheism*, senses Freud's trauma at the loss of a common legal language. For Bickerman there was no ultimate truth. Historical challenges bred creative responses. In the time of earlier persecutions, Jews seeped in Greek culture elaborated an anachronistic narrative of the law before the law as a defensive strategy. German Jews, Bickerman implied, would need to invent their own creative cultural responses. Freud's Sinai and Bickerman's pre-Sinai stand in opposition to each other. But both drew upon the same triptych of rupture-trauma-recovery. Law giving means rupture, and so much of what law experiences afterwards can be understood as the struggle against rupture. Jacob Burckhardt once remarked that history is the one field of study in which one cannot begin at the beginning.[8] This verity may very well hold true for law as well.

Notes

1. Robert Cover, "Nomos and Narrative" in Martha Minow, Michael Ryan, and Austin Sarat, eds. *Narrative, Violence, and the Law: The Essays of Robert Cover* (Ann Arbor: University of Michigan Press, 1992), 96.

2. Bernard M. Levinson, *Deuteronomy and the Hermeneutics of Legal Innovation* (Oxford University Press, 1997), 150.

3. Albert I. Baumgarten, "Elias J. Bickerman's Contributions to Jewish History: An Initial Assessment," forthcoming. Arnaldo Momigliano, "The Absence of the Third Bickerman," in *Essays on Ancient and Modern Judaism*, transl. Maura Masella-Gayley (Chicago: University of Chicago Press, 1994), pp. 217-21. Martha Himmelfarb, "Elias Bickerman on Judaism and Hellenism," in David N. Myers and David B. Ruderman, eds, *The Jewish Past Revisited: Reflections on Modern Jewish Historians* (New Haven: Yale University Press, 1998), 199-211.

4. Elias J. Bickerman, *The Jews in the Greek Age* (Cambridge: Harvard University Press, 1988), pp. 294-95; Elias J. Bickerman, *God of the Maccabees*, trans. Horst R. Moehring (Leiden: Brill Academic Press, 1979), 82-113.

5. Hindy Najman, *Seconding Sinai: The Development of Mosaic Discourse in Second Temple Judaism* (Leiden: Brill Academic Press, 2003), 15.

6. The idea of Moses as split between Egyptian and Semitic versions appears to be quite similar to the discussion of the need to unpack mythological figures such as Heracles. Herodotus, *The History*, trans. David Greene (Chicago: University of Chicago Press, 1987), 150-51.

7. Sigmund Freud, *Moses and Monotheism*, Trans. Katherine Jones (New York: Vintage, 1939), p. 32. Jan Assmann, *Moses the Egyptian: The Memory of Egypt in Western Monotheism* (Cambridge: Harvard University Press, 1997) suggests that it was not guilt over the homicide, but the very denial of the Egyptian role in monotheism which was most striking about the remembered origins of Jewish law. For a general examination of the importance of the figure of Moses in *fin-de-siècle* Europe, *see* Bluma Goldstein, *Reinscribing*

Moses: Heine, Kafka, Freud, and Schoenberg in a European Wilderness (Cambridge: Harvard University Press, 1992). Jacques Derrida, *Archive Fever: A Freudian Impression*, trans. Eric Prenowitz (Chicago: University of Chicago Press, 1995) discusses the tension between collective memory and personal memory. Yosef Hayim Yerushalmi, *Freud's Moses: Judaism Terminable and Interminable* (New Haven: Yale University Press, 1993). Freud's Moses operated within the tradition of biographical studies, non-fiction and fictional—such as Thomas Mann's *Joseph and His Brothers*. However, its timing as Nazi persecutions were in the ascendent, and the fact that his presumed Jewish role in patricide looked uncannily like Christian antisemitic traditions of the Jewish part in the murder of Christ, made *Moses and Monotheism* seem particularly subversive. Peter Gay, *Freud: A Life for Our Time* (New York: Norton Publishing, 1988), 645-47.

8. Quoted in M.I. Finley, *The World of Odysseys* (London: Chatto & Windus, 1956), 12.

Bibliography

Abraham Ibn Ezra, *Yesod Morah ve-Sod Torah*. Edited by Yosef Cohen and Uriel Simon. Ramat-Gan: Bar Ilan University Press, 2002.

Adler, Elchanan. "Be-Inyan ha-Miẓvot she-Nitnu be-Marah," *Or Mizraḥ* 4 (2003): 18-41.

Agus, Aharon. *The Binding of Isaac and Messiah: Law, Martyrdom, and Deliverance in Early Rabbinic Religiosity*. Albany: State University of New York Press, 1988.

Aharon Ha-Levi. *Sefer Ha-Ḥinukh*. Jerusalem: Eshkol, 1977/78.

Albani, Matthias. Frey, Jörg, and Lange, Armin. *Studies in the Book of Jubilees*. Tübingen: Mohr Siebeck, 1997.

Albeck, Theodore. *Das Buch der Jubiläen und die Halacha*. Berlin, 1930.

Alsheikh, Moshe. *Torat Moshe*. 5 vols. Jerusalem: Wagshall Publishers, 1989/1990.

Albo, Joseph. *Sefer Ha-Ikkarim, Book of Principles*. Translated by Isaac Husik. Philadelphia: Jewish Publication Society, 1929.

Alter, Yehuda Leib. *Sefat Emet*. 2 vols. Jerusalem: n.p., 1970/71.

Anderson, Gary A. "The Status of the Torah before Sinai: The Retelling in the Damascus Covenant and the Book of Jubilees," *Dead Sea Discoveries* 1 (1994): 1-29.

——. "The Status of the Torah in the Pre-Sinaitic Period: St. Paul's Epistle to the Romans." In *Biblical Perspectives: Early Use and Interpretation of the Bible in Light of the Dead Sea Scrolls*. Edited by Michael E. Stone and Esther G. Chazon. Leiden: Brill, 1998.

Arama, Yiẓḥak. *Sefer Akedat Yiẓḥak*. Israel: n.p., n.d.

Aristotle. *Nicomachaean Ethics*. Translated by Terence Irwin. Indianapolis: Hackett Publishing Company, 1985.

Assmann, Jan. *Moses the Egyptian: The Memory of Egypt in Western Monotheism*. Cambridge: Harvard University Press, 1997.

Austin, John. *The Province of Jurisprudence Determined*. Edited by Wilfrid E. Rumble. Cambridge: Cambridge University Press, 1995.

Baḥyya ben Asher, *Rabenu Baḥya Beur al Ha-Torah*. Edited by Ḥayim Dov Chavel. Jerusalem: Mosad Ha-Rav Kook, 1994.

Baḥya ibn Paquda, *The Book of the Direction to the Duties of the Heart*. Translated by Menahem Mansoor. London: Littman Library, 1973.

Batnitzky, Leora, *Idolatry and Representation: The Philosophy of Franz Rosenzweig*. Princeton: Princeton University Press, 2000.

Baumgarten, Albert I. "Elias J. Bickerman's Contributions to Jewish History: An Initial Assessment," forthcoming.

———. "Elias Bickerman on the Hellenizing Reformers: A Case Study of an Unconvincing Case," *Jewish Quarterly Review* 97 (2007): 149-71.

Benamozegh, Elijah. *Israël et l'Humanité: Etude sur le problème de la religion universelle et sa solution*. Paris: Ernest Leroux, 1914.

Benjamin, Walter. "On the Concept of History." In *Selected Writings*. Edited by Michael W. Jennings. 4 vols. Cambridge: Harvard University Press, 2003.

Bialik, Ḥayim. "Halacha and Aggada." Translated by Leon Simon. Jerusalem: Ibis Editions, 2000.

Bickerman, Elias. *From Ezra to the Last of the Maccabees: Foundations of Post-Biblical Judaism*. New York: Schocken Books, 1962.

———. *The God of the Maccabees*. Translated by Horst R. Moehring. Leiden: Brill Academic Press, 1979.

———. *The Jews in the Greek Age*. Cambridge: Harvard University Press, 1988.

Bleich, J. David. "Judaism and Natural Law," *The Jewish Law Annual* 7 (1988): 5-42.

Blidstein, Gerald. "Rabbinic Judaism and General Culture: Normative Discussion and Attitudes." In *Judaism's Encounter with Other Cultures: Rejection or Integration. Jerusalem*. Jerusalem: Jason Aronson, 1997.

Bloch, Maurice. *Prey into Hunter: The Politics of Religious Experience*. Cambridge: Cambridge University Press, 1992.

Boyarin, Daniel. "Inner Biblical Ambiguity, Intertextuality, and the Dialectic of Midrash: The Waters of Marah," *Prooftexts* 10 (1990): 29-48.

Brague, Rémi. *La loi de Dieu: Histoire philosophique d'une allinance*. Paris: Éditions Gallimard, 2005.

Breuer, Isaac. *Concepts of Judaism*. Edited by Jacob S. Levinger. Jerusalem: Israel Universities Press, 1974.

Brody, Robert. *The Geonim of Babylonia and the Shaping of Medieval Jewish Culture*. New Haven: Yale University Press, 1998.

Bruckner, James K. *Implied Law in the Abraham Narrative: A Literary and Theological Analysis*. London: Sheffield Academic Press, 2001.

Cassuto, U. *A Commentary on the Book of Exodus*. Translated by Israel Abrahams. Jersusalem: Magnes Press, 1997.

Chajes, Ẓevi Hirsch. *Torat Avot*. Zulkew: Saul Meyerhoffer, 1836.

Charles, R.H. *The Book of Jubilees or the Little Genesis*. London: Adam and Charles Black, 1902.

Cohen, Jeremy. *"Be Fertile, and Increase, Fill the Earth and Master It": The Ancient and Medieval Career of a Biblical Text*. Ithaca: Cornell University Press, 1989.

Cohen, Shaye J.D. *The Beginnings of Jewishness: Boundaries, Varieties, Uncertainties*. Berkeley: University of California Press, 1999.

Connerton, Paul. *How Societies Remember*. Cambridge: Cambridge University Press, 1989.

Constable, Marianne. *Just Silences: The Limits and Possibilities of Modern Law*. Princeton: Princeton University Press, 2005.

Cover, Robert. "Nomos and Narrative." In *Narrative, Violence, and the Law: The Essays of Robert Cover*. Edited by Martha Minow, Michael Ryan, and Austin Sarat. Ann Arbor: University of Michigan Press, 1992.

———. *Justice Accused: Antislavery and the Judicial Process*. New Haven: Yale University Press, 1975.

D'Entrèves, A.P. *Natural Law: An Introduction to Legal Philosophy*. London: Hutchinson's University Library, 1951.

Davis, David Brion. *The Problem of Slavery in the Age of Revolution 1770-1823*. Ithaca: Cornell University Press, 1975.

Derrida, Jacques. *Archive Fever: A Freudian Impression*. Translated by Eric Prenowitz. Chicago: University of Chicago Press, 1995.

Eisen, Robert, *The Book of Job in Medieval Jewish Philosophy*. Oxford: Oxford University Press, 2004.

Eisenberg, Melvin Aaron. *The Nature of the Common Law*. Cambridge: Harvard University Press, 1988.

Elon, Menaḥem. *Ha-Mishpat Ha-Ivri*. 3 vols. 3rd ed. Jerusalem: Magnes Press, 1988.

The Fathers According to R. Nathan. Edited by Judah Goldin. New Haven: Yale University Press, 1955.
Feiner, Shmuel Feiner. *Haskalah and History: The Emergence of a Modern Jewish Historical Consciousness*. Oxford: Littman Library, 2002.
Finley, M.I. *The World of Odysseus*. London: Chatto & Windus, 1956.
Fishbane, Michael. *Biblical Interpretation in Ancient Israel*. Oxford: Oxford University Press, 1985.
Fraade, Steven D. *From Tradition to Commentary: Torah and its Interpretation in the Midrash Sifre to Deuteronomy*. Albany: State University of New York Press, 1991.
———. "Navigating the Anomalous: Non-Jews at the Intersection of Early Rabbinic Law and Narrative." In *The Other in Jewish Thought and History: Constructions of Jewish Culture and Identity*. Edited by Laurence J. Silberstein and Robert L. Cohen. New York: New York University Press, 1994.
———. "Nomos and Narrative Before Nomos and Narrative," *Yale Journal of Law & the Humanities* 17 (2005): 81-96.
Freud, Sigmund. *Moses and Monotheism*. Translated by Katherine Jones. New York: Vintage, 1939.
Fröhlich, Ida. *Time and Times and Half a Time: Historical Consciousness in the Jewish Literature of the Persian and Hellenistic Eras*. Sheffield: Sheffield Academic Press, 1996.
Gager, John. *Reinventing Paul*. Oxford: Oxford University Press, 2000.
Gay, Peter. *Freud: A Life for Our Time*. New York: Norton Publishing, 1988.
Ginzburg, Carlo. *Wooden Eyes: Nine Reflections on Distance*. Translated by Martin Ryle and Kate Soper. New York: Columbia University Press, 2001.
Glenn, H. Patrick. *Legal Traditions of the World: Sustainable Diversity in Law*. Oxford: Oxford University Press, 2000.
Goldberg, Sylvie-Anne. *La Clepsydre: Essai sur la pluralité des temps dans le judaïsme*. Paris: Albin Michel, 2000.
Goldstein, Bluma. *Reinscribing Moses: Heine, Kafka, Freud, and Schoenberg in a European Wilderness*. Cambridge: Harvard University Press, 1992.
Halbertal, Moshe. *Al Derekh Ha-Emet: Ha-Ramban ve-Yirata shel Mesoret*. Jerusalem: Shalom Hartman Institute, 2006.

———. *Concealment and Revelation: Esotericism in Jewish Thought and its Philosophical Implications*. Translated by Jackie Feldman. Princeton: Princeton University Press, 2007.

———. *Mehafakhot Parshaniut be-Hithaveten*. 2nd revised ed. Jerusalem: Magnes Press, 1999.

———. *People of the Book: Canon, Meaning, and Authority*. Cambridge: Cambridge University Press, 1997.

——— and Avishai, Margalit. *Idolatry*. Cambridge: Harvard University Press, 1992.

Halbwachs, Maurice. *On Collective Memory*. Translated by Lewis A. Coser. Chicago: University of Chicago Press, 1992.

Ha-Levi, Judah. *Sefer Ha-Kuzari*. Edited by Yehudah Even Shmuel. Tel Aviv: Dvir Publishing Co., 1972.

———. *The Kuzari*. Translated by H. Hirschfeld. New York: Schocken Books, 1964.

Halivni, David Weiss. *Revelation Restored: Divine Writ and Critical Responses*. Boulder: Westview Press, 1997.

———. *The Book and the Sword: A Life of Learning in the Shadow of Destruction*. New York: Farrar, Strauss, and Giroux, 1996.

Hampshire, Stuart. *Justice is Conflict*. Princeton: Princeton University Press, 2000.

Hart, H.L.A. *The Concept of Law*. Oxford: Oxford University Press, 1961.

Hartman, David. *Israelis and the Jewish Tradition: An Ancient People Debating its Future*. New Haven: Yale University Press, 2000.

Ḥayim of Volozhin. *Nefesh Ha-Ḥayim*. Bnei Brak: n.p., 1987/88.

———. *Ruaḥ Ḥayim*. Jerusalem: n.p., 1993/4.

Hecht, N.S., Jackson, B.S. Passamaneck, S.M., Piattelli, D., and Rabello, A.M. *An Introduction to the History and Sources of Jewish Law*. Oxford: Clarendon Press, 1996.

Heinemann, Yitzhak. *Ta'amei Ha-Miẓvot be-Sifrut Yisrael*. Jerusalem: Orei Publishers, 1992/3.

Herodotus. *The History*. Translated by David Greene. Chicago: University of Chicago Press, 1987.

Herzog, Isaac. *The Main Institutions of Jewish Law*. 2 vols. London: Soncino Press, 1936.

Himmelfarb, Martha. "Elias Bickerman on Judaism and Hellenism." In *The Jewish Past Revisited: Reflections on Modern Jewish Historians*.

Edited by David N. Myers and David B. Ruderman. New Haven: Yale University Press, 1998.

Hirsch, Samson Raphael. *The Pentateuch*. Translated by Isaac Levy. 6 vols. Gateshead: Judaica Press, 1973.

Hobbes, Thomas. *Leviathan*. Edited by Richard Tuck. Cambridge: Cambridge University Press, 1991.

Hobsbawm, Eric and Ranger Terence Ranger. *The Invention of Tradition*. Cambridge: Cambridge University Press, 1983.

Idel, Moshe. *Golem: Jewish Magical and Mystical Traditions on the Artificial Anthropoid*. Albany: State University of New York Press, 1990.

Isserles, Moshe. *Shealot u-Teshuvot Ha-Rema*. Edited by Asher Siev. Jerusalem: Feldheim Publishing House, 1970.

Jackson, Bernard S. *Wisdom-Laws: A Study of the Mishpatim of Exodus 21:1–22:16*. Oxford: Oxford University Press, 2006.

Jolowicz, H.F. *Historical Introduction to the Study of Roman Law*. Cambridge: Cambridge University Press, 1932.

Josephus, Flavius, *Judean Antiquities*. Leiden: Brill Academic Publishers, 1999.

Judah Loew ben Beẓalel (Maharal). *Derekh Ḥayim*. Edited by Ḥayim Pardes. Tel-Aviv: Machon Mordecai, 1980.

———. *Ḥumash Gur Aryeh ha-Shalem*. 9 vols. Jerusalem: Machon Yerushalayim, 1989.

———. *Tiferet Yisrael*. Edited by Ḥayim Pardes. Tel-Aviv: Yad Mordecai, 1984/5.

Katz, Jacob. *Divine Law in Human Hands: Case Studies in Halakhic Flexibility*. Jerusalem: Magnes Press, 1998.

———. *Exclusiveness and Tolerance: Studies in Jewish-Gentile Relations in Medieval and Modern Times*. Oxford: Oxford University Press, 1961.

Kaufmann, Yehezkel. *Toldot ha-Emuna ha-Yisraelit*. Tel Aviv: Dvir Publishers, 1969.

Kelly, J.M. *A Short History of Western Legal Theory*. Oxford: Oxford University Press, 1992.

Kisska, Anthony J. *Aquinas's Theory of Natural Law: An Analytic Reconstruction*. Oxford: Clarendon Press, 1996.

Kook, Abraham Isaac. *Igerot Ha-Rayah*. 4 vols. Jerusalem: Mosad Ha-Rav Kook, 1984.

Kugel, James L. *In Potiphar's House: The Interpretive Life of Biblical Texts*. New York: HarperCollins, 1990.

———. *The Bible as It Was*. Cambridge: Harvard University Press, 1997.

———. *How to Read the Bible: A Guide to Scripture, Then and Now*. New York: Free Press, 2007.

———. *The Ladder of Jacob: Ancient Interpretations of the Biblical Story of Jacob and his Children*. Princeton: Princeton University Press, 2006.

———. *Traditions of the Bible: A Guide to the Bible as it was Read at the Start of the Common Era*. Cambridge: Harvard University Press, 1998.

Lamm, Norman. *Torah Lishmah: Torah for Torah's Sake in the Works of Rabbi Hayyim of Volozhin and his Contemporaries*. New York: Yeshiva University Press, 1989.

Legendre, Pierre. *L'Inestimable objet de la transmission: Etude sur le principe généalogique en Occident*. Paris: Librarie Fayard, 1983.

Leibowitz, Yeshayahu. *Judaism, Human Values, and the Jewish State*. Edited by Eliezer Goldman. Cambridge: Harvard University Press, 1992.

Levinson, Bernard M. *Deuteronomy and the Hermeneutics of Legal Innovation*. Oxford University Press, 1997.

Levinson, Jon D. "The Conversion of Abraham to Judaism, Christianity, and Islam." In *The Idea of Biblical Interpretation: Essays in Honor of James L. Kugel*. Edited by Judith H. Newman, Hindy Najman, and James L. Kugel. Leiden: Brill, 2003.

Lévi-Strauss, Claude. *The Raw and the Cooked*. Translated by John and Doreen Weightman. New York: Harper & Row, 1970.

Lichtenstein, Aaron. "Noahide Law from the Genizah: The Thirty Laws of Samuel ben Hophni Gaon," *Hebrew Studies* 28 (1987): 113-16.

Luẓatto, Shmuel D. *Perush ShaDaL al Ḥamishah Ḥumshei Torah*. Tel Aviv: Dvir, 1971.

Mack, Michael. *German Idealism and the Jew: The Inner Anti-Semitism of Philosophy and German Jewish Responses*. Chicago: University of Chicago Press, 2003.

Magid, Shaul. *Hasidism on the Margin: Reconciliation, Antinomianism, and Messianism in Izbica/Radzin Hasidism*. Madison: University of Wisconsin Press, 2003.

Maimonides, Moses. *The Guide of the Perplexed*. Translated by Shlomo Pines. 2 vols. Chicago: University of Chicago Press, 1963.

Malbim, Meir Leibush. *Sefer Torat Elohim*. 6 vols. New York: M.P. Press, n.d.

Margalit, Avishai. *The Ethics of Memory*. Cambridge: Harvard University Press, 2002.

Martens, John W. "Unwritten Law in Philo: A Response to Naomi G. Cohen," *Journal of Jewish Studies* 43 (1992): 38-45.

Martyn, J. Louis. *Galatians: A New Translation with Introduction and Commentary* [Anchor Bible]. New York: Doubleday, 1998.

Martyr, Justin. *Dialogue with Trypho, 16 Writings of Saint Justin Martyr*. Washington: Catholic University of America Press, 1977.

Meir Simḥa ha-Cohen of Dvinsk. *Meshekh Ḥokhmah*. Edited by Judah Cooperman. 5 vols. Jeruslaem: Michlalah, n.d.

Menaḥem Naḥem of Chernobyl. Meor Enayim. New Square: Meor Torah Institute, 1997.

Mendelssohn, Moses. *Jerusalem or On Religious Power and Judaism*. Translated by Allan Arkush. Hanover: Brandeis University Press, 1983.

Momigliano, Arnaldo. "The Absence of the Third Bickerman," in *Essays on Ancient and Modern Judaism*. Translated by Maura Masella-Gayley. Chicago: University of Chicago Press, 1994.

Morgan, David. *The Sacred Gaze: Religious Visual Culture in Theory and Practice*. Berkeley: University of California Press, 2005.

Myers, David N. *Resisting History: Historicism and its Discontents in German-Jewish Thought*. Princeton: Princeton University Press, 2003.

Nadler, Alan. *The Faith of the Mithnagdim: Rabbinic Responses to Hasidic Rapture*. Baltimore: The Johns Hopkins University Press, 1997.

Nachmanides, Moses. *Kitvei Rabbenu Moshe ben Naḥman*, Edited by Ḥayim Dov Chavel. 2 vols. Jerusalem: Mosad Ha-Rav Kook, 1984.

———. *Perush HaRamban al ha-Torah*. Edited by Ḥayim Dov Chavel. 2 vols. Jerusalem: Mosad Ha-Rav Kook, 1967.

———. *Sefer Ha-Miẓvot le-ha-Rambam ve-Hasagot Ha-Ramban*. Edited by Ḥayim Dov Chavel. Jerusalem: Mosad Ha-Rav Kook, 1981.

Najman, Hindy. "The Law of Nature and the Authority of Mosaic Law, *Studia Philonica Annual* 11 (1999) 55-73.

———. *Seconding Sinai: The Development of Mosaic Discourse in Second Temple Judaism*. Leiden: Brill Academic Press, 2003.

Neher, André. *The Exile of the Word: From the Silence of the Bible to the Silence of Auschwitz*. Translated by David Meisel. Philadelphia: Jewish Publication Society, 1981.

Nora, Pierre. *Realms of Memory: Rethinking the French Past*. Translated by Arthur Goldhammer. New York: Columbia University Press, 1992.

Novak, David. *Natural Law in Judaism*. Cambridge: Cambridge University Press, 1998.

——. *The Image of the Non-Jew in Judaism: An Historical and Constructive Study of the Noahide Laws*. Queenston: Edwin Mellon Press, 1983.

Pardes, Ilana. *The Biography of Ancient Israel: National Narratives in the Bible*. Berkeley: University of California Press, 2000.

Philo, *Works of Philo* [Loeb Classical Library]. 10 vols. Translated by F.H. Colson et. al. Cambridge: Harvard Univesity Press, 1929.

Plaskow, Judith. *Standing at Sinai: Judaism from a Feminist Perspective*. San Francisco: Harper & Row Publishers, 1990.

Rappaport, Uriel. *Sefer Ha-Makabim*. 2 vols. Jerusalem: Yad Ben Zvi, 2004.

Raokover, Nahum. *Law and the Noahides: Law as a Universal Value*. Jerusalem: Library of Jewish Law, 1998.

Rokeah, David. *Justin Martyr and the Jews*. Leiden: Brill Publishers, 2002.

Rosanes, Judah. *Parshat Derakhim*. Jerusalem: Yitzhak Ochana, 1995/6.

Rosenblatt, Jason. *Renaissance England's Chief Rabbi: John Selden*. Oxford: Oxford University Press, 2006.

Rosenblum, H. *Ha-Malbim: Parshanut, Filosofiah, mada, u-Mistorin be-Kitvei HaRav Meir Leibush Malbim*. Jerusalem: Mosad Ha-Rav Kook, 1988.

Rosenzweig, Franz. "The Builders," in *On Jewish Learning*, edited by Nahum Glazer. New York: Schocken Books, 1955.

——. *The Star of Redemption*. Translated from the German by William W. Hallo. Notre Dame: University of Notre Dame Press, 1985.

Ross, Tamar. *Expanding the Palace of the Torah: Orthodoxy and Feminism*. Boston: Brandeis University Press, 2004.

Rubenfeld, Jed. *Freedom and Time: A Theory of Constitutional Self-Government*. New Haven: Yale University Press, 2001.

Saadia Gaon. *Emunot ve-De'ot*, Translated by Joseph Kapaḥ. Jerusalem: Makhon Mishnat Ha-Rambam, 1994/5.

——. *The Book of Beliefs and Opinions*. Translated by Samuel Rosenblatt. New Haven: Yale University Press, 1948.

———. *Perushei Rabenu Saadia Gaon al Ha-Torah.* Translated by Yosef Kapaḥ. Jerusalem: Mosad Ha-Rav Kook, 1984.

Sacco, Rudolfo. "Mute Law," *American Journal of Comparative Law* 43 (1995): 455-68.

Safran, Bezalel. "Rabbi Azriel and Nachmanides: Two Views of the Fall of Man." In *Isadore Twersky, Rabbi Moses Nachmanides (Ramban): Explorations in his Religious and Literary Virtuosity*. Cambridge: Harvard University Press, 1983.

Schultz, Joseph P. "Two Views of the Patriarchs: Noahides and Pre-Sinai Israelites." In *Texts and Responses: Studies Presented to Nahum N. Glazer on the Occasion of his Seventieth Birthday by his Students*. Edited by Michael A. Fishbane and Paul R. Flohr. Leiden: Brill, 1975.

Schwartzchild, Steven S. "Do Noachites Have to Believe in Revelation? A Passage in Dispute Between Maimonides, Spinoza, Mendelssohn, and Hermann Cohen: A Contribution to a Jewish View of Natural Law," In *Pursuit of the Ideal: Jewish Writings of Steven Schwarzschild*, edited by Menachem Kellner. Albany: State University of New York Press, 1990.

Seeskin, Kenneth. *Searching for a Distant God: The Legacy of Maimonides*. Oxford: Oxford University Press, 2000.

Seforno, Obadiah. *Beur Ha-Seforno al Ha-Torah.* Jerusalem: Mosad Ha-Rav Kook, 1987.

Segal, Alan F. *Paul the Convert: The Apostolate and Apostasy of Saul the Pharisee*. New Haven: Yale University Press, 1990.

Shapiro, Marc. *Between the Yeshiva World and Modern Orthodoxy: The Life and Works of Rabbi Jehiel Jacob Weinberg*. London: Littman Library, 1999.

Shmuel ben Ḥofni Gaon, *Perush Shmuel ben Ḥofni Gaon*. Edited by A. Greenbaum. Jerusalem: Mosad Ha-Rav Kook, 1979.

Siev, Asher. *Shealot u-Teshuvot Ha-Rema.* Jerusalem: Yeshiva University, 1970.

Skinner, Anthony David. *Gershom Scholem: A Life in Letters 1914-1982.* Cambridge: Harvard University Press, 2002.

Sklare, David E. *Samuel ben Hofni Gaon and his Cultural World: Texts and Studies*. Leiden: E.J. Brill, 1996.

Soloveitchik, Joseph B. *Shiurim le-Zekher Aba Mari z'l,* 2 vols. Jerusalem: 1983/4.

———. *Ḥamesh Derashot*. Jeruaslem: Makhon Orot, 1973/4.

———. "Kol Dodi Dofek." In *Ish Ha-Emunah*. Jerusalem: Mosad Ha-Rav Kook, 1980/1.

Sparks, H.F.D. *The Apocryphal Old Testament*. Oxford: Oxford University Press, 1984.

Sperling, Avraham. *Sefer Ta'amei Ha-Minhagim*. Jerusalem: Eshkol, 1981/2.

Spiegel, Shalom. *The Last Trial: On the Legends and Lore of the Command to Offer Isaac as a Sacrifice: The Akedah*. Translated by Judah Goldin. Philadelphia: Jewish Publication Society, 1967.

Stahl, Nanette. *Law and Liminality in the Bible*. Sheffield: Sheffield Academic Press, 1995.

Stern, Sacha. *Calendar and Community: A History of the Jewish Calendar 2nd Century BCE to the 10th Century CE*. Oxford: Oxford University Press, 2001.

———. *Time and Process in Ancient Judaism*. Oxford: Littman Library, 2002.

Sternbuch, Moshe. *Sefer Ta'am ve-Daat*. 3 vols. Jeusalem: n.d.

Stone, Suzanne Last, "In Pursuit of the Counter-Text: The Turn to the Jewish Legal Model in Contemporary American Legal Theory," *Harvard Law Review* 106 (1993): 813-94.

Strenski, Ivan. *Durkheim and the Jews of France*. Chicago: University of Chicago Press, 1997.

Sutcliffe, Adam. *Judaism and Enlightenment*. Cambridge: Cambridge University Press, 2003.

Torat Ḥayim. 7 vols. Jerusalem: Mosad Ha-Rav Kook, 1986.

Twersky, Isadore. *Rabad of Posquieres: A Twelfth-Century Talmudist*. Cambridge: Harvard University Press, 1980.

———, "Religion and the Law." In Studies in Jewish Law and Philosophy. Edited by Isadore Twersky. New York: KTAV Publishing House, 1982.

Urbach, Ephraim E. *The Sages: Their Concepts and Beliefs*. 2 vols. Jerusalem: Magnes Press, 1975.

Van Ruiten, J.T.A.G. M. *Primaeval History Interpreted: The Rewriting of Genesis 1-11 in the Book of Jubilees*. Leiden: Brill, 2000.

Van Seters, John. *A Law Book for the Diaspora: Revision in the Study of the Covenant Code*. Oxford: Oxford University Press, 2003.

VanderKam, J.C. *The Book of Jubilees*. 2 vols. (Leuven: Peeters, 1989).

Veyne, Paul. Les Grecs ont-ils cru à leurs mythes? Paris: Editions du Seuil, 1983.

Walzer, Michael. Exodus and Revolution. New York: Basic Books, 1985.
Weiler, J.J.H.H. "On Being a Judge—Jethro's Lesson," 2 *Green Bag* 291-96 (1999).
Weinberg, Jehiel Jacob. *Shealot u-Teshuvot Seridrei Eish*. 2 vols. Jerusalem: Jehiel Weinberg Institute, 1998/9.
Weinreich, Max. *History of the Yiddish Language*. Translated by Shlomo Noble. Chicago: University of Chicago Press, 1980.
Weisbrod, Carol. *Emblems of Pluralism: Cultural Differences and the State*. Princeton: Princeton University Press, 2002.
Weitzman, Steven. *Surviving Sacrilege: Cultural Persistence in Jewish Antiquity*. Cambridge: Harvard University Press, 2005.
White, R.S. *Natural Law in English Renaissance Literature*. Cambridge: Cambridge University Press, 1996.
Wolfson, Harry Austryn. *Philo: Foundations of Religious Philosophy in Judaism, Christianity, and Islam*. 2 vols. Cambridge: Harvard University Press, 1982.
Yaakov ben ha-Rosh. *Baal Ha-Turim Perush al Ha-Torah*. 2 vols. Jerusalem: Feldheim, 1995.
Yerushalmi, Yosef Hayim. *Freud's Moses: Judaism Terminable and Interminable*. New Haven: Yale University Press, 1993.
———. *Zakhor: Jewish History and Jewish Memory*. Seattle: University of Washington Press, 1982.
Yonah ben Avraham of Gerona, *Shaarei Teshuva*. Jerusalem: Eshkol Publishing House, 1977/8.

Index

About the Author

Steven Wilf was born in Philadelphia. He was educated at Yale University, where he received both his doctorate in history and his law degree, and currently teaches at the Law School of the University of Connecticut. He has been a visiting scholar at New York University Law School, the University of Chicago, Brown University, the Freie Universität Berlin, and the Law Faculty of the Hebrew University in Jerusalem. He clerked for the United States Court of Appeals for the Second Circuit in New York. The author of numerous articles on legal history, intellectual property law, and historical jurisprudence, he lives with his wife and children in New Haven.

www.ingramcontent.com/pod-product-compliance
Ingram Content Group UK Ltd.
Pitfield, Milton Keynes, MK11 3LW, UK
UKHW040909190926
475560UK00008B/56

9 780739 123133